T0074933

Microsoft® Azure®

2nd Edition

by Jack Hyman

A Wiley Brand

Microsoft® Azure® For Dummies®, 2nd Edition

Published by: **John Wiley & Sons, Inc.,** 111 River Street, Hoboken, NJ 07030-5774, www.wiley.com

Copyright © 2023 by John Wiley & Sons, Inc., Hoboken, New Jersey

Media and software compilation copyright © 2023 by John Wiley & Sons, Inc. All rights reserved.

Published simultaneously in Canada

For general information on our other products and services, please contact our Customer Care Department within the U.S. at 877-762-2974, outside the U.S. at 317-572-3993, or fax 317-572-4002. For technical support, please visit https://hub.wiley.com/community/support/dummies.

Wiley publishes in a variety of print and electronic formats and by print-on-demand. Some material included with standard print versions of this book may not be included in e-books or in print-on-demand. If this book refers to media such as a CD or DVD that is not included in the version you purchased, you may download this material at http://booksupport.wiley.com. For more information about Wiley products, visit www.wiley.com.

Library of Congress Control Number: 2022948948

ISBN 978-1-119-89806-1 (pbk); ISBN 978-1-119-89807-8 (ebk); ISBN 978-1-119-89808-5 (ebk)

SKY10069071_030624

Contents at a Glance

Table of Contents

Introduction

Microsoft Azure is a public cloud service in which you rent compute services from Microsoft that run in Microsoft's data centers. You pay only for the resources you use over the course of your billing period.

Microsoft Azure For Dummies is intended to provide you with a gentle yet thorough introduction to Microsoft Azure. In this updated second edition, I cover the must-know features you are likely to encounter as you begin the Azure journey. I show you how things work and why it makes sense to use specific features. Undoubtedly, cloud computing can be complex at first, but it also has the potential to save you or your organization money, time, and effort.

About This Book

Many books on Microsoft Azure have been published, yet most cover laser-focused areas: analytics, security, machine learning, systems administration, app development, and so on. And certification texts generally cover just enough to pass a focused exam and are not a general reference on all core Azure capabilities. With the constant feature rollouts in the Azure platform, it can be hard to keep up, which is why in this edition of *Microsoft Azure For Dummies*, I cover the new features and those that have undergone drastic change since the first edition of this book was published in 2019.

I've worked with Azure for close to a decade. Here's a bit of a secret: Whether you are the most experienced Azure Cloud Engineer or just starting out, you'll experience some technical challenges every now and then. Even Microsoft Most Valued Professionals (MVPs) find it labor-intensive to stay current with the constant changes introduced by the Azure product management team.

Thus, I wrote this book with the intention of helping you with the following:

>> **Becoming comfortable with Microsoft Azure:** I give you this comfort by sticking to what Microsoft calls the "80 percent scenarios," or Azure deployments used by 80 percent of its customer base.

- » **Gaining skill with programmatic deployment:** Along the way, I show you how to use Azure PowerShell, Azure Command-Line Interface (CLI), and Azure Resource Manager (ARM) templates to get your Azure work done. These Azure access methods change less frequently than the Azure portal graphical user interface (GUI).

- » **Becoming comfortable with tools and staying current:** You can expect the Azure portal to change such that what you see on your screen may not match what's in this book. Why is that? Because no two Azure users deploy the same resources or configure their user experience the same way. So don't be alarmed! I updated both chapters in Part 6 of the book ("The Part of Tens") to help you plan for the future of Azure and how to optimize your environment.

In addition, I include many web addresses throughout this book. If Microsoft changes a page address and the link I provide no longer works, don't fret! Simply run a Google search for the article title and you'll find the updated page address nearly instantly.

Throughout this book, you'll also find dozens of step-by-step procedures. I want you to keep the following points in mind as you work through them:

- » You need an Azure subscription to follow the steps. If you haven't already done so, you can create a free Azure account (https://azure.microsoft.com/free) that gives you 30 days to spend $200 USD on any Azure service. This quota should get you through this book's material as long as you delete your deployments when you finish using them.

- » I often provide sample values that work in my environment but may not be supported in yours based on geography and resources utilized. You should customize these procedures to suit your requirements.

- » You'll likely need a few additional tools along the way. All of these tools are available from the Microsoft website as *Azure utilities*.

Finally, most of the Azure administration and development tools discussed are available for Windows, macOS, and Linux. (I'm using a Windows 10 or 11 Enterprise workstation.)

Foolish Assumptions

I wrote this book with several types of readers in mind. See whether you can place yourself roughly or exactly in any of the following descriptions:

>> You're an experienced IT professional who may or may not already be using Azure for future initiatives at work.

>> You might be preparing for an Azure certification.

>> You're an IT newcomer who wants to know Azure to future-proof your career.

>> You're proficient in other public cloud platforms, such as Amazon Web Services or Google Cloud Platform, and you want to see how Azure compares.

>> You need a quick reference, not a hundred Azure books, to lead you in the right direction for business and technical success.

Regardless of your present attitude and orientation toward Azure, I hope that by studying this book and applying its methods you become more knowledgeable about Azure and thereby excel in your profession.

Icons Used in This Book

If you've read a *For Dummies* book before, then you're probably familiar with the icons. If not, or if you want a formal description of each, then read on!

TIP

The Tip icon marks tips (duh!) and shortcuts that you can use to make working with Azure easier.

REMEMBER

Remember icons mark especially important information. To siphon off the most important information in each chapter, skim the paragraphs that have these icons.

TECHNICAL STUFF

The Technical Stuff icon marks information of a highly technical nature. You'll be digging into the weeds a bit more. You can skip if you like, though!

WARNING

The Warning icon tells you to watch out! It marks important information that may save you headaches.

ON THE WEB

When you see the On the Web icon, it points to valuable Azure-related websites. Most of these URLs direct you to more detailed information on the Microsoft website.

Beyond the Book

Beyond what's included between the covers of this book, I created a Cheat Sheet that includes tips, tricks, and shortcuts for the Azure services you use over the course of the book. You can find the Cheat Sheet and other information related to this book (such as errata) by visiting https://www.dummies.com and searching for "Azure For Dummies" in the search box.

Where to Go from Here

Although I'd read this book in order starting with Chapter 1, you may not prefer to use that method. You can dip into any chapter with no formal dependency on those that come before it, so flip to the chapter that you want to begin with and let's get to work!

1

Getting Started with Microsoft Azure

IN THIS CHAPTER

» **Introducing the cloud**

» **Differentiating among the cloud computing models**

» **Introducing the major Microsoft Azure services**

» **Starting your Azure subscription**

» **Learning how Azure deploys product updates**

Chapter **1**

Introducing Microsoft Azure

elcome to cloud computing, and welcome to Microsoft Azure! I'm not sure what occurred in your professional or personal life to lead you to read this book, but I'm glad you're here with me. In this chapter, I cover ground-level terminology, beginning with precisely what buzzwords *the cloud* and *cloud computing* mean.

By the end of this chapter, you'll have your very own Azure subscription running at the free tier. Are you excited? I hope so!

What Is Cloud Computing?

Ask one hundred people to define cloud computing and I am confident the responses may make you laugh, cry, or think a bit. You see, many people at first think cloud technology is anything but shared compute capacity and resources using a common interface.

Most people use cloud services whether they're aware of doing so or not. Think of your smartphone. Where do you think your photos, media, files, and settings are being backed up? What is behind your ability to retrieve your content wherever you are in the world, provided you have an internet connection?

Do you use a web-hosting company to host your personal website? Where is the physical server that houses your website? How about accessing that digital video service or music heard over the Internet?

These scenarios are examples of cloud computing, in which you simply rent resources on another organization's infrastructure.

The resources you rent consist of the following hardware and software components:

>> **Compute:** *Compute* is raw computing power — the central processing unit (CPU) and random-access memory (RAM) that form the platform for applications and data.

>> **Storage:** *Persistent storage* means you have a place on Microsoft's servers to store your files and other data. When you save a file to a cloud-hosted storage account, the file should remain in place forever, or at least until you move or delete it.

>> **Network:** Azure provides a software-defined network infrastructure on which you can host your virtual machines and other Azure services. Because the cloud almost always involves an internet connection, *online* and *cloud* are essentially synonymous. I say almost always because a business can create a private cloud that shares most attributes of a public cloud but is local to its private network environment. Microsoft also sells a private, portable version of Azure called Azure Stack.

>> **Analytics:** You'll never get to touch the cloud provider's compute, storage, or network resources. The closest you'll get is viewing its telemetry data in your web browser or from a management app. Thus, Azure and other public cloud providers give you tools to see precisely how much of their services you consume each minute. Cloud analytics also gives you valuable troubleshooting and performance-tuning advice for your cloud infrastructure.

Businesses are interested in using the cloud because it allows them to offload a lot of what's scary, annoying, and/or expensive about maintaining an on-premises data center, such as the following:

>> **Power:** It's potentially very expensive to provide electricity to all the equipment necessary to host your applications and services. And what happens if your on-campus data center experiences a utilities outage? When you move your data into the cloud, your provider takes on the risk of these issues.

- >> **Capital expenditure:** When you run an on-premises data center, you either rent your physical servers or purchase them outright. As such, you're responsible for all hardware upgrades and repairs. All that hardware can be expensive, too.

- >> **Security and configuration overhead:** If you can't afford local systems administrators, or if your existing resources are stretched thin, it can be too easy to leave a vulnerability in place on an on-premises server that can be compromised by bad actors. By contrast, when you use a public cloud service like Azure, you rely upon Microsoft's human and machine learning–based threat intelligence to help keep your applications, services, and data safe.

Do you see the trend here? Cloud computing is popular because it's convenient for the end user and cheaper for the enterprise business. Before I go any further, however, I want to codify what I mean by *cloud computing*.

NIST definition

The National Institute of Standards and Technology (NIST, pronounced *nihst*), a research laboratory in the United States, developed the standard definition of cloud computing. According to NIST, the five essential characteristics of cloud computing are

- >> **On-demand self-service:** Cloud customers can provision services at any time and are charged only for the resources they consume.

- >> **Broad network access:** Cloud services are ordinarily offered globally, and the customer is encouraged to place services as geographically near its consumers as possible.

- >> **Resource pooling:** Cloud services are *multitenant,* which means that different customers' environments are isolated. You should never, ever see another Azure customer's data, and vice versa.

- >> **Rapid elasticity:** A cloud services customer can accommodate variable traffic patterns by configuring their services to scale accordingly. For instance, you can configure Azure to automatically duplicate your web servers to accommodate traffic spikes and then remove servers automatically when they are no longer needed.

- >> **Measured service:** The cloud offers services on demand, which are metered; once again, customers pay only provisioned resources.

ON THE WEB

If you want to read the source material, check NIST Special Publication 800-145, *The NIST Definition of Cloud Computing*, which you can download from https://csrc.nist.gov/publications/detail/sp/800-145/final.

Cloud computing benefits

As I mention earlier in this chapter, cloud computing is attractive to both businesses and consumers because of its convenience, high availability, and potential cost savings. Whereas organizations had to once buy expensive hardware with limited capacity, also known as a capital expenditure (CapEx), Microsoft Azure uses a consumption-based spending model that's classified as an operational expenditure (OpEx).

So why is OpEx so attractive? The fairly predictable, recurring cost model of OpEx is appealing to cost-conscious organizations. (And which organization isn't cost-conscious nowadays?)

The cloud's rapid scalability and elasticity are capabilities that only the largest companies in the world can afford to manage on their own. Microsoft Azure enables smaller companies and individuals to replicate an SQL database between geographical regions with a couple of mouse clicks. (See Figure 1-1.) Making high availability this accessible to customers is an enormous benefit of cloud computing.

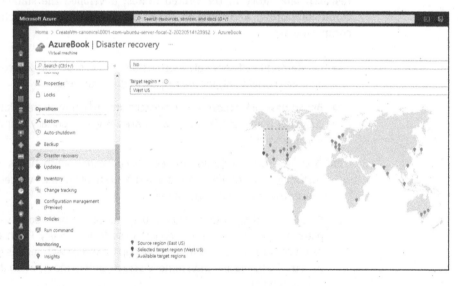

FIGURE 1-1: In Azure, you can ensure that a virtual machine includes disaster recovery in one or several locations around the world with only a couple of clicks.

Economies of scale

The term *economies of scale* means that a business that purchases its internal resources at a larger volume can pass along savings to its customers.

OTHER CLOUD PROVIDERS

For completeness, I want you to know that although this book's focus is Microsoft Azure, other major public cloud providers also take advantage of economies of scale. These public cloud providers include, but aren't limited to, the following:

- Alibaba Cloud
- Amazon Web Services (AWS)
- Google Cloud Platform (GCP)
- IBM Cloud
- Oracle Cloud
- Salesforce

At this writing, Microsoft has its Azure product portfolio spread across 78 regions worldwide. Within each region are two or more physical data centers. Each data center has untold numbers of server racks, blade servers, storage arrays, routers, switches, and so forth — an immense physical capacity. To further elaborate, while there may be 78 regions worldwide, several regions such as the United States might have many physical data centers. Because there are over 200 physical data centers with compute capacity globally, businesses can be assured their data has a home. I think we can reasonably assume that Microsoft gets a discount from the original equipment manufacturers (OEMs) because it purchases in such huge volume. Microsoft's purchase discounts means that the company in turn extends the savings to its Azure customers. It's as simple as that.

Understanding Cloud Computing Models

The working definition of *cloud computing* is a subscription arrangement under which a person or business rents a cloud service provider's infrastructure and pays only for the services consumed. That definition is fine. In this section, however, I want to sharpen your general understanding of cloud computing by explaining the deployment and service delivery models.

Deployment models

In Azure nomenclature, *deployment* refers to your provisioning resources in the Azure public cloud. You may be saying, "What's this? Why is Microsoft Azure called a public cloud? I thought you said that different Azure customers can never see each other's resources by default." Hang on; hang on. Let me explain.

Public cloud

Microsoft Azure is a public cloud because its global data center fabric is accessible by the general public. Microsoft takes Azure's multitenant nature very seriously; therefore, it adds layer after layer of physical and logical security to ensure that each customer's data is private. In fact, in many cases, even Microsoft doesn't have access to customers' data encryption keys!

Other major cloud service providers — including AWS and GCP (see the sidebar "Other cloud providers") — are also considered to be public cloud platforms.

TECHNICAL
STUFF

Microsoft has three additional, separate Azure clouds for exclusive governmental use and restricted country usage. You might read Microsoft literature that contains references to Azure Cloud, which refers to its public cloud, and to Azure Government Cloud, which refers to its sovereign, special-access clouds for the U.S. government. No member of the general public can access an Azure Government Cloud without being associated with a government body. The same is true with other country-specific sovereign clouds such as China and Germany. If you are interested in learning more about Azure Government Cloud, including a list of resellers, go to https://docs.microsoft.com/azure/azure-government/documentation-government-csp-list.

Private cloud

As I mention earlier, very, very few businesses have enough financial, capital, and human resources to host their own cloud environments. Typically only the largest enterprise organizations can afford having their own private cloud infrastructure with redundant data centers, storage, networking, and compute, but they may have security prohibitions against storing data in Microsoft's (or any other cloud provider's) physical data centers. Example organizations include financial institutions and healthcare organizations.

Microsoft has two private cloud options, and the one you choose is often dictated by your security needs. For those who no longer want to deal with a hardware footprint, a Microsoft Azure customer can create a dedicated hosting environment whereby computing resources are exclusively owned and managed by a single enterprise. Accessing such computing resources requires the use of a private internal network. Because you are asking Microsoft for dedicated capacity, the costs are understandably higher. That said, most organizations needing dedicated capacity utilize this private cloud offering. Microsoft sells a portable version of the Azure cloud, Azure Stack, which consists of a server rack that a company leases or purchases from a Microsoft-affiliated hardware or service provider. The idea is that you can bring the hallmarks of cloud computing — on-demand self-service, resource pooling, elasticity, and so forth — to your local environment without involving either the Internet or an external cloud provider, unless you want to.

Your administrators and developers use the same Azure Resource Manager (ARM) application programming interface (API) to deploy resources locally to Azure Stack as they use to deploy to the Azure public cloud. This API makes it a snap to bring cloud-based services on premises, and vice versa. ARM is discussed in more detail in Chapter 2.

Hybrid cloud

When you combine the best of on-premises and cloud environments, you have a hybrid cloud. If you are part of any enterprise organization, I can almost guarantee you that some facet of the business operates in a hybrid cloud. Why am I so certain of this? A hybrid cloud allows the business to salvage (read: continue to use) the on-premises infrastructure that it's already paid for while leveraging the hyper scale of the Azure public cloud. It often takes time to transition from a legacy system to a cloud infrastructure.

Take a look at Figure 1-2. In this topology, the on-premises network is extended to a virtual network running in Azure. You can do all sorts of nifty service management here, including

» Joining the Azure virtual machines (VMs) to your local Active Directory domain.

» Managing your on-premises servers by using Azure management tools.

» Providing nearly instant failover disaster recovery (DR) by using Azure as a DR site. *Failover* refers to having a replicated backup of your production servers available somewhere else so that you can shift from your failed primary environment to your backup environment within minutes. Failover is critical for businesses that cannot afford the downtime involved in restoring backups from a backup archive.

By the end of this book, you'll understand how to deploy the environment you see in Figure 1-2, but here's an overview of what's going on:

» On the left side is a local business network that connects to the Internet via a virtual private network (VPN) gateway.

» On the right (Azure) side is a three-VM deployment in a virtual network. A site-to-site VPN connects the local environment to the virtual network.

Finally, an Azure load balancer spreads incoming traffic equally among the three identically configured web servers in the web tier subnet. As a result, the company's internal staff can access the Azure-based web application over a secure VPN tunnel and get a low-latency, reliable, always-on connection to boot.

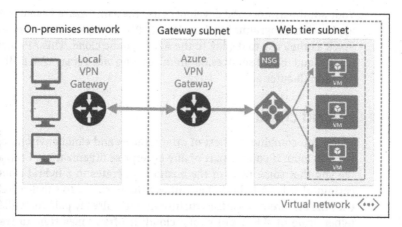

FIGURE 1-2:
A hybrid cloud in which the on-premises corporate network extends to Azure.

REMEMBER

In this book, I refer to a local, physical network environment as an *on-premises environment*. In the wild, you'll see stray references to "on premise" — sadly, even in Microsoft's Azure documentation. Don't make this mistake. A *premise* is an idea; *premises* refers to a location.

Service delivery models

Organizations deploy applications in three primary ways: Software as a Service, Platform as a Service, and Infrastructure as a Service.

Software as a Service (SaaS)

An SaaS application is a finished, customer-facing application that runs in the cloud. Microsoft Office 365 is a perfect example. As shown in Figure 1-3, you can use Word Online to create, edit, and share documents with only a web browser; an internet connection; and an Office 365 subscription, which you pay for each month on a subscription basis.

With SaaS applications, you have zero visibility into the back-end mechanics of the application. In the case of Word Online, you neither know nor care how often the back-end servers are backed up, where the Office 365 data centers are geographically located, and so forth. All you care about is whether you can get to your cloud-hosted documents and whether Word Online behaves as you expect.

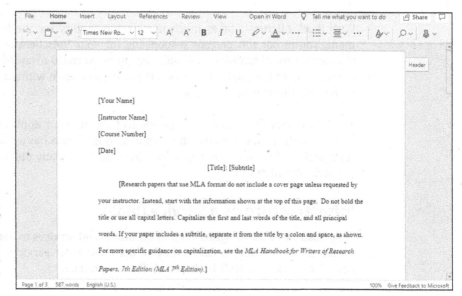

FIGURE 1-3:
Microsoft Word
Online, part of
the Microsoft
Office 365
product family, is
an example of an
SaaS application.

Platform as a Service (PaaS)

Consider a business that runs a three-tier on-premises web application with VMs. The organization wants to move this application workload to Azure to take advantage of the benefits of cloud computing. Because the organization has always done business by using VMs, it assumes that the workload must by definition run in VMs in Azure.

Not so fast. Suppose that the workload consisted of a Microsoft-stack application. Maybe the business should consider using PaaS products such as Azure App Service and Azure SQL Database to leverage autoscale and pushbutton georeplication.

REMEMBER

I discuss both Azure App Service and Azure SQL Database in Part 3. For now, understand that *georeplication* means placing synchronized copies of your service in other geographic regions for fault tolerance and placing those services closer to your users.

Or maybe the workload is an open-source project that uses PHP and MySQL. No problem. Azure App Service can handle that scenario. Microsoft also has a native hosted database platform for MySQL called (appropriately enough) Azure Database for MySQL.

With PaaS, Microsoft takes much more responsibility for the hosting environment. You're not 100 percent responsible for your VMs because PaaS products abstract all that plumbing and administrative overhead away from you. Sounds dreamy, right? The goal is to develop the best application without focusing on the system administration overhead.

The idea is that PaaS products free you to focus on your applications and, ultimately, on the people who use those applications. If PaaS has a trade-off, it's that relinquishing full-stack control is an adjustment for many old-salt systems and network administrators.

Infrastructure as a Service (IaaS)

Most businesses that migrate their applications and services to Azure use the IaaS model at first, if only because they've delivered their services via VMs in the past — the old "if it ain't broke, don't fix it" approach.

In large part, IaaS is where the customer host one or more VMs in a cloud. The customers remain responsible for the full lifecycle of the VM, including

>> Configuration

>> Data protection

>> Performance tuning

>> Security

By hosting your VMs in Azure rather than in your on-premises environment, you save money because you don't have to provision the physical and logical resources locally. You also don't have to pay for the layers of geographic, physical, and logical redundancy included in Azure out of the box.

Thus, whereas SaaS is a service that's been fully abstracted in the cloud and the customer simply uses the application, IaaS offers a split between Microsoft's responsibility (providing the hosting platform) and the customer's responsibility (maintaining the VMs over their lifecycles).

TIP

To sum up the major distinction between IaaS and PaaS, IaaS gives you full control of the environment but you sacrifice scalability and agility. PaaS gives you full scalability and agility, but you sacrifice some control. To be sure, the cloud computing literature contains references to other cloud deployment models, such as community cloud. You'll also see references to additional delivery models, such as Storage as a Service (STaaS) and Identity as a Service (IDaaS). This chapter focuses on the most commonly used cloud deployment and delivery models.

WARNING

Cloud computing in general, and Microsoft Azure in particular, uses what's called the *shared responsibility model*. In this model, Microsoft's responsibility is providing the tools you need to make your cloud deployments successful — Microsoft's data centers, the server, storage and networking hardware, and so on. Your responsibility is to use those tools to secure, optimize, and protect your deployments. Microsoft isn't going to configure, back up, and secure your VMs automatically; those tasks are your responsibility.

Introducing Microsoft Azure Services

The Microsoft Azure service catalog has hundreds of services. In fact, the number of services increase on a rolling basis, generally quarterly, and the list is constantly evolving. Microsoft maintains a services directory at `https://azure.microsoft.com/services`, but in this chapter, I give you a high-level tour of what Microsoft calls 80 percent services — the Azure products that 80 percent of the customer base uses.

Azure history

In October 2008, Microsoft announced Windows Azure at its Professional Developers Conference. Many people feel that this product was a direct answer to Amazon, which had already begun unveiling AWS to the general public.

The first Azure-hosted service was SQL Azure Relational Database, announced in March 2009. Then came support for PaaS websites and IaaS virtual machines in June 2012. Figure 1-4 shows what the Windows Azure portal looked like during that time.

Satya Nadella became Microsoft's chief operating officer in February 2014. Satya had a vision of Microsoft expanding its formerly proprietary borders, so Windows Azure became Microsoft Azure, and the Azure platform began to embrace open-source technologies and companies that Microsoft formerly considered to be hostile competitors.

TIP

Microsoft Azure provides first-class support for Linux-based VMs and non-Microsoft web applications and services, which is a huge deal. Did you ever expect Microsoft to promote another vendor's products besides its own? I surely didn't once upon a time.

Finally, Microsoft introduced the RM deployment model at Microsoft Build 2014. The API behind Windows Azure was called Azure Service Management (ASM), and it suffered from several design and architectural pain points. ASM made it super-difficult to organize deployment resources, for example, and it was impossible to scope administrative access granularly. So changes were bound to come from Azure's Product Development team.

FIGURE 1-4:
The Windows Azure portal, circa 2012.

The ARM API is modeled closely on the AWS API (you know the old saying "Imitation is the sincerest form of flattery"), with core architectural concepts such as resource groups and role-based access controls that were direct analogs of features in the AWS cloud.

To support old customers with old deployments, ARM still offers limited support for ASM deployments in the Azure portal (see Chapter 2). These resources are tagged with the suffix Classic. This book is committed to the ARM API, however, and because few organizations still utilize these services, I won't be addressing ASM IaaS products.

Azure Virtual Machines is Microsoft Azure's meat and potatoes IaaS product. Specifically, the Azure Marketplace in the Azure portal lists thousands of precon-figured VM images from Microsoft, endorsed Linux distributions, and third-party solution providers. You can see the gallery of VM images in Figure 1-5.

You can migrate your on-premises physical and virtual machines to Azure, of course, as well as create custom VM images. I get to those topics in time; I promise.

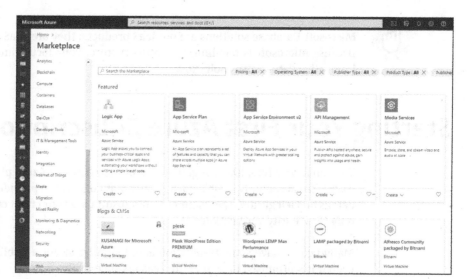

FIGURE 1-5:
The Azure
Marketplace
includes prebuilt
Windows and
Linux VM images.

PaaS products

The Azure product portfolio is filled with powerful, cost-saving PaaS offerings. The following are some of the more high-profile Azure PaaS products:

>> **App Service:** Web Apps, Mobile Apps, API Apps, Logic Apps, and Function Apps

>> **Databases:** Cosmos DB, Azure SQL Database, Azure Database for MySQL, and Azure Cache for Redis

>> **Containers:** Azure Container Instances, Azure Container Registry, and Azure Kubernetes Service

>> **DevOps:** Azure DevOps and Azure DevTest Labs

>> **Internet of Things (IoT):** Azure IoT Hub, Azure IoT Edge, Azure Sphere, and Azure Digital Twins

>> **Machine learning:** Azure Machine Learning Service, Azure Bot Service, Cognitive Services, and Azure Search

>> **Identity:** Azure Active Directory (AD), Azure AD Business-to-Business, and Azure AD Business-to-Consumer

>> **Monitoring:** Application Insights, Azure Monitor, and Azure Log Analytics

>> **Migration:** Azure Site Recovery, Azure Cost Management, Azure Database Migration Service, and Azure Migrate

REMEMBER

Microsoft Database solutions are not IaaS products; they are PaaS products. Why? Because Microsoft is handling the infrastructure, your focus can be on building innovative data-centric solutions.

Starting Your First Azure Subscription

You can have a free, low-obligation trial of the Microsoft Azure platform with the Azure free account. *Low-obligation* means that you have to provide some personal details and a legitimate payment type. Microsoft uses your credit card information only for identity verification.

Many people have some trepidation about signing up for a public cloud service, even if it's promised to be free, for reasons such as these:

>> Does Microsoft begin to charge my credit card when the free trial period expires?

>> What if I accidentally leave an Azure service running? Will Microsoft ding my credit card for it?

I address these and other perfectly reasonable concerns, starting by explaining how Azure subscriptions work.

Understanding subscription types

When you sign up for an Azure free account, you receive $200 (or the equivalent in your local currency) to spend on any Azure service over a 30-day period. At the end of the 30 days, Microsoft does not convert your account to pay as you go (PAYG), the typical paid subscription offer.

Instead, any running services you have are stopped, and to restart your services, you need to convert your trial account manually to a PAYG account or other subscription offer in the Azure portal.

That said, the Azure free account provides 12 months of free availability to several IaaS and PaaS services, including the following:

>> 750 hours of B1ms General Purpose VMs running Windows Server or Linux

>> 5GB locally redundant hot-tier blob storage

>> 10 web, mobile, or API apps with 1GB storage

>> 25GB Cosmos DB instance

>> 15GB outbound data transfer from Azure

ON THE WEB

You can see a full list of Azure free tier services by looking up the Free services blade in the Azure portal or by visiting the Azure Free Account FAQ page at https://azure.microsoft.com/free/free-account-faq.

REMEMBER

A *blade* refers to a *pane* in the Azure portal. I use the word a lot in this book, and you'll see it all the time in the Azure documentation.

Additionally, several Azure services run on an always-free tier; you'll need to check https://azure.microsoft.com for specifics. Remember, however, that the free tier services aren't there for you to run production workloads. The tier exists to give you an opportunity to test Azure, to see whether it may fit your professional or personal needs.

Pay-As-You-Go (PAYG for short) is the most common standard subscription offer. Each month, you receive an invoice stating charges for the Azure resources you consume outside the Azure free-tier services.

The Enterprise Agreement (EA) is a special-purpose contract intended for larger businesses that are willing to commit to a one or three-year Azure subscription. Microsoft offers EA customers special discounts on Azure services and provides them a special management portal for analyzing spending, creating budgets, tracking use, and so forth. Discounts are often as high as 75 percent.

REMEMBER

Under EA, you pay your yearly fee up front and must use it or lose it. If you commit to $12,000 for the first year and spend only $9,000 by December 31, for example, you lose the remaining $3,000. At the end of each contract year, however, you can adjust your fee for the upcoming year to better match your use and expectations. If you spend more than the $12,000, Microsoft provides you with a discount similar to the upfront commitment under an EA exclusively.

Several other Azure subscription offers grant recurring monthly credits, including these:

>> **Visual Studio:** Given to those who have a Visual Studio Online subscription

>> **Action Pack:** Given to Microsoft Partner Network members

>> **Azure for Students:** A free credit ($100) over 12 months for students with a verified academic email address

>> **Azure Pass:** Normally granted by Microsoft to Azure user groups and educational institutions and intended for free distribution

Creating a free Azure account

To sign up for an Azure free account, you need an internet connection and any modern web browser.

TIP

I suggest that you perform this procedure (and all procedures in this book) on a desktop or laptop computer rather than a tablet or smartphone. Microsoft makes the Azure portal as mobile-friendly as possible but given the amount of typing you'll be doing, I recommend using a larger computer. Also, the mobile form facts are purpose-built for analytics rendering and basic administrative actions, not heavy coding or configuration.

Follow these steps to create your account:

1. **Browse to** `https://azure.microsoft.com` **and look for a free-account.**

   Microsoft changes the Azure website regularly, so I hesitate to ask you to look in a particular spot for the link or a button. Somewhere on the page, you'll find the link or button to click.

2. **Sign in with your Microsoft account, or create a new one.**

   The Azure free account is a Microsoft account, which powers all of the company's online services including Xbox and Office 365. If you already have a Microsoft account, however, you may want to create a new one exclusively for Azure use. I suggest this because you probably want to keep your Azure business completely isolated from, say, your Xbox leisure.

3. **In the About You section, provide your contact details, and click Next.**

   Microsoft needs this information to set up your Azure subscription. It also uses your telephone number, email address, and payment details to verify your identity.

4. **In the Identity Verification by Card section of the next page, provide valid credit card details.**

   Note that you can't use a prepaid credit card or gift card; the card has to be a legitimate credit or debit card with your name and billed to your address. Microsoft won't charge your account unless you upgrade to a paid subscription offer. That said, Microsoft may put a $1 verification hold on your credit card account; this hold is lifted within three to five business days.

   You can have only one Azure free account, and Microsoft performs the identity verification in part to prevent fraud.

5. **In the Agreement section, confirm that you agree to the subscription agreement, offer details, and privacy statement; then click Sign Up.**

6. **On the You're Ready to Start with Azure page that appears, click Go to the Portal.**

   You're done and ready to rock. That was easy, wasn't it?

You should now see the Azure portal, along with a Welcome to Microsoft Azure message, as shown in Figure 1-6.

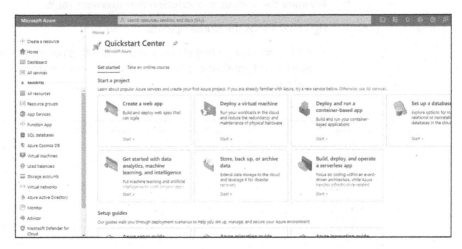

FIGURE 1-6:
Signing in to the
Azure portal for
the first time.

I formally introduce the Azure portal in Chapter 2. For now, bookmark this address (`https://portal.azure.com`), because you'll be using it a lot from now on.

Click Start Tour to take a spin around the Azure portal. In the background of Figure 1-6, you see the Quickstart Center; you can return to this blade at any time by typing **quickstart center** in the search box on the top navigation bar. The Quickstart Center contains links to the documentation and to Microsoft Learn, Microsoft's free Azure education portal.

Viewing subscription details

Follow these steps to view your Azure free-account subscription details:

1. **Type subscriptions in the global search box in the Azure portal.**

   The Subscriptions option should appear almost instantly.

TIP

As you'll quickly learn in Azure, there are hundreds of products available. Frankly, it's tough to find some of them in one or two clicks. Using the global search box at the top of the Azure Portal can get you to your destination in a matter of minutes.

2. **In the Subscriptions blade, select your Free Trial subscription.**

Before you click Free Trial, notice the information that the Subscriptions blade gives you: Your account role is Account Admin, and the status of the account is Active. So far, so good.

3. **Examine the various subscription management tools.**

Figure 1-7 shows the following tools:

- *A:* The Overview setting shows you the Essentials panel (shown on the right side of the figure), where you see details on your subscription status and metadata.

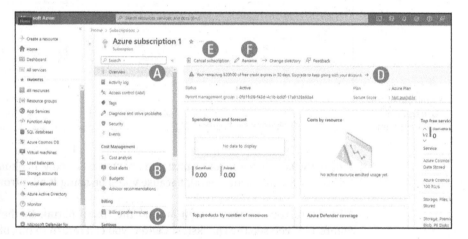

FIGURE 1-7: Viewing your Free Trial subscription in the Azure portal.

- *B:* The Cost Management settings enable you to report on the Azure service you've consumed and/or are currently consuming.

- *C:* The Payment Methods setting enables you to change the payment method associated with your subscription.

- *D:* Upgrade Subscription enables you to convert your free trial to a PAYG subscription. If you convert before you spend the $200 or reach the 30 days, you keep your credit before the cost meter starts ticking.

- *E:* The Manage button takes you to the Azure Account Center, where you can print past service invoices, set billing alerts, and change the account that owns the subscription.

- *F:* The Cancel Subscription button enables you to . . . well, cancel your subscription. What else?

- *G:* The Rename button enables you to change the logical name of your subscription from Free Tier to something more meaningful to you and your organization.

If you decide to upgrade your subscription, Microsoft asks whether you want to buy a monthly support plan. As with the PAYG subscription, you can cancel a support plan at any time with no penalty. The three support tiers, each of which has a fixed monthly cost, are

>> **Developer plan:** Support for trial and nonproduction environments. You can interact with Azure support staff members from 9 a.m. to 5 p.m. in your time zone, with an initial response time of less than 8 business hours. As of this writing in August 2022, the monthly cost is $29.

>> **Standard plan:** Support for production environments. You receive 24/7 technical support and a response within 2 hours. As of this writing, the Standard plan costs $100 per month.

>> **Professional Direct plan:** Support for businesses that rely heavily on Azure. You get 24/7 technical support and a response for critical issues within one hour. As of this writing, Microsoft charges $1,000 per month for this support plan.

>> **Premier plan:** This support tier is aimed at large enterprises that require extensive support and service globally within minutes. Microsoft also provides architectural support not available in any other tier. Acquiring a Premier plan requires you reach out to Microsoft or an authorized partner.

REMEMBER

Unless you have an EA with Microsoft, you can cancel your Azure subscription at any time. Be aware, however, that you're required to delete all your resources before Microsoft will let you cancel the subscription.

Staying Current with Azure

Unlike the old days of installing a piece of software on your computer and waiting a year (or longer) for the latest update — that you had to purchase — cloud computing infrastructure updates are transparent. Suppose your organization decides to suddenly upload 2TB of data to one of its databases. Back when folks used CDs and DVDs to maintain backups, you'd need to make sure that there was enough capacity for what is now an insignificant storage change. Because cloud computing platforms such as Azure are elastic, your storage needs can go up and down quickly, and the user can focus on other system responsibilities. Sure, you will certainly get an invoice for the extra capacity, but you'll never have to worry about not having enough space.

Also constantly evolving are those core applications and resources that Microsoft is responsible for within the cloud. Microsoft introduces updates to its cloud almost daily. Most changes are to fix development bugs or patch up security snafus. The nice thing for you, the cloud consumer, is that you don't have to wait for these changes; they just happen transparently. Your monthly service charges include the constant updates.

Customizing the Azure user experience

Each time you add a new resource or service, the Azure portal user experience changes. You'll see new icons, dashboards, KPIs, and blades to navigate between features. For example, notice that Figure 1-1 had a completely different user experience than when you opened the new subscription. The account shown in Figure 1-1 has been operating for several years versus the one shown in Figure 1-7. In addition, the user experience was personalized.

You can create a personalized look and feel by following these steps:

1. **Click the gear icon located in the top-right corner of the Azure portal.**

   A page titled Portal Settings is launched.

2. **On the left side, locate the secondary navigation.**

   Several options are available in this list including Appearance + startup views and Language + region. These two options enable you customize the look and feel of the portal as well as the display language.

3. **Click the Appearance + startup view.**

   Once the Appearance + startup view appears, you can configure the Menu Behaviors, Theme, Contrast, Focus Navigation, and Startup View, as shown in Figure 1-8.

   You can modify the user experience to best suit your desired portal environment.

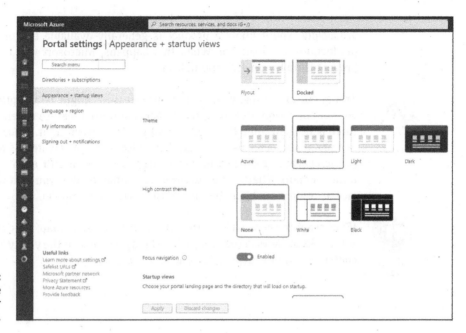

FIGURE 1-8:
Configuring the
Azure portal user
experience.

Rolling with the Azure updates

I've already established that when you use a cloud provider such as Microsoft Azure, your hosting environment is updated frequently. The frequency of updates is determined by criticality and features. The term *service lifecycle* is more appropriate to describe the frequency, as there is a methodology used before features become fully available for public consumption. Of course, Microsoft won't put the emergency security patches or critical bug fixes through a long-haul process. But when there is a new service or resource offering being introduced, the cycle is regimented.

**TECHNICAL
STUFF**

Every Azure resource or service starts with a development phase formally called a *private preview.* The Azure Development team collects and defines the requirements on a rolling basis to support a viable product. Most users will not have access to development-level work, as Microsoft selects targeted cloud workloads to evaluate such features. Once the development team is confident in a feature, the service is released to the public as a beta. Also known as *public preview,* the public can access and experience the feature in its entirety and are given the opportunity to provide feedback. During the public preview, Microsoft does not charge users to use and test the feature, as the community and development team use that feedback to work out product kinks. The final step in the Azure update cycle is *general availability.* You'll know a product is generally available because it becomes a production-ready service. When this happens, Microsoft will indicate that the product is no longer free and in beta.

WARNING

Trying out and integrating a shiny new feature might be tempting for you and your organization. However, remember that until a feature is generally available, there is no guarantee the product will get the "green light." Make sure to check out any products terms and conditions. Also, any preview item is excluded from a Service Level Agreement. In some cases, previews aren't even covered by customer support. That's why Microsoft recommends that you wait to deploy a service or resource publicly for any mission-critical workload.

ON THE WEB

If you want to see what's on the Microsoft Azure road map, check out the Microsoft Books of News, a road map of features presented at the yearly Microsoft Ignite conference. Go to `https://aka.ms/ignite-book-of-news`.

IN THIS CHAPTER

» Getting to know Azure Resource Manager

» Familiarizing yourself with Azure regions

» Learning the Azure management tools

» Connecting to Azure from the desktop

Chapter **2**

Exploring Azure Resource Manager

I n this chapter, I take you on a quick drive through the nuts and bolts of the back-end services that make up the Microsoft Azure public cloud. As you read this chapter, you may find the discussion of REST APIs a bit overwhelming (and too much in the coding weeds). But stay with me, please! No matter what level Azure professional you are — Azure newbie, Microsoft MVP, or somewhere in between — you will be exposed to APIs in the Azure Resource Manager. After all, the API is the underpinning to all Azure-based services.

Introducing Azure Resource Manager

Azure Resource Manager (most often abbreviated ARM and pronounced like the body part) is the deployment and management service underneath Microsoft Azure. Every action you take in Azure, regardless of the tool you use, calls the ARM REST APIs. The Azure portal is simply a web front end that abstracts ARM REST API requests and responses.

"What's a REST API, Jack?" you rightly ask. I answer that question next.

REST APIs

An application programming interface (API) is a software specification that allows interaction with other software applications. Twitter, for example, publishes its API specification to allow software developers to tap Twitter services for use in their own applications (fetching tweets, making posts, and so forth).

Representational state transfer (REST) is a software development methodology that defines how web-based APIs can communicate by using Hypertext Transfer Protocol (HTTP).

HTTP has five primary methods (also called *operations* or *verbs*) that a REST API call can undertake:

>> GET: Retrieve resource details

>> POST: Create a new resource

>> PUT: Update a resource (replace the existing resource)

>> PATCH: Incrementally update a resource (modify existing resource)

>> DELETE: Remove a resource

TECHNICAL STUFF

Four of the aforementioned HTTP methods deal with the four primary data operations in information technology: Create, Read, Update, and Delete. Because we in IT like puns and juvenile humor, we call these operations CRUD for short.

Hey, at this point don't get bogged down with the HTTP verbs. I describe them here only to give you fuller context.

Now I'll relate this REST API stuff to Microsoft Azure. ARM's REST API fundamentally defines Azure products and services, and specifies how you can use them within your subscriptions. Every individual artifact you deploy in Azure represents a resource. Thus, virtual machines (VMs), web applications, databases, storage accounts, and key vaults are defined in the ARM REST API as discrete resource types.

Resource providers

In the ARM REST API definition, a *resource provider* is a service that delivers a specific Azure product. The Azure resource provider's namespace is arranged hierarchically.

To illustrate this namespace, consider the resource ID for one of my Azure storage accounts, named az4dum:

```
/subscriptions/e08e12eb-bf01-4a01-aef3-74544faccc21/resourceGroups/DummiesBook/
    providers/az4dum/Microsoft.Storage/storageAccounts/az4dum
```

First of all, notice the forward slashes and the way the resource path resembles a Uniform Resource Identifier (URI). That's intentional because all REST APIs are web-based and use HTTP or HTTPS URIs exclusively. You can read the storage-account resource ID from left to right to traverse the ARM REST API namespace:

>> subscriptions: The node below slash (/), which is the top-level root of the ARM REST API hierarchy.

>> e08e12eb ...: The subscription ID of the subscription that hosts my storage account.

>> resourceGroups: The resource group namespace. The resource group is the primary deployment unit in Azure.

>> DummiesBook: The resource group that hosts my storage account.

>> providers: The resource provider level.

>> Microsoft.Storage: The resource provider that governs Azure storage services (of which the storage account is but one service).

>> storageAccounts: The resource group that hosts my storage account.

>> az4dum: A reference to the actual storage account.

TIP

If you've worked with REST APIs, you may want to use a third-party product such as Postman (https://www.getpostman.com) to interact with the ARM REST API. If you haven't, point your browser to https://resources.azure.com, sign in with your subscription owner account, and browse the ARM REST API and your Azure subscription resources graphically. Figure 2-1 shows the interface.

As I mention earlier, I have a storage account called az4dum located in a resource group named DummiesBook. Here's how to "walk the tree" by using Azure Resource Explorer:

1. **On the left navigation bar, expand Subscriptions, and then expand your subscription.**

   In Figure 2-1, I've expanded my subscription.

2. **Expand resourceGroups and then expand your target resource group.**

3. **Expand providers, expand Microsoft.Storage, and then select your storage account.**

4. **In the main screen, browse the JavaScript Object Notation (JSON) output that defines your storage account.**

   In Figure 2-1, the az4dum storage account is the only resource in my DummiesBook resource group, so it's easy to find the resource definition in the JSON output. Note the references to the HTTP verbs at the top of the screen: GET, PUT, POST, and DELETE.

FIGURE 2-1:
The Azure
Resource
Explorer allows
you to view the
ARM REST API
directly.

WARNING

Although Azure Resource Explorer puts you in read-only mode by default, note the Read Only button at the top of the interface. If you have sufficient privilege, you could go beyond simple GET requests and perform PUTs, POSTs, and DELETEs on your Azure resources, so be careful!

JSON

RESTful APIs use JSON (ordinarily pronounced *jay-sahn*) data format to encode all request and response data, which is certainly true in ARM.

Douglas Crockford invented JSON in 2001 as a way to represent data in a relatively compact, human-readable form. JSON documents are plain-text and can be opened in any text editor.

TIP

If you're an Azure professional, I recommend using Visual Studio Code as your text editor.

JSON elements consist of a comma-separated list of key/value pairs. Check out this JSON snippet from the Azure storage account I discussed previously. Pay attention to how much you can learn about this resource by viewing a small amount of code. Don't worry about understanding it yet — you're just getting started!

```
"sku": {
  "name": "Standard_LRS",
  "tier": "Standard"
},
"kind": "StorageV2",
"id": "/subscriptions/e08e12eb-bf01-4a01-aef3-74544faccc21 /resourceGroups/
  DummiesBook/
            providers/Microsoft.Storage/
            storageAccounts/az4dum",
  "name": "az4dum",
  "type": "Microsoft.Storage/storageAccounts",
  "location": "eastus",
```

All deployments in Azure are recorded in JSON format. These ARM templates, as they're known, make it much easier to create reliable, repeatable Azure environments.

In the Azure portal in Figure 2-2, for example, you can see the az4dum storage account I created in my testing environment. I then select the Export template setting, and click Download to capture the storage account's ARM template definition. You can see this process in action in Figure 2-2.

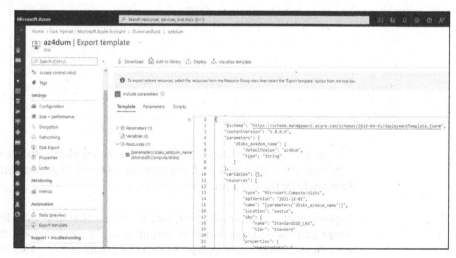

FIGURE 2-2: You can locate and download the JSON source code behind every Azure resource.

I can't overstate how important it is to get comfortable with JSON in general and ARM templates in particular. The good news is that over the course of this book, you'll get lots of practical experience with both.

ARM management scopes

In a computer's file system, you have a defined hierarchy: volume, folder, sub-folders, and files. Permissions you set at a higher scope flow by inheritance to lower scopes. Giving an assigned user read-only access to your server's E drive, for example, results in that user inheriting read-only access to all the E drive's folders, subfolders, and files.

Inheritance and multilayer scopes work much the same way in Azure. All your resource groups are contained within an Azure subscription, and you can roll one or more subscriptions up into a management group. These management scopes (see Figure 2-3) simplify granting role-based access control authorization assignments and governance policies to your resources and, ultimately, their users.

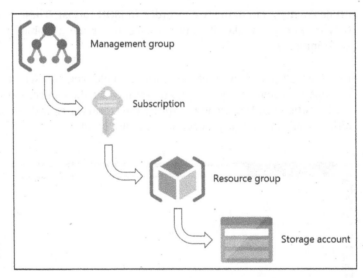

FIGURE 2-3: Azure management scopes.

Let me give you an example of how an Azure administrator can combine these management scopes. Roll with me here for now; you'll understand these concepts intimately by the time you finish the book.

Suppose that an administrator needs to ensure that any VMs deployed by other Azure admins occur within only corporate authorized regions. But I'm going to complicate this scenario by saying that the organization's VMs are spread across

44 resource groups in 6 subscriptions. Whoa! Even with inheritance, the management overhead here would be a smidge overwhelming

But the situation isn't as complex as it seems. Why? The administrator creates a single management group that includes the six corporate subscriptions. The same administrator can then create single Azure policy defining the resource deployment rule and overarching security requirements. After, you can then associate the policy with the management group. The Azure Policy flows by inheritance through its enclosed subscriptions and resource groups to the existing and future VMs, which is powerful and efficient management.

Getting Familiar with Azure Regions

In public cloud computing, you store your resources in Microsoft's physical infrastructure. (See Chapter 1.) This infrastructure consists of an enormous data-center network spread around the world.

This worldwide web (as it were) of Azure data centers means that you can place your cloud resources geographically close to your customers, thereby giving them low-latency, high-performance connections to your applications. As of July 2022, Microsoft Azure had 59 regions in operation and a further 19 under development, totaling 78 by the end of 2022. The Microsoft Azure regions operate over 200 physical data centers in various global locations. In terms of geography, the sprawl currently stands at more than 140 countries.

ON THE WEB

Want to find the perfect Azure geography for your cloud project, go to https://azure.microsoft.com/global-infrastructure/geographies.

Availability zones

When you host customer-facing services in Azure, high availability should be uppermost in your mind. What plans do you have if a failure occurs in your home region's data center?

Microsoft has been gradually rolling out availability zones throughout its region map. Essentially, an *availability zone* allows you to place replica VMs in different data centers in the same region. In other words, availability zones represent separate locations within a single Azure region.

Figure 2-4 illustrates this concept, with two identically configured web server VMs are placed in two availability zones in my home region. An Azure load balancer in front of the VMs makes both of them available under the same IP address or Domain Name System host name. With this setup, if one of my VMs goes offline (through my own error or a Microsoft data-center outage), my service remains online and functional.

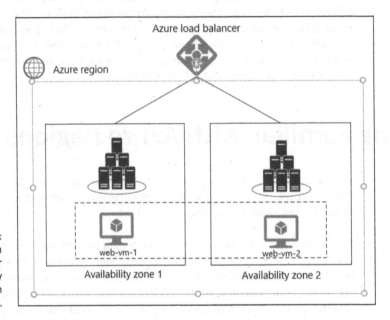

FIGURE 2-4: Providing high availability for replica VMs by placing them in availability zones.

In Azure nomenclature, *region* and *location* are interchangeable.

REMEMBER

TECHNICAL STUFF

OPERATIONAL SECURITY

You may notice that I'm being intentionally vague in describing the network of data centers that make up Microsoft's global regions. This vagueness is by design, due to an information security principal known as *operational security*. Customers trust Microsoft to keep its regional data centers secure on physical and logical levels, so the company doesn't publish any more information on data-center internals than required to be worthy of trust.

In my career, I can count on two hands the number of Microsoft employees I've met who have visited an Azure data center. The practical guidance is that you should place your Azure resources in the regions that are physically closest to your customers. Furthermore, for high availability and to reach different audiences, you can redundantly host resources across multiple regions.

Geographies

Microsoft organizes its regions into geographies to support corporate compliance and data residency requirements.

Sovereign regions

Azure is called a public cloud service because most of its regions and services are available for purchase by the general public. That said, Microsoft hosts special regions called government clouds or sovereign clouds for exclusive use by particular governmental bodies around the world (see Chapter 1). In order to procure services and gain resource commitments within a sovereign region, you must be affiliated with a government agency. Additionally, a limited number of Microsoft partners are able to sell cloud services in sovereign regions.

Azure Government regions are inaccessible (invisible) to nongovernment employees. Examples of Microsoft sovereign regions, availability zones, and data centers for the governments include the United States, China, and Germany.

Paired regions

Earlier in this chapter, I mention that you can place redundant copies of your Azure services in more than one region for failover redundancy. When you do so, you should first determine Microsoft's designated paired region to ensure minimal latency. Microsoft builds additional high-speed network connectivity between paired regions, which assures customers that their multiregional deployments won't suffer undue latency.

ON THE WEB

Search `https://docs.microsoft.com/azure` for the article "Business continuity and disaster recovery (BCDR): Azure Paired Regions," which includes the master list of paired regions.

TIP

In my Azure consultancy, I recommend that customers test the latency between their location and Azure by visiting Azure Speed Test 2.0 at `https://azurespeedtest.azurewebsites.net`. You may find that the lowest-latency Azure region wasn't what you thought it was.

Introducing the Azure Management Tools

It's time to become familiar with the most common Azure management tools. All the step-by-step procedures I describe in this book assume that you're working on a Windows 10 workstation, but you can accomplish nearly every task in this book on a macOS or Linux system.

Azure portal

The Azure portal (https://portal.azure.com) is a responsive web application that forms the basic graphical administration platform in Azure. Figure 2-5 shows the Azure portal.

>> **Page header (A):** The top navigation bar is sometimes called *global navigation* because these controls are available everywhere in the Azure portal. Open the Favorites menu.

>> **Global search (B):** Search for any Azure resource. The search results include documentation links.

>> **Cloud Shell (C):** Open Azure Cloud Shell to perform command-line Azure work.

>> **Global subscription filter (D):** Display a subset of your Azure subscriptions to make your Azure portal view lists easier to browse.

>> **Notifications (E):** Check the progress of current and past deployments.

>> **Your account (F):** Log out, switch directories, and edit your account profile.

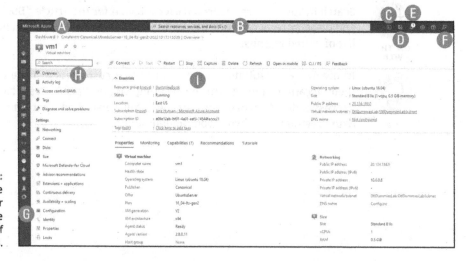

FIGURE 2-5: The Azure portal is your administrative base of operations.

>> **Favorites (G):** Load up your most frequently used Azure services.

>> **Resources pane (H):** Use the search box to find the setting that you need to configure.

>> **Configuration blade (I):** *Blade* refers to the detail screens in which you do your Azure work. The horizontal scroll bar helps you move from side to side.

REMEMBER

Your Azure portal customization affects only your user account. Your colleagues will have their own favorites lists, subscription filters, custom dashboards, and so forth.

TIP

Responsive web applications rearrange themselves dynamically to accommodate different web browsers and screen sizes. Accessing the full portal on a smartphone usually isn't fun, however. Microsoft makes mobile versions of the Azure portal available for iOS and Android mobile devices. You can perform most administration tasks in this mobile app, including accessing Cloud Shell.

Azure PowerShell

The Azure portal is fun, but what if you're asked to deploy 10, 100, or 1,000 VMs? You certainly don't want to perform repetitive actions by clicking-clicking-clicking in the Azure portal. For administrative automation, use Azure PowerShell. PowerShell is an automation language that you can use to perform any repetitive task in Windows Server, macOS, Linux, Azure, AWS . . . you get the picture.

If you haven't begun to skill up on PowerShell, today's the day; you need to have at least intermediate-level PowerShell skills to be fully productive in Azure. Follow these steps to get the Az modules installed on your Windows 10 or 11 workstation:

1. **Open an elevated PowerShell console.**

   In Windows, open the Start menu, type PowerShell, right-click the icon, and choose Run as Administrator from the shortcut menu.

2. **Install the Az modules from the PowerShell Gallery.**

   Microsoft operates a curated PowerShell module repository called (appropriately enough) the PowerShell Gallery. Run the following command to download and install Azure PowerShell:

   ```
   Install-Module -Name -Az -Verbose -Force
   ```

   Technically, the -Verbose and -Force switch parameters are optional, but I suggest using -Verbose so that you can read detailed command output, and -Force to upgrade the modules if you already have them installed on your computer.

3. **Update your local help.**

   PowerShell doesn't ship with local help by default because the documentation changes so rapidly. Make sure that you have the most recent PowerShell command help at your disposal by using this command:

   ```
   Update-Help -Force -ErrorAction SilentlyContinue
   ```

   The `-ErrorAction SilentlyContinue` bit suppresses any errors or glitches that may occur during the help-file download. For a variety of reasons, you should expect to see an occasional error when running `Update-Help`. (Someone on the PowerShell team may have forgotten to create a help article for a command, for example.)

4. **Sign into your Azure subscription.**

   Run the following command to generate a Sign In to Your Account dialog box. After you authenticate, you'll be brought back to the PowerShell console, all logged in and ready to rock.

   ```
   Connect-AzAccount
   ```

5. **To close your PowerShell connection, close the console window.**

TIP

You'll need to use the aforementioned steps every time you want to manage Azure with PowerShell. However, you can automate Azure PowerShell sign-in by using a special Azure Active Directory (AD) account called a service principal. For details, see the Azure documentation article "Create an Azure Service Principal with Azure PowerShell" at https://docs.microsoft.com/powershell/azure/create-azure-service-principal-azureps?view=azps-8.0.0.

Azure CLI and Azure Cloud Shell

As a cloud administrator, you'll quickly gain a handle on how to utilize the command-line interface within Azure. Unlike other public cloud-hosting platforms, Microsoft offers two options: one inside the Azure portal and a desktop-based alternative. The Azure command-line interface (CLI) is your nifty, cross-platform command-line interface for Azure. Some Azure administrators and developers prefer the Azure CLI to the traditional use of Azure PowerShell. The predominant reason is the speed at which changes can be made, especially in interactive mode. Another reason is that the learning curve is a smidgen easier given that your tool is inside the Azure portal, not another tool in the kitchen sink.

In this book, you work with the Azure CLI from within Azure Cloud Shell. Cloud Shell is a browser-based command-line environment that gives you access to

PowerShell, Azure CLI, and a bunch of other administrative and development tools. For those of you who are still interested in learning how to install Azure CLI on the desktop, don't fret! I show you how to do so later in this chapter.

Follow these steps to start getting acquainted with Azure Cloud Shell and the Azure CLI:

1. **On the global navigation bar in the Azure portal, click Cloud Shell.**

   The You Have No Storage Mounted dialog box opens.

2. **Select your Azure subscription, and click Create Storage.**

   The first time you start Cloud Shell, you're required to specify a storage account. You use the storage account to store all your Cloud Shell resources (modules, scripts, and so forth).

   Click Show Advanced Settings if you want to use an existing storage account or if you desire full control of the storage account's name and region.

   You need to specify whether you want to start with Bash or PowerShell. I suggest that you go with PowerShell.

3. **On the Cloud Shell toolbar, ensure that PowerShell is the current environment.**

   You can do this by inspecting the first element on the Azure Cloud Shell toolbar. Note that you can switch between the Bash and PowerShell environments simply by making a choice from this menu.

   You can start your Cloud Shell session from a PowerShell session or a bash shell session. These steps are in the PowerShell environment.

4. **Run Get-CloudDrive to see your cloud drive information.**

   The command tells you everything you need to know about where your Cloud Shell files are. Your cloud drive points to a file share in the designated Azure storage account.

5. **Type az interactive to start an interactive Azure CLI session.**

6. **Answer yes or no to the request to send telemetry information to Microsoft.**

   Be patient the first time you start the Azure CLI interactive environment. It normally takes a minute or longer to fully initialize.

7. **Type the following command to view your available storage accounts:**

   ```
   az storage account list -o table
   ```

As you type, pay attention to the following behaviors in Azure CLI, which I think are extraordinarily helpful:

- Azure CLI provides autocomplete drop-down menus that help you complete commands. Take advantage of these menus. Press Tab to accept the highlighted option, or use the arrow keys to select an alternative.

- In the middle of the screen, Azure CLI provides inline documentation as you type.

- Azure CLI provides JSON output by default, but in this case, specify tabular format instead. Then run az configure to specify table or another default output format that better suits your comfort.

8. **To exit Cloud Shell, close the pane.**

TECHNICAL STUFF

Cloud Shell is so fast because Microsoft stages Docker containers in its global content delivery network. Azure uses your client IP address and geolocation to connect you to the Cloud Shell container nearest you, which offers the fastest connection.

Azure SDKs

As discussed earlier in this chapter, a REST API is an HTTP-based interface that allows two software systems to communicate, and the Azure portal, PowerShell, and the Azure CLI are ways to *abstract* (hide the details of) the underlying ARM REST API.

For software developers, software development kits (SDKs) represent yet another API abstraction layer. As of this writing, actually, Azure SDKs are available for the following programming languages and frameworks:

» Android	» PHP
» Go	» Python
» iOS	» Ruby
» Java	» Swift
» .NET	» Windows
» Node.js	» Xamarin

An Azure SDK provides the project templates and code libraries you need to interact with Azure services. In this book, I use Visual Studio 2022 to work with Azure SDKs. As shown in Figure 2-6, all you have to do is enable the Azure development workload; Visual Studio takes care of the rest of the setup.

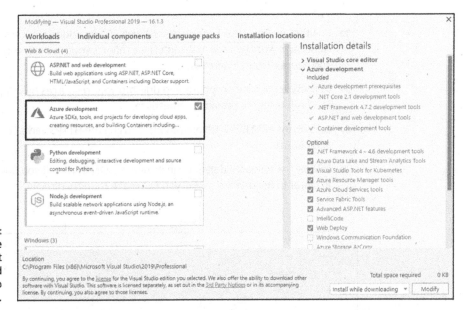

FIGURE 2-6:
Enable the Azure
development
workload
in Visual Studio
2022.

ON THE WEB

If you're new to Visual Studio, you may want to get more detailed instructions on modifying installed workloads. See the Microsoft documentation article "Modify Visual Studio" at https://docs.microsoft.com/visualstudio/install/modify-visual-studio?view=vs-2019.

Incidentally, if you're thinking, "Hey, I'm not a developer; I don't want to pay for Visual Studio!" hang on a second. Microsoft makes Visual Studio 2022 Community Edition free of charge for testing and development. Both Windows and macOS versions are available.

ARM REST API

You can get down to the "bare metal" of the ARM REST API if you want to. Figure 2-7 shows Azure Resource Explorer (https://resources.azure.com), a browser-based interface to the ARM REST API.

The annotations are as follows:

» **A:** Choose the Azure AD to which you want to attach.

» **B:** Set the environment to Read Only (the default) or Read/Write. Be careful when you work in Read/Write mode, because you're operating directly on your Azure resources.

>> **C:** Although Resource Explorer uses a well-known address, access is authenticated, and what you see in the interface reflects your user account's Azure AD and Azure resource permissions.

>> **D:** Browse your subscriptions and drill into your resources by using the ARM REST API resource provider namespace.

>> **E:** Perform ARM REST API operations by using the HTTPS verbs GET, PUT, POST, and DELETE.

>> **F:** View the resource definition in its native JSON format. If you put Resource Explorer in Read/Write mode, you can make changes directly.

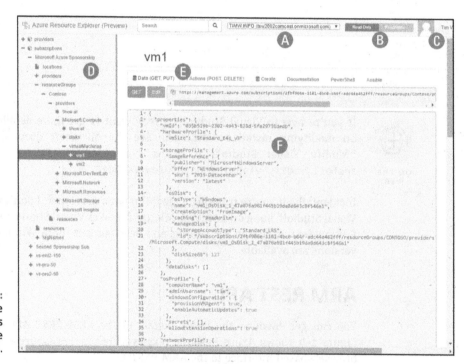

FIGURE 2-7:
Azure Resource
Explorer gives
you access to the
ARM APIs.

WARNING

As many people, including the folks in the open-source community, often say, "with great power comes great responsibility."

You may wonder when and why you'd ever need to interact with Azure at the basic REST API level. This type of interaction is more common than you think, however. Maybe you'll be troubleshooting resource behavior and can't reach the control you need in the Azure portal or another abstraction layer. Or perhaps you're writing your own API and need to know how to structure ARM REST API calls for your own use.

Azure Storage Explorer

It should not surprise you that the secret sauce in Azure is storage. Microsoft Azure Cloud Administrators sometime obsess over how to handle storage. If many people have their hand in the proverbial Azure pot, containing the environment can be just as difficult as managing the old rusty filing cabinet in your office. One of the most significant requests within the Microsoft enterprise community was for a tool that allows IT to oversee storage operations. Microsoft answered these requests with the introduction of Azure Storage Explorer, a GUI-based tool that an IT professional can use to handle the storage operations in the cloud.

Storage Explorer lets an administrator manage their cloud accounts on a Windows, macOS, and Linux desktop. If you've used an FTP GUI-style interface, then you should be familiar with how to connect. Notice in Figure 2-8 that there are a variety of resource types an administrator can use to create a data connection to review the contents of the storage. The type of storage is not just limited to that on Azure, either; it can be local, attached, or an Azure account. An administrator can even review the contents of a data lake if configured.

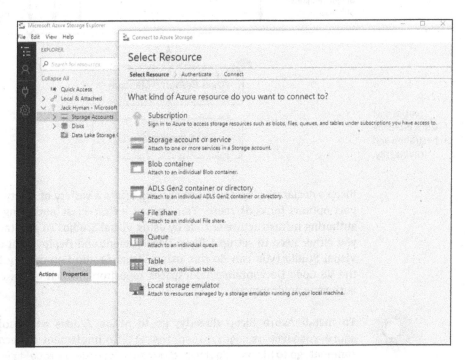

FIGURE 2-8:
Azure Storage
Explorer.

ON THE WEB

Interested in downloading and how to configure the Azure Storage Explorer for your environment? Go to `https://azure.microsoft.com/features/storage-explorer`.

Azure Bicep

What is a Microsoft product without some sort of specialized language, right? Microsoft created a domain-specific language (DSL) for Azure called Bicep. With Bicep, the administrator applies a declarative syntax to deploy those Azure resources (you guessed it, the APIs among the resources), to Azure-specific infrastructure. You or other administrators on your team can use the repeatable file as needed in the development lifecycle of your Azure instance to stand up resources, literally on a whim. The best part is that the resources are deployed consistently — not as one-offs. Notice in Figure 2-9 how a single Azure Bicep file consumes various nontemplated infrastructure as code assets that would be a part of Azure Resource Manager and potentially several providers. The Bicep file, though, handles the deployment as a single asset.

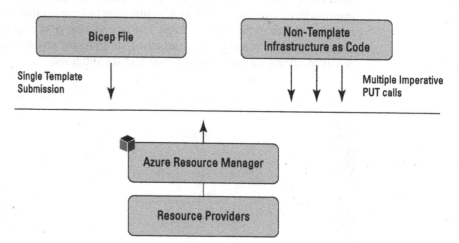

FIGURE 2-9: Azure Bicep file orchestration and modularity.

Bicep's declarative syntax is concise and offers a variety of safety types and support options for code reuse. You can get a first-class authoring experience for authoring infrastructure as code by using Visual Studio. To get started with Bicep, you either need to set up a Bicep Development and Deployment environment in Visual Studio (you can do this using Visual Studio Community Edition) or use the VS Code Devcontainer/Codespaces repository, which offers a preconfigured authoring environment.

TIP

To install Azure Bicep directly, go to `https://docs.microsoft.com/azure/azure-resource-manager/bicep/install`. To implement a preconfigured environment, go to `https://github.com/Azure/vscode-remote-try-bicep`.

REMEMBER

Bicep is not your general-purpose programming language. It is called domain-specific for a reason. It is not intended to write fancy applications. Bicep code does one thing: declare Azure resources and resource properties without having to write a whole sequence of commands to create an itty-bitty resource.

Installing Azure CLI on the Desktop

Some cloud administrators prefer to connect to Azure and execute administrative commands for Azure resources on their local systems versus using the Azure Cloud Shell. You can always use the Azure CLI for Windows from a browser or run CLI from inside a Docker container. When trying to minimize the use of the web browser but still get the functionality of command line (Cmd), Bash, Windows PowerShell, and PowerShell, an administrator can resort to the Azure CLI for Desktop. There are several flavors including a Windows distribution installed via MSI, a Linux distribution installed via Windows Subsystem, or a Mac installation.

ON THE WEB

Looking to download the Azure CLI Desktop Installer? Go to `https://docs.microsoft.com/cli/azure/install-azure-cli`.

TIP

Just because you are getting a 4-for-1 deal doesn't mean all tools are equal. If you are looking to access resources using a syntax similar to Bash scripting or primarily working with Linux, Azure CLI is more suitable for your needs. PowerShell is the perfect fit for those users who use Windows system commands because the syntax follows a verb-noun naming scheme. Data is returned as an object.

2

Deploying Infrastructure Services to Microsoft Azure

Chapter 3

Managing Storage in Azure

S torage is an example of a universal service in the Microsoft Azure Cloud. Regardless of what kind of workload you're running — virtual machines (VMs), app service, functions, machine learning, or whatever — you're likely to require persistent object storage. By the end of this chapter, you'll have a solid grasp of the Azure storage account: what it is, how it works, how to deploy it, and how to store and retrieve different data types.

Understanding Azure Storage Data Types

The Azure storage account represents a multipurpose container resource that provides highly available, persistent storage for three primary data types: unstructured, semistructured, and structured.

Unstructured data

Unstructured data is data that has no schema enforcing it. Think of *binary large objects* (blobs) as you would files, virtual hard drives, document files, and media files. All these objects are file-storage objects with any particular format and contents.

Although the term *blob* encompassed the word *large*, a blob object is a file of any size, whether it's a 1K text file or a 120GB virtual hard disk file.

Semistructured data

Semistructured data doesn't have the column-row arrangement that relational data does, but it's not as freeform as pure binary unstructured data. The table service in the Azure storage account is semistructured in the form of key/value data pairs.

NoSQL databases are an example of semistructured data. As I discuss in Chapter 9, Cosmos DB is Azure's principal NoSQL database product.

Structured data

If you've worked with any relational database system, you understand *structured data* — data that is decomposed into one or more tables in which a particular data type binds each column. So far, I've explained that an Azure storage account stores unstructured and semistructured data. But what about structured data?

As it happens, the Azure storage account doesn't have a structured data storage option. Instead, you need to use one of Microsoft's relational databases. Azure has placed all relational database solutions into the Platform as a Service (PaaS) products bucket if you utilize the database as a dedicated resource. If you utilize a database inside your VM, it becomes Infrastructure as a Service (IaaS).

Examples of structured databases in the Azure ecosystem include Azure SQL Database and Azure Database for MySQL Servers. And I will talk about these platforms at length later in Chapter 9.

At this point, you understand that an Azure storage account blob service is used for unstructured data, and table service is used for semistructured data. But you should be aware of two additional storage account services:

>> **Queue:** Supports asynchronous message delivery among application components. The service is fast and scalable, with low overhead.

>> **File:** Creates Server Message Block (SMB) and Network File System (NFS)-compatible file shares and accesses them from within or outside Azure.

Working with a Storage Account

Now consider how to plan for Azure storage. The Azure general-purpose storage account includes several configuration options, so you want to make the right decisions for cost savings and security.

Creating a storage account

Before you create your first storage account, you should understand some key facts. First, you need to determine what kind of storage account you need. Here are your choices:

>> **General-purpose v2:** Unless you have a compelling reason to choose otherwise, you should often choose this type because it's the most robust option. It includes all four storage account services: blob, table, queue, and file.

>> **General-purpose v1:** This option mainly supports classic Azure deployments and has fewer features than v2. If you are looking for DevTest storage options to save a few bucks, consider v1.

>> **Blob storage:** This storage account supports only the blob service. You once needed this type to specify access tiers, but now you don't need to choose this storage account type for new deployments.

Next, you have to address the question of performance tiers. Standard storage is less expensive and slower because it uses traditional mechanical hard drives on the Azure back end. Premium storage is more expensive and much faster because the Azure storage fabric uses solid-state drives with no moving parts.

Whether you want to pay extra money for a faster storage account depends on what data you plan to store. If you plan to place database data and log files in a storage account, you probably need the robust, predictable performance of premium storage. For most other data, the standard performance tier should be fine.

 You will want to invest in premium storage if speed and reliability are essential. Why, you ask? You are almost guaranteed to experience superior performance with premium over standard storage when large datasets are involved.

TIP

Finally, you have to determine which storage-account replication option you need. Azure storage is highly available because Microsoft *replicates* (creates exact copies of) your storage account at least three times. Here are your options, from least to most expensive:

>> **Locally redundant storage (LRS):** Microsoft makes three copies of your storage account within a single data center in your home region.

>> **Zone-redundant storage (ZRS):** The three storage account copies are spread among different data centers in your home region.

>> **Georedundant storage (GRS):** Three storage account copies are spread across data centers in your home region, and another three copies are placed in a secondary region chosen by Microsoft. (See Chapter 2 for more information about paired regions.)

>> **Read-access georedundant storage (RA-GRS):** This option is GRS, but you get read-only access to the contents of your secondary storage account.

Your replication option depends on your availability needs, compliance requirements, and so forth.

WARNING

Azure storage provides high availability, which means that your data is durable and not susceptible to loss or deletion. You still need to back up your storage account data, however. Microsoft doesn't do that for you. Just because Azure storage accounts are highly available doesn't mean they're highly recoverable by default.

ON THE WEB

I decided not to discuss Azure resource pricing because that topic is beyond the scope of the book and because prices can change more often than products. For price information, visit https://azure.microsoft.com/pricing.

Table 3-1 summarizes the protection offered by each storage-account replication option.

TABLE 3-1

Replication Protection

Replication Option	Protects
LRS	Storage array within a single data center in your home region
ZRS	A single data center in your home region
GRS	Your home region

When you know which type of storage account you need, you can create a new storage account in the Azure portal. Go to https://portal.azure.com, log in with your subscription owner account, and then follow these steps:

1. **In the Azure portal, navigate to the Storage Accounts blade.**

   You can do this in various ways, but I recommend typing **storage accounts** in the global search box and selecting the appropriate link.

   Don't select Storage Accounts (Classic), which concerns Azure Service Management. This book deals with Azure Resource Manager (ARM).

2. **On the Storage Accounts blade, click Add.**

3. **On the Basics page, specify a subscription and a new or existing resource group.**

4. **Complete the form below Instance details (see Figure 3-1), and click Next to continue.**

   - *Storage Account Name:* This name needs to be globally unique and to contain only lowercase letters and numbers. The maximum length is 24 characters.

   - *Location:* Place the storage account closest to the users who need its resources.

FIGURE 3-1: Creating a general purpose storage account.

- *Performance:* Standard is lower-speed storage, whereas Premium is higher-speed (and more expensive) storage. If you need more predictable input/output performance, choose Standard.

- *Account Kind:* You always want to select general-purpose v2.

- *Replication:* Unless you have a business need for higher availability, locally redundant storage (LRS) is a good starting choice. You can always change your mind later by visiting the storage account's Configuration blade.

- *Access Tier* (default): The Access Tier option may give you a price break, depending on whether you access the storage account data frequently (Hot tier) or infrequently (Cold tier). I talk more about tiers later in this chapter.

5. **On the Networking page, click Next to continue.**

   The Network connectivity blade allows you to configure a service endpoint for the storage account, which integrates the storage account into an Azure virtual network. I talk about service endpoints in Chapter 4.

6. **Complete the form on the Advanced page, as shown in Figure 3-2:**

FIGURE 3-2: Configuring advanced storage account options.

- *Secure Transfer Required:* Leave this option set to Enabled to ensure that you use encrypted HTTPS, not unencrypted HTTP, to access your storage account data.

- *Allow Access From:* Leave this option set to All Networks. Optionally, you can use service endpoints to integrate a storage account into a virtual network.

- *Blob Soft Delete:* Enable this option to create a recycling bin for your deleted blob objects.

- *Hierarchical Namespace:* Leave this option set to Disabled.

7. **On the Tags screen, click Next: Review + Create.**

   Using taxonomic tags is a great way to categorize related Azure resources, but you don't need to worry about tags now.

8. **If validation passes, click Create to submit the deployment to ARM.**

   If you receive a validation error, check the configuration-blade tabs; the one that contains the error should have a dot next to it.

REMEMBER

Don't freak out if the procedures I provide don't match what you see in the Azure portal. The reason is simple: Microsoft is continually tinkering with the portal, updating the user interface and adding or modifying services and settings. The important thing is to understand what you're configuring.

Figure 3-3 shows details on ARM deployment.

FIGURE 3-3:
Watching a
Microsoft Azure
deployment.

The following are some key features to note:

>> Open the Notification menu (A) to check the status of current and recent deployments.

>> Gain access to the deployment's underlying ARM template (B), which is useful for future automated deployments.

>> The Redeploy button (C) is helpful if a deployment fails; you can fix the errors in the ARM template and pick up the deployment where it left off. This important ARM characteristic is called *idempotence*.

>> You can open the resource group associated with the deployment (D) and navigate to the Deployments setting to review this and other deployments, download template definitions, and so forth.

>> This list of granular deployment operations (E) is tremendously helpful for troubleshooting failed deployments.

Using the blob service

Although general-purpose storage accounts have four discrete services intended for different data and object types, most of this chapter focuses on the blob service. However, I briefly discuss each service's value later in the chapter.

The reason for focusing on blob almost exclusively is twofold:

>> This is a beginner's book, and the other three services are intended for a more advanced audience.

>> The blob service is the most frequently used Azure storage account service.

Installing Azure Storage Explorer

Azure Storage Explorer is a free, closed-source, cross-platform desktop application that enables you to interact with your Azure storage accounts.

Go to `https://azure.microsoft.com/features/storage-explorer` (or search for *Azure Storage Explorer* in your favorite search engine), download the program, and install it on your computer. Follow these steps to configure Storage Explorer:

1. **In the Connect to Azure Storage dialog box, select Add an Azure Account, set the Azure environment to Azure, and click Next.**

If the dialog box doesn't appear the first time you start Storage Explorer, click the Add Account button on the Storage Explorer sidebar. (The button's icon looks like an electrical plug.)

2. **Authenticate to Azure, using your administrative account.**

3. **In the Show Resources from These Subscriptions filter, ensure that your target Azure subscription is selected, and click Apply.**

   Because I manage multiple subscriptions, I decided to show you a single account for this example.

Figure 3-4 shows Storage Explorer and the following features:

» Click the Explorer button (A) to browse your storage account(s).

» Click the Manage Accounts button (B) to filter Storage Explorer's subscriptions in Explorer view.

» Click the Add Account button (C) to simultaneously sign in with more than one Azure Active Directory (AD) account.

» Expand general-purpose storage accounts to see their services (D). The navigation works like a File Transfer Protocol client application.

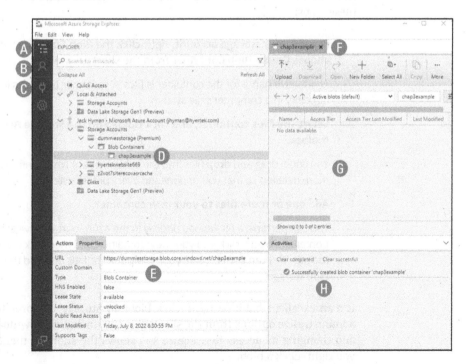

FIGURE 3-4:
Azure Storage
Explorer.

» View the properties of the current selection (E). By default, storage accounts use the following public endpoints for each service:

- Blob service: `https://<storage-acct-name>.blob.core.windows.net/`
- File service: `https://<storage-acct-name>.file.core.windows.net/`
- Queue service: `https://<storage-acct-name>.queue.core.windows.net/`
- Table service: `https://<storage-acct-name>.table.core.windows.net/`

» Each service has its own toolbar (F). The blob service toolbar shown in Figure 3-4 is used for containers and file uploads/downloads, whereas the table service toolbar is used for data import/export and queries.

» This pane (G) provides granular interaction with your storage account.

» The Activities pane (H) shows error, warning, and information messages from Storage Explorer.

TIP

Storage Explorer is also available in the Azure portal. Browse to your storage account, and select the Storage Explorer setting.

Uploading blobs

Now it's time to create a blob container and upload some files to Azure. Follow these steps:

1. **Expand your storage account, right-click the Blob Container node, and choose Create Blob Container from the shortcut menu.**

    An intuitive name for the container is files. A container functions like a directory in a computer's file system.

2. **Select the files container, and click Upload on the Storage Account toolbar.**

    You could drag and drop files into the container, but I'm intentionally being more detailed so that you understand every process step.

3. **Add one or more files to your new container.**

    You can perform a file upload directly in the Azure portal. Navigate to the Containers blade, click into your new container, and then click Upload from the toolbar. You can then browse your computer for files and add them to Azure blob storage.

It's an excellent habit to right-click blobs in Storage Explorer to access handy administrative options from the shortcut menu, including downloading the object and changing its access tier. Figure 3-5 shows the shortcut menu you see when you right-click a blob.

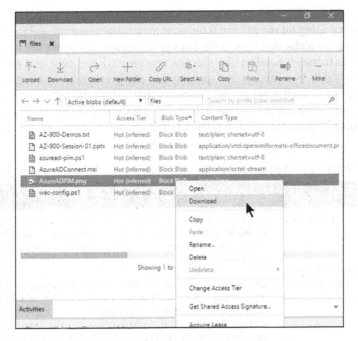

FIGURE 3-5:
Try right-clicking
everything in
Azure Storage
Explorer to see
available options.

TIP

Practice working with blob upload, download, and deletion by using keyboard shortcuts (which you can find at `https://docs.microsoft.com/azure/vs-azure-tools-storage-explorer-accessibility#shortcut-keys`) as well as Storage Explorer's menu and toolbar system. However, make sure to practice with test files and not production resources.

Changing blob access tiers

This section returns to the Azure portal so that you can modify a blob object's access tier. First, it's instructive to understand how Microsoft prices standard-tier storage accounts. You're charged for

>> **Storage volume:** Storage volume represents the amount of data in your blob service.

>> **REST API transactions:** Every time you interact with the blob service, that interaction translates into a read, write, update, or delete REST API call, and Microsoft charges you for each call.

>> **Data egress network traffic:** There's no charge for ingress (upload or inbound) traffic into the storage account, but you pay for egress (download or outbound) data transfer.

Depending on the pricing scheme, it may make sense for you to change the access tier for blobs that have different use scenarios. Azure applies a three-tiered system to how it handles blob storage. The tiers are hot, cool, and archive, as outlined in Table 3-2. Access and pricing are often assumed to be the only difference between each storage tier. However, that is just the difference from the surface. Depending on your stage within the data lifecycle, you'll want to consider the most affordable and accessible pricing option.

TABLE 3-2

Storage Tiers

Storage Tier	Description
Hot access	Hot access is intended for frequently accessed applications and data. Access in this tier is tied to the highest read/write activity volume. While the cost is the highest in the hot access tier, access costs over time are much less expensive.
Cool access	Cool access is intended for data that will be stored for a minimum of 30 days but is likely to be accessed within 3 to 6 months. Examples of data stored in this tier include media files, backup and recovery data, and log files. The price is a bit less than for the hot access tier, but so is instant accessibility and availability of resources. If a user decides to migrate data from the hot to cold tier and vice versa, there is a cost associated with the transfer to the premium tier.
Archive access	Archive access is intended for data that is needed once in a while. If you intend to access the data every 6 to 12 months and don't need to view data on demand, archive storage may be the best option. There are trade-offs for getting affordable storage, though. If you don't intend to access your files for a minimum of 180 days and are willing to pay a sizable surcharge to unthaw your data (especially with large blobs), archive storage may be the best option.

WARNING

While Microsoft has a 99.9 percent availability commitment for hot and cool tier storage, the same is not true for archival storage. Similarly, if you need to access data at a moment's notice, Microsoft commits to providing access within milliseconds. That is far from the case with archival storage, as there is a need to rehydrate data (which is needed when you access data that is not used frequently). Access to archive data may take hours for even the first bit of data to transfer.

TIP

Don't automatically count out archival storage because of its lack of flexibility. Archival storage indeed has a purpose. If you don't intend to access files frequently (say once a year) and you can wait a bit to get your hands on the data, you can save quite a bit. But, your usage patterns over the long term, including storage growth, data access costs, transactional activity, georeplication support, and egress/ingress (outbound/inbound) transfer, should dictate the best storage tier for your blob storage strategy.

To modify the access tier for one of the blobs you uploaded into your files blob container, follow these steps:

1. **In the Azure portal, locate your storage account, and select the Containers setting.**

2. **Browse to the files container, select one of your blobs, and click Change Tier from the toolbar.**

   When you select a blob, Azure shows you all the blob's metadata.

3. **From the Access Tier drop-down menu, choose Archive, and click Save to confirm your changes.**

   I show you the interface in Figure 3-6. The Azure portal should display a message informing you that marking the blob as Archive makes it inaccessible until you explicitly return it to the Hot or Cool tier.

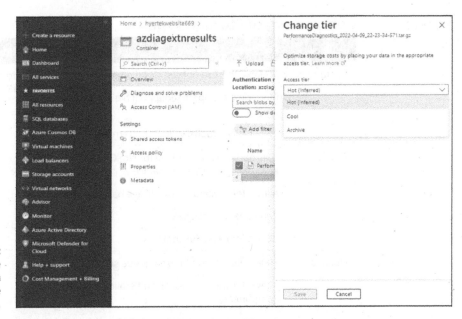

FIGURE 3-6: Changing the access tier of a blob in an Azure storage account.

Archived blobs are inaccessible unless you take them out of the Archive tier. This is a process Microsoft calls "rehydrating." Repeat these steps to rehydrate an archived blob but choose Cool or Hot as the blob's new access tier.

Understanding the file, table, and queue services

So far I've covered blob storage at great lengths. But, blob storage is not the only type of storage service available when using Microsoft Azure. Blob storage may not be the best option for your solution depending on your use case. For example, when you intend to use storage against a REST API, there are alternatives beyond blob such as table and queue storage. All three options are commonly used when implementing a PaaS application. You'll find these storage types behind the scenes in websites and mobile applications, microservices, and serverless applications.

Dedicated or shared storage to run a VM or network running on Windows or Linux is required, and the storage use case is tied to IaaS, which aligns with disk and file storage, not blobs, tables, or queues. Table 3-3 provides a comparison of the different storage types.

TABLE 3-3   ## Comparison of Storage Types

Type	Features	Cloud Architecture
Containers	Scalable REST API-based cloud object storage	Platform as a Service (PaaS)
	Block blobs support sequential file input and output	
	Page blobs support written pattern data	
Tables	Appropriate when looking for NoSQL autoscaling for massive datasets	
	Allows for dynamic data storage based on load	
	Can scale to Petabytes	
	Allows for key/value lookups	
Queues	100% reliable cloud-based queue service	
	Allows for the decoupling and scaling of components	
	Provides message visibility, including timeout alternatives	
	Update messages can protect poor queue data	

Type	Features	Cloud Architecture
Disks	Persistent disk for all Azure IaaS VM types Architecture is based on page blobs Different types of storage available include premium, SSD-based, high IOPS, and low latency options	Infrastructure as a Service (IaaS)
Files	Fully managed cloud-based file shared Maps to a semantic-based file system structure Used most often with legacy applications	

File service

I consider the Azure Files service a sort of Swiss Army knife with numerous use cases. For one thing, you store your Cloud Shell home folder environment in a file share. To get started with Cloud Shell, follow these steps:

1. **On the Azure portal top navigation bar, click Cloud Shell.**

2. **In the You Have No Storage Mounted dialog box, verify your Azure subscription, and click Show Advanced Settings.**

3. **Specify your cloud drive settings.**

   Feel free to reuse your existing storage account. Create a file share with an intuitive name such as cloud-drive. (**Note:** No spaces are allowed in file-share names.)

4. **Click Create Storage to continue.**

5. **When Cloud Shell loads, ensure that you're in the PowerShell environment.**

   If you're not in the PowerShell environment, open the session menu and make the change. The session menu is the first button on the toolbar; it's a drop-down list with two entries: PowerShell and Bash.

6. **Run the command Get-CloudDrive.**

   This command shows the storage account and file share in which your Cloud Shell cloud drive exists.

7. **On the Cloud Shell toolbar, click the Upload/Download Files button, and choose Manage File Share from the drop-down list.**

   Click the Upload button (see Figure 3-7) to upload script files, web pages, and other project artifacts, and then access them from anywhere in the world via Cloud Shell.

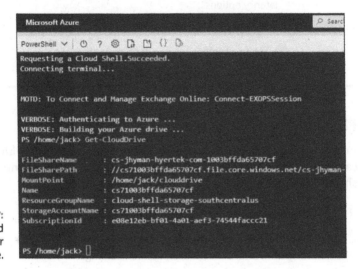

FIGURE 3-7:
Azure Cloud
Shell and your
cloud share.

TIP

Just because you can upload unlimited files does not mean that you want to do so in one fell swoop. Be deliberate as the upload process takes a bit longer than your ordinary file upload/download.

Table service

The Azure storage account table service is a NoSQL key-value store representing semistructured data. As mentioned earlier in this chapter, many developers like programming against table storage because it's easy to work with and is a fast, scalable, and cost-effective way to temporarily or permanently store application data.

ON THE
WEB

Azure table storage is aimed at high-capacity NoSQL storage within a single region. Check the Azure Cosmos DB table API if you're looking for georeplication and worldwide scale. For more information, visit https://docs.microsoft.com/ azure/cosmos-db/table-introduction.

Queue service

Message queuing may seem foreign to you if you're not a software developer. The idea is that if you've separated your application into modular services (so-called *microservices* software architecture), you need a mechanism that enables these services to send and receive message data asynchronously.

Queue storage is a fast, scalable, yet relatively simple messaging platform. If developers need more advanced features (higher scale, guaranteed message delivery, transaction support, and so forth), refer them to the storage queue service's bigger sibling, Azure Service Bus.

Introducing Azure Disk Storage

Before Microsoft introduced Managed Disks, VM virtual hard drives (VHDs) were used in blob service for storage accounts. This arrangement wasn't ideal for many reasons:

>> Mixing VHDs with other, random blobs made the organization more complex.

>> An administrator could quickly delete VM disks accidentally while cleaning out blob storage containers.

>> It's possible to grant the world anonymous access to blob containers. If the container stores VM VHDs, it creates a potentially catastrophic security problem.

>> Storage accounts have a fixed request rate of 20,000 input/output operations per second. If you put too many VHDs in a single storage account, your VM performance is crippled.

With Managed Disks, your VM operating system and data disks are stored and maintained by Microsoft. You're free to do whatever you want with your VHDs, but you don't have to deal with the headaches involved in storage account–based storage.

Before Managed Disks, VM disks were stored in general-purpose storage accounts. This was a recipe for all sorts of potentially dangerous outcomes.

To illustrate how to work with Managed Disks, follow these steps to use Azure Cloud Shell and Azure CLI to create a resource group and VM. Don't worry about the VM details here; I deep-dive into VM care and feeding in this book in Chapter 5.

1. **In the Azure portal, open Cloud Shell.**

   For this exercise, it doesn't matter whether you're in the Bash or PowerShell environment.

2. **Use the Azure command-line interface (CLI) to create a new resource group.**

   You don't have to use the same name and region that I do. Be creative. Don't worry about cost, because you're setting up this environment only for practice. When you finish using it, you can delete it. Here's the code:

   ```
   az group create --name SimpleVM --location eastus
   ```

   Don't be surprised to see the Azure CLI output in JSON (JavaScript Object Notation), the default output format.

TIP

   Run az configure to change your Azure CLI defaults, including specifying table as your default output format.

3. **Run az vm create to create a Windows Server 2016 VM quickly.**

   Usually, I don't recommend this method, because Azure CLI doesn't provide any administrative flexibility. For purposes of this step, however, it's okay.

   In the following code, myPassword is a placeholder; use a strong password instead. Also, type the following command on one line, and ignore my backslashes. The backslashes are visual indications that the command has been broken into multiple lines to make it easier to read:

   ```
   az vm create \
   --resource-group SimpleVM \
   --name WindowsVM \
   --image win2016data center \
   --admin-username azureuser \
   --admin-password myPassword
   ```

4. **When deployment is complete, navigate to the Disks blade.**

   A fast way is to type **disks** in the Azure portal's global search box.

5. **Select your disk in the list, and inspect its properties.**

   Figure 3-8 shows some of the cool things you can do with VM disks on the Disks blade in the Azure portal:

   - Set the account type (A). Surprisingly, the quick-create operation chose the more expensive but higher-performing Premium SSD option.
   - Download the VHD to your computer (B).
   - Make a backup copy of the disk (C).

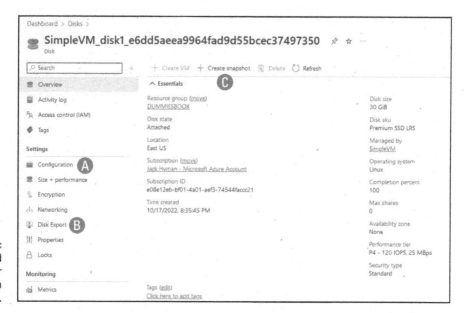

FIGURE 3-8:
Use Managed
Disk storage for
your VMs in
Azure.

WARNING

The associated VM has to be stopped and deallocated for most VM disk activities. Consider this requirement if you need to perform VHD configuration on a production VM.

IN THIS CHAPTER

» Differentiating Azure's virtual
network building blocks

» Deploying and configuring virtual
networks

» Connecting virtual networks

» Configuring Azure Firewalls and VPN
Gateways

» Learning about Azure ExpressRoute

Chapter 4

Planning Your Virtual Network Topology

M icrosoft has invested billions of its dollars into building networking features within Azure. Surprising, right? It shouldn't be for a few reasons:

» Ethernet and TCP/IP internetworking is a complicated subject that's deep enough to build an entire career as a networking professional.

» Software-defined networking in the Azure Cloud differs from on-premises hardware networking.

» The costs and consequences of making a mistake with Azure networking are high.

In this chapter, I cover the foundational concepts of Azure networking. I don't provide the most complete explanation, as there are plenty of long tomes specifically written about Azure Network infrastructure. Here, I talk about the virtual networks options, which form the boundary in which you place your virtual machine (VM) and potentially other Azure services. I also describe the Azure Firewall and Virtual Private Network options, which are critical to the enterprise.

Understanding Virtual Network Components

The *Azure Virtual Network* (VNet) is Azure's strong isolation and communications boundary. A common beginner's mistake is placing VMs on separate VNets and expecting communication between them to be possible by default — because, say, the VNets are in the same Azure region and subscription.

Not true! Although VMs within a single VNet can communicate fine by default (barring firewall deny rules, naturally), no direct communication is possible between VNets without additional administrative intervention.

For now, let's get started with the VNet discussion by looking at the various components of such a network. But first, let's take a quick detour and review all the networking options before we dive too far. Table 4-1 outlines the virtual network communication approaches and their required networking components.

TABLE 4-1   **Types of Network Connectivity**

Networking Approach	Description
Internet	The baseline of all network communications, the Internet is where all resources in a VNet can communicate on an outbound basis. Inbound communication requires that a public IP address be assigned. You are likely going to require a load balancer.
Azure Virtual Network (VNet)	VNets enable you to deploy Azure resources such as a VM, App Service, Azure Kubernetes Service (AKS) container, or a VM Scale Set to a targeted audience.
VNet service endpoints	VNet service endpoints enable you to extend the VNet using a private address space. They identify the specific network connection or any Azure service resource over a direct connection. The big difference here is the ability to secure critical resources such as storage and database VNets.
VNet peering	Peering is a way to connect VNets and enable resources on either side of a VNet to communicate. Network connections can be in the same or different Azure regions.
Point-to-site (P2S) virtual private network (VPN)	A VPN is, by default, an actual P2S network. You can establish a connection between the virtual network and a single computer. You must configure a separate connection if a computer wants to establish connectivity with the virtual network. A P2S connection is appropriate for making a few modifications to existing network infrastructure because your primary objective is to communicate between a single computer instance and the virtual network, which allows for encrypted tunneling.

Networking Approach	Description
Site-to-site VPN	Unlike a P2S connection, a site-to-site connection allows for a connection between an on-premises VPN and a single Azure VPN Gateway using a virtual network. It is ideal for hybrid configurations. For example, if you have an on-premises resource that requires authorization to connect to a virtual network, you are likely to configure a site-to-site VPN. Like a P2S VPN network, connectivity is encrypted through an Internet tunnel.

Address space

The *address space* is the top-level private IPv4 (Internet Protocol version 4) address range you define for your VNet. Microsoft's best-practice guidance here is to ensure that you have no IP address overlap among your VNets or your on-premises networks.

All network communications within a VNet take place only in Azure; thus, your address space must come from the private, nonroutable IPv4 address ranges defined in Request for Comments (RFC) 1918:

>> 10.0.0.0–10.255.255.255 (/8 prefix)

>> 172.16.0.0–172.31.255.255 (/12 prefix)

>> 192.168.0.0– 92.168.255.255 (/16 prefix)

ON THE WEB

To learn more about the private IP address ranges, read the RFC 1918 source document at https://tools.ietf.org/html/rfc1918.

IPv6

TECHNICAL STUFF

Let's chat for a moment about Internet Protocol version 6, called IPv6 for short. The public IPv4 address space has long since been exhausted, and the world has slowly embraced IPv6. Most businesses that use IPv6 do so in a *dual-stack* configuration, using both IPv4 and IPv6.

The long story short is that Azure VNets and public load balancers support IPv6. To learn more about IPv6 in Azure, go to https://docs.microsoft.com/azure/virtual-network/ip-services/ipv6-overview.

Subnets

Your VNet address space is worthless until you define one or more subnets. What's cool about subnets is that Azure system routing takes care of directing traffic among the subnets of a single VNet. No router is required.

The most common architectural pattern places each application tier in its subnet — perhaps one subnet for the web front-end tier, one for the business logic tier, and one for the data tier. This way, you can sculpt your traffic rules more quickly because the VMs on each subnet can have the exact same network traffic requirements.

Azure always reserves five IP addresses from each subnet for its use. Suppose you create a subnet that uses the address 192.168.10.0/24. Here's what happens:

>> 192.168.10.0 is reserved because it's the subnet's network ID.

>> 192.168.10.1 through 192.168.10.3 are reserved for Azure's private use.

>> 192.168.10.4 is the first usable IP address in the subnet and is distributed by Azure's Dynamic Host Configuration Protocol.

>> 192.168.10.255 is reserved for protocol conformance.

WARNING

Azure is a metered service, and every service has a predefined capacity limit. In a single subscription in a single region, you can define up to 1,000 VNets and 3,000 subnets per virtual network. Those capacities seem to be absurdly high at first blush. The day will come when you'll run into one of these service limits, especially if you have a high-traffic website or application that takes over the world! So prepare yourself if you expect to scale your solution for mass consumption. For more details, visit the Azure docs article "Azure subscription and service limits, quotas, and constraints" at https://docs.microsoft.com/azure/azure-subscription-service-limits.

Creating a Virtual Network

Figure 4-1 shows the environment deployed in this chapter.

The topology has the following notable features:

>> The VNet is divided into two subnets to reflect standard application tiers.

>> Each VNet is protected by a single network security group (NSG).

>> A service endpoint links a storage account to a VNet.

>> VNet peering logically connects VNet1 and VNet2.

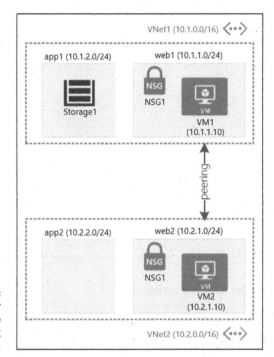

Deploying with the Azure portal

When you're signed into the Azure portal with your administrative account, follow these steps to deploy your first Azure virtual network:

1. **Either create a new resource group or add to an existing resource group.**

2. **Use the global search box in the Azure portal to browse to the Virtual Networks blade.**

3. **Click Add.**

4. **Fill out the Create Virtual Network Configuration blade and click Create to submit the deployment.**

   To complete this configuration, you'll need to click through several screens like that shown in Figure 4-2.

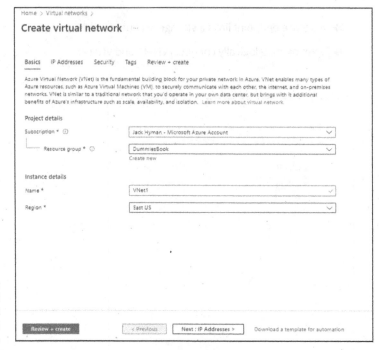

Create virtual network

Basics   IP Addresses   Security   Tags   Review + create

Azure Virtual Network (VNet) is the fundamental building block for your private network in Azure. VNet enables many types of Azure resources, such as Azure Virtual Machines (VM), to securely communicate with each other, the internet, and on-premises networks. VNet is similar to a traditional network that you'd operate in your own data center, but brings with it additional benefits of Azure's infrastructure such as scale, availability, and isolation. Learn more about virtual network.

Project details

Subscription * ⓘ   Jack Hyman - Microsoft Azure Account

     Resource group * ⓘ   DummiesBook
                                      Create new

Instance details

Name *   VNet1

Region *   East US

Review + create   < Previous   Next : IP Addresses >   Download a template for automation

FIGURE 4-2:
The Create virtual network configuration screen.

For practice, use the following values:

- *Name:* VNet1

- *Address Space:* 10.2.0.0/16

- *Subscription:* [your subscription]

- *Resource Group:* [your selected resource group]

- *Location:* Whichever Azure region is closest to you. (These examples use East US 2.)

- *Subnet Name:* Default

- *Subnet Address Range:* 10.2.1.0/24

- *DDoS Protection:* Basic

- *Service Endpoints:* Disabled

- *Firewall:* Disabled

After Azure deploys the new VNet, you must revisit its configuration settings to define the second subnet. Follow these steps to accomplish that goal:

1. **Navigate to the VNet1 Configuration blade.**

2. **In the VNet's Settings list, select Subnets; then click the Subnet button.**

3. **Fill out the form on the Add Subnet blade, and click Create to complete the configuration.**

   Use the following values:

   - *Name:* app1
   - *Address Range:* 10.1.2.0/24
   - *Network Security Group:* None
   - *Route Table:* None
   - *Service Endpoints Services*: 0 selected
   - *Delegate Subnet to a Service:* None

Software-defined networking can become abstract and difficult to envision. In the VNet1 Settings list, under Monitor click Diagram, as shown in Figure 4-3. Azure creates a vector diagram that depicts your virtual network; clicking an element in the graphic takes you to that resource's settings.

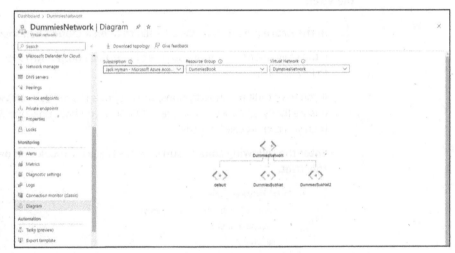

FIGURE 4-3:
Azure generates
nifty network
diagrams for you.

I find these diagrams invaluable for figuring out how my VNets are laid out. What's even cooler is that you can

>> Click any of the diagram shapes in the Azure portal to go to their configuration blades.

>> Click Download Topology to download a scalable vector graphics (SVG) format image for use in your architectural documentation.

TIP

If you don't own a Microsoft Visio license, consider getting one. Visio makes creating Azure diagrams simple. I highly recommend that anyone with work that involves Azure invest in Visio so they can make visualizing cloud-based resources easier.

Specifically, import the VNet topology image into Visio, right-click it, and choose Group ⇨ Ungroup from Visio's shortcut menu. Now you have access to all the shapes. You should also download the Azure Visio stencils at https://www.microsoft.com/download/details.aspx?id=41937.

Deploying with PowerShell

You can deploy the second VNet by using Cloud Shell and PowerShell. Because limited space is available on this page, I've broken the code in the following steps across multiple lines, but you should type the code as single lines. I've used a backtick (`) as a line-continuation character to make the PowerShell code easier to understand, but you shouldn't add it in Cloud Shell. Follow these steps to deploy the VNet:

1. **In the Azure portal, click Cloud Shell to open a Cloud Shell session.**

   If the session opens in Bash, use the Cloud Shell's drop-down menu to switch to PowerShell.

   If you have multiple subscriptions, you may need to run Set-AzContext to ensure that you're focused on the right one. If you have only one subscription, then you can proceed directly.

2. **Enter the following code to run New-AzVirtualNetwork and define the VNet:**

   ```
   New-AzVirtualNetwork `
       -ResourceGroupName DummiesBook `
       -Location EastUS2 `
       -Name VNet2 `
       -AddressPrefix 10.3.0.0/16
   ```

   Note the backtick (`) characters in my code. The backtick is not the single quotation mark but the key above the Tab key on the keyboard. In PowerShell, you use the backtick to continue a code line to the next line. To make the code a bit more readable for the book, I use this convention. You can certainly omit them if you don't mind having the code lines run long in Cloud Shell.

3. **Run Add-AzVirtualNetworkSubnetConfig to define the web2 and app2 subnets.**

   Variables in PowerShell start with a dollar sign. Here's the code:

```
$subnetConfig1 = Add-AzVirtualNetworkSubnetConfig `
    -Name web2 `
    -AddressPrefix 10.3.1.0/24 `
    -VirtualNetwork 'VNet2'
$subnetConfig2 = Add-AzVirtualNetworkSubnetConfig `
    -Name app2 `
    -AddressPrefix 10.3.2.0/24 `
    -VirtualNetwork 'VNet2'
```

4. **Use the PowerShell pipeline and the `Set-AzVirtualNetwork` command to commit the configuration.**

   The PowerShell pipeline allows you to feed the output from one command to a subsequent command. Here's the code:

```
$subnetConfig1 | Set-AzVirtualNetwork
$subnetConfig2 | Set-AzVirtualNetwork
```

TIP

5. One reason performing Azure deployments programmatically is considered more efficient than doing it in the Azure portal is that you can specify all deployment aspects in one fell swoop. In the preceding example, both subnets are defined simultaneously. The Azure portal form allows you to specify only your first subnet.

Configuring Virtual Networks

Thus far, this chapter has laid the foundation for future VM and Azure service internetworking. Before populating your VNet, you need to make some tweaks to ensure it's behaving the way you want.

Deciding on a name resolution strategy

Azure-provided name resolution, enabled by default in your VNets, ensures that your VMs can communicate via a short hostname and IP address. However, the problem some businesses have is they want their cloud VMs to use a custom DNS domain name (company.com, for example).

If you need VMs in different VNets to resolve one another's host names, or if you want to use a custom, fully qualified domain name for your cloud VMs, then you need to configure custom name resolution. For instance, you can do either of the following:

>> Deploy a private Azure Domain Name System (DNS) zone and link the zone to both subnets.

>> Deploy DNS server VMs in each VNet and configure them to forward name resolution queries to each other.

In your VNets, browse to the DNS servers setting. You should see the default (Azure-provided) setting. If you need to override DNS, select Custom and then supply one or more custom DNS server IPv4 addresses. These addresses might point to

>> On-premises DNS servers (if you're running in a hybrid cloud)

>> A DNS server VM(s) running in the local VNet

>> An Azure-provided virtual IP address (168.63.129.16)

TIP

168.63.129.16 is a good IP address to know because you may want your VMs to fall back to an Azure-provided DNS if a recursive name lookup fails with the prescribed list of custom DNS servers.

WARNING

Never attempt to configure TCP/IP properties from within a VM in Azure. If you do so, you'll immediately lose a network connection to your VM. Remember that you're dealing with cloud-based software-defined networking here, not your local physical or virtual servers. You must perform all your VM networking configuration in Azure Resource Manager (ARM), whether you use the Azure portal, PowerShell, or the Azure command-line interface (CLI).

Configuring network security groups

NSGs are traffic filters you can associate with VM virtual network interface cards or VNet subnets. I recommend that you associate NSGs with subnets to reduce future troubleshooting and apply the same inbound and outbound traffic rules to multiple VMs simultaneously.

An NSG consists of one or more access rules that have the following properties:

>> **Priority:** Lower-priority values are evaluated first. As you add rules, leave space between them to allow room for future growth.

- **Name:** I suggest that you name your NSG rules as descriptively as possible (such as HTTP-in-Allow).

- **Port:** This property is the Transmission Control Protocol (TCP) or User Datagram Protocol (UDP) port assignment.

- **Protocol:** This property is TCP, UDP, or both.

- **Source:** This property is where the traffic stream originates.

- **Destination:** This property is where the traffic stream is going.

- **Action:** This property is Allow or Deny.

An NSG runs each traffic stream through its inbound or outbound rules list, depending on the direction of traffic. The first rule that applies becomes the effective rule. Unless you have a catch-all rule to deny all unclassified traffic, you open the possibility of connection types you don't want, which could compromise your VM's security.

Tables 4-2 and 4-3 summarize the default inbound and outbound rules for NSGs.

TABLE 4-2   Default Inbound Security Rules

Rule	Description
AllowVnetInBound	Allows inbound traffic originating in this VNet and any peered VNets
AllowAzureLoadBalancer InBound	Allows health-probe traffic inbound from any Azure load balancer IP address
DenyAllInBound	Catch-all rule ensuring that any inbound traffic not caught by a previous rule is denied

TABLE 4-3   Default Outbound Security Rules

Rule	Description
AllowVnetOutBound	Allows outbound traffic from this VNet and to any peered VNets
AllowInternetBound	Allows VMs to reach the public Internet from within the VNet
DenyAllInBound	Catch-all rule ensuring that any outbound traffic not caught by a previous rule is denied

Although Microsoft created the default inbound and outbound NSG security rules for your convenience, you're not obligated to use them. I feel that they open the door to way too many opportunities to attack your cloud infrastructure (hence being too permissive), so I suggest that you create DenyAllInbound and DenyAllOutBound rules manually and don't use the other default rules.

The VNet shown in Figure 4-1 earlier in this chapter includes NSG1 for filtering traffic and contains the default inbound and outbound rules.

Because you have the exact access requirements in VNet2, you associate NSG1 with both subnets.

To create the NSG and allow inbound HTTP traffic (TCP port 80), follow these steps:

1. **Use the Azure portal's global search to find the Network Security Groups blade; then click Add on the toolbar.**

   Don't select the Network Security Groups (Classic) option. The focus of this book is ARM.

2. **Complete the Create Network Security Group blade form and click Create.**

   Use these properties:

   - *Name:* NSG1
   - *Subscription:* [your subscription]
   - *Resource Group:* [your resource group]
   - *Location:* East US (use your home region; these examples use mine)

3. **After deployment, select your NSG and browse the Inbound Security Rules setting in the Settings list.**

   Note that there are separate settings for inbound and outbound security rules. The Default Rules button toggles their state. Leave both settings enabled for this exercise.

4. **Click Add.**

5. **Complete the add Inbound Security Rule blade form and click Create.**

   By default, Azure places you in Advanced view, where you want to be. (If you like, click Basic to see the simplified view.)

Use these configuration properties for NSG1:

- *Source:* Service Tag, Internet

  Your source can be a comma-separated list of IP addresses or address ranges, a service tag, or an application security group. For now, understand that this rule applies to inbound traffic from the public Internet.

- *Source Port Ranges:* Any (denoted by the asterisk)

- *Destination:* VirtualNetwork (service tags to the rescue)

- *Destination Port Ranges:* 80

- *Protocol:* TCP

- *Action:* Allow

- *Priority:* 100

- *Name:* HTTP-In-Allow

- *Description:* (add if you want to)

6. **Create a new outbound (I repeat, *outbound*) security rule for NSG1.**

    This rule allows traffic from the default subnet to the storage account you'll place on the app1 subnet.

    Use these properties:

    - *Source:* Virtual Network

    - *Source Port Ranges:* Any

    - *Destination:* Service tag, Storage

    - *Destination Port Ranges:* Any

    - *Protocol:* Any

    - *Action:* Allow

    - *Priority:* 100

    - *Name:* Storage-Out-Allow

    - *Description:* (fill in if you want to)

Figure 4-4 shows my completed NSG1 configuration on the NSG1 Overview page.

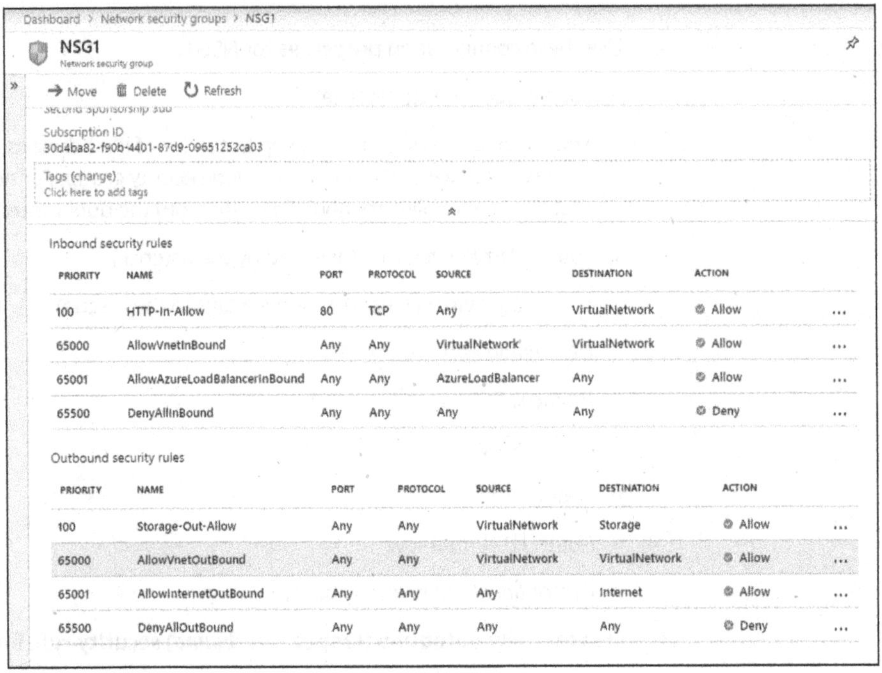

Dashboard > Network security groups > NSG1

NSG1
Network security group

→ Move 🗑 Delete ↻ Refresh

second sponsorship sub

Subscription ID
30d4ba82-f90b-4401-87d9-09651252ca03

Tags (change)
Click here to add tags

Inbound security rules

PRIORITY	NAME	PORT	PROTOCOL	SOURCE	DESTINATION	ACTION	
100	HTTP-In-Allow	80	TCP	Any	VirtualNetwork	⊘ Allow	...
65000	AllowVnetInBound	Any	Any	VirtualNetwork	VirtualNetwork	⊘ Allow	...
65001	AllowAzureLoadBalancerInBound	Any	Any	AzureLoadBalancer	Any	⊘ Allow	...
65500	DenyAllInBound	Any	Any	Any	Any	⊘ Deny	...

Outbound security rules

PRIORITY	NAME	PORT	PROTOCOL	SOURCE	DESTINATION	ACTION	
100	Storage-Out-Allow	Any	Any	VirtualNetwork	Storage	⊘ Allow	...
65000	AllowVnetOutBound	Any	Any	VirtualNetwork	VirtualNetwork	⊘ Allow	...
65001	AllowInternetOutBound	Any	Any	Any	Internet	⊘ Allow	...
65500	DenyAllOutBound	Any	Any	Any	Any	⊘ Deny	...

FIGURE 4-4:
NSG1
configuration.

Adding service tags and application security groups

Service tags are labels that aggregate pools of IP address prefixes and make crafting accurate NSG rules much more accessible. Some familiar service tags are

- » **VirtualNetwork:** All virtual network address spaces, for both local and peered VNets

- » **Internet:** All public IP addresses, both Azure-owned and public

- » **AzureLoadBalancer:** The virtual IP addresses of your deployed Azure load balancers

- » **AzureCloud:** Azure public IP address space

- » **Storage:** IP address range for the Azure Storage service

Application security groups (ASGs) are in effect user-created service tags. With them, you can group resources in an administrator-defined way to ease NSG rule assignment. For example, you might create an ASG called "webservers" that applies to the web-server VMs in your deployment.

Sadly, using the default inbound and outbound rules is an all-or-nothing proposition: You can't selectively delete individual default inbound or outbound rules. Thus, instead of using the default rules, you should plan to re-create what you need.

For more information on ASGs, read the Azure docs article "Security Groups" at https://docs.microsoft.com/azure/virtual-network/security-overview.

Associating the NSG with the appropriate subnets

Follow these steps to link your new NSG with the default subnet on VNet1 and the web2 subnet on the VNet2 subnet:

1. **On the NSG1 Configuration blade, select Subnets.**

2. **On the Subnets blade, click Associate.**

3. **On the Associate subnet blade, choose the appropriate virtual network and subnet.**

   You need to complete this procedure twice: once for VNet1/default and once for VNet2/default2

Understanding service endpoints

Service endpoints secure certain Azure services by limiting their connectivity to a virtual network. You might have a storage account containing sensitive data that should be accessed only by VMs on a particular VNet. In this case, creating a service endpoint for the service account on the appropriate virtual network accomplishes your goal.

Other Azure products bound to VNets via service endpoints include SQL Database, Cosmos DB, Key Vault, and App Service.

This section walks you through the configuration. To create a Microsoft.Storage service endpoint on the Vnet1 app1 subnet, follow these steps:

1. **In the Azure portal, browse to VNet1, and select the Service Endpoints setting.**

2. **On the toolbar, click Add.**

3. **On the Add Service Endpoints blade, select Microsoft.Storage as the service and app1 as the subnet; then click Add to complete the configuration.**

You're not finished with your work, however: You need to associate a storage account with the app1 subnet. Defining the service endpoint on the VNet opens up the possibility of integrating a storage account into the network. You next need to go to the storage account to complete the configuration. Service endpoint policies allow you to filter VNet traffic to Azure services.

4. **Open Storage Explorer and ensure that you can connect to a storage account.**

   If you created a storage account in Chapter 3, you can use that storage account. You should be able to access the files' blob container and the blobs inside.

5. **Back in the Azure portal, browse to the VNet1 resource, and select the Service Endpoints setting.**

6. **From the Microsoft.Storage context menu (the ellipses at the end of the row; see Figure 4-5), choose Configure Virtual Networks in a storage account.**

7. **Select your storage account and the Firewalls and Virtual Networks setting on the Storage Accounts blade.**

8. **In the Allow Access From section, select Selected Networks.**

9. **In the Virtual Networks section, choose Add Existing Virtual Network.**

10. **Browse the VNet1 virtual network and app1 subnet, and click Add.**

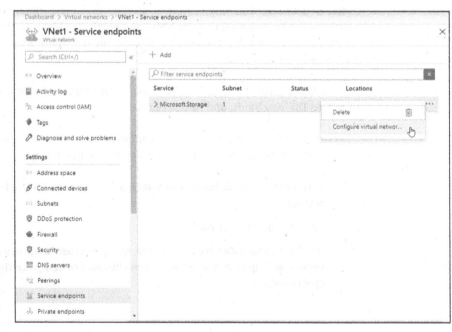

FIGURE 4-5: In the Azure portal, most resources have a context menu from which you can select configuration options.

11. Click Save to complete the configuration.

The storage account's Firewalls and Virtual Networks blade contains some additional options once you've enabled service endpoints:

- *Add Your Client IP Address:* If you don't select this option, you won't be able to access the storage account from your current workstation.

- *Allow Trusted Microsoft Services to Access This Storage Account:* Enable this option to ensure other Azure services (such as Key Vault, Azure AD, and so on) can reach the storage account and vice versa.

12. Close and reopen Storage Explorer.

13. Test connectivity to your storage account.

You should expect to see an error message. Don't panic, this is expected!

Connecting Virtual Networks

Here are two ways to logically link two VNets to support topologies that require it:

» With production/development VNets that support inter-VNet communication

» With hub-spoke VNet architectures in which the hub VNet has a link to the on-premises environment

Azure provides two options for linking VNets, which I describe next.

Configuring VNet peering

VNet peering is one way to connect two Azure virtual networks. Until late 2018, virtual network gateways and a VNet-to-VNet virtual private network (VPN) were needed to connect VNets in different regions. Nowadays, VNets in different regions and even in different Azure subscriptions can peer.

Network traffic across a VNet peering is private, occurring over the Azure network backbone and using private IP addresses. No VPN expense or overhead is required for peering, although you can deploy a VNet-to-VNet VPN if your security needs dictate. You can also configure both sides of peering from the perspective of only one VNet.

Follow these steps to configure a VNet peering between your VNet1 and VNet2 virtual networks:

1. **In the Azure portal, browse to VNet1, select the Peerings setting and click Add (see Figure 4-6).**

2. **Fill out the form on the Add Peering blade and click OK.**

    Use these configuration properties:

    - *Name of the Peering from VNet1 to Remote Virtual Network:* vnet1-to-vnet2-peering

    - *Virtual Network Deployment Model:* Resource manager

    - *Subscription:* [your subscription]

    - *Virtual Network:* VNet2

    - *Name of the Peering from Remote Virtual network to VNet1:* vnet2-to-vnet1-peering

      (Not too long ago, you had to configure the peering in both VNets; it's nice to have the convenience to define both sides in one configuration blade now.)

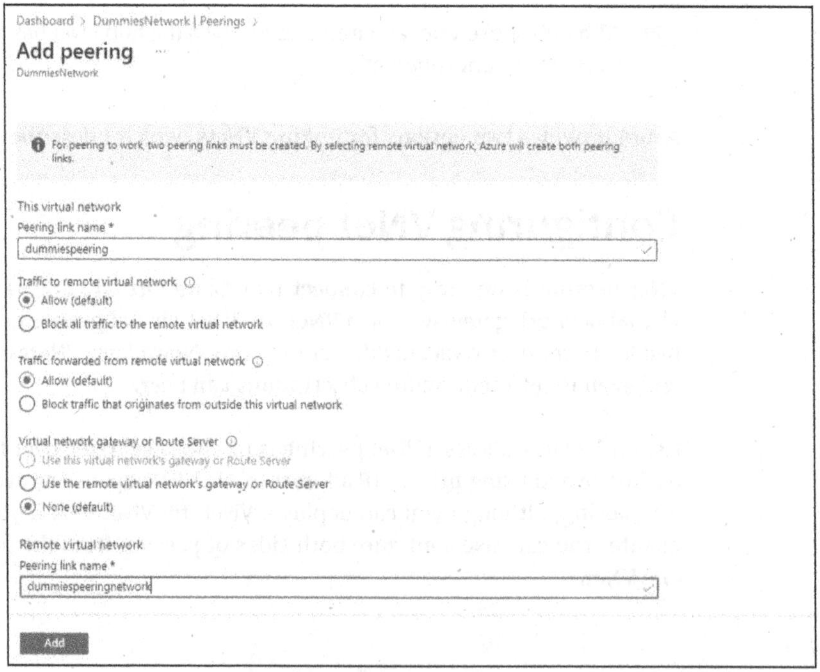

FIGURE 4-6: Configuring VNET Peering.

- *Allow Virtual Network Access (Both Directions):* Enabled

- *Configure Forwarded Traffic Settings (Both Directions):* Disabled

- *Allow Gateway Transit:* Not selected

3. **Click OK to submit the configuration to ARM.**

   Eventually, the VNet1 and VNet2 Peerings blades should show the peering status as Connected. It does take a few minutes to create the connection, so patience is of the essence. You now have a routing path between the two VNets that involves only Azure — no public Internet (or VPN connection).

Understanding service chaining

When you select peering in the Azure portal, you can customize the peering relationship to accomplish routing goals. For example, you may have a spoke VNet that must reach your on-premises environment by transiting through a hub VNet.

It's vital for you to know that VNet peerings are not transitive. Figure 4-7 shows a common hub-and-spoke VNet topology.

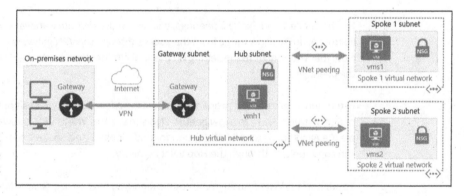

FIGURE 4-7:
A hub-and-spoke
virtual network
topology.

In the figure, the Hub virtual network serves as a transit point between Azure and the business's local network environment.

Figure 4-7 also shows two peerings to Spoke 1 and Spoke 2. The no-transitivity property means that vms1 in Spoke 1 can't communicate directly with vms2 in Spoke 2 through the hub by default. To fix this problem, you can do one of the following:

>> Create a third peering between Spoke 1 and Spoke 2.

>> Configure a network virtual appliance and route traffic explicitly.

Do you see what I'm talking about here? Many businesses require more than one virtual network in Azure, and you often need to configure connectivity between them. For instance, a business might use peering to link development and production VNets.

Another use case is placing a network virtual appliance such as an enterprise firewall in the Hub network and sharing that device for traffic in other, linked VNets. This is what Microsoft means by the term *service chaining*.

A route table is necessary for Azure when you need to control how traffic flows within and between VNets. The route table defines one or more "next hop" destination IP addresses; if you've worked with static IP routing in your local environment, then the Azure route table should be easy for you to pick up.

TECHNICAL STUFF

CONFIGURING PEERING

Before continuing, I must address how to allow the Hub virtual network to forward traffic from either spoke to the other or through the VPN tunnel to an on-premises network.

For the Spoke 1 and Spoke 2 peerings, enable the Use Remote Gateways option to instruct Azure to allow traffic from the spokes through the VPN gateway in hub. Note that you configure the setting on the spoke rather than on the Hub sides of the peerings.

In the Hub VNet's peering properties, enable the Allow Gateway Transit option. This option instructs Azure to allow peered VNets to use this VNet's VPN gateway. Also enable the Allow Forwarded Traffic option for both Spoke 1 and Spoke 2 so that the spokes can communicate through the Hub VNet in theory.

To support full VNet transitive communication, you have to use *service chaining*, in which you deploy a network virtual appliance to your Hub VNet and implement user-defined routes.

The figure shows an NVA virtual machine configured as a router that can forward IP traffic from other VNets. You associate a user-defined route (also known as an Azure route table) with each Spoke VNet to provide a next-hop routing address of 10.1.1.100: the network virtual appliance. In so doing, you override Azure system routes with your custom routes.

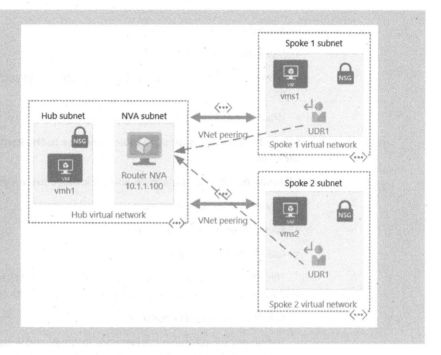

WHAT IS AN NVA?

A *network virtual appliance* (NVA) is an ordinary VM that runs in Azure but has a fundamentally different purpose from most VMs. Typically, an NVA has more than one virtual network interface card attached to multiple subnets within a VNet. The NVA configured for IP forward, and runs a third-party network traffic management application.

Leading providers of enterprise load balancers, firewalls, proxy servers, and other devices publish preconfigured NVAs to the Azure Marketplace, for example. These VMs run a thin, specialized Linux version and are configured via a web interface. To browse the NVAs in the Azure Marketplace, visit https://azure.microsoft.com/solutions/network-appliances.

Follow these steps to create a sample route table, assuming that the NVA listens for traffic on the private IP address 10.1.1.100:

1. Use the global search in the Azure portal to find the Route Tables blade.

2. On the Route Tables blade, click Add.

3. Complete the Create Route Table blade form and click Create.

Here are the properties to use:

- *Name:* nva-next-hop
- *Subscription, Resource Group, Location:* Use the values you've been using thus far
- *Virtual Network Gateway Route Propagation:* Disabled

4. **Select the nva-next-hop route table, navigate to the Routes blade, and click Add.**

5. **Fill in the Add Route blade form and click OK to submit your configuration.**

   Specify the following properties:

   - *Route Name:* nva-default-route
   - *Address Prefix:* 0.0.0.0/0.

     This IP address range, known as a default route, applies to every traffic bit outbound from the subnet(s) associated with this route table.

   - *Next Hop Type:* Virtual Appliance.

     The other options are Virtual Network, Internet, and Virtual Network Gateway. Remember when you learned about service tags and network security groups? That's what these identifiers are as well.

   - *Next Hop Address:* 10.1.1.100

   A note from ARM reminds you to enable IP forwarding on the NVA. You configure this forwarding as a property of the NVA's network interface card settings.

6. **Associate the route table with the appropriate subnet(s).**

   To do this, open the Subnets blade in the route table's Settings list, and select Associate. As shown in Figure 4-6 earlier in this chapter you need to associate your new route table with the Spoke 1 and Spoke 2 subnets to force their outbound traffic through the NVA in the Hub VNet.

The hub-and-spoke VNet design pattern and service chaining are not uncommon scenarios. User-defined route tables allow you to move from Azure-provided routing, which works well enough, to custom routing, in which you granularly shape how traffic flows within VNets, between VNets, and between a transit VNet and your on-premises networks.

REMEMBER

Don't forget about your NSGs and their inbound and outbound rules. When you create more complex VNet topologies, such as service chaining and peering, you'll most likely need to tweak existing NSG rules or create new ones to accommodate the new traffic flows.

User-defined routes

As I mention earlier in this section, when you create subnets, Azure also creates system routes like the proverbial highway to communicate along the way. You may want to override these predefined system routes by creating user-defined routes (UDRs). Think of implementing a UDR as overriding your GPS system's predefined directions; with a UDR, you are calling the shots.

For example, suppose you have two networks that consist of two subnets and you need to add a VM used as a DMZ with a firewall. Your mission is simple: Push the traffic to go only through the firewall and not the two subnets. That's where the UDR and IP forwarding come in. You'll want to create a routing table in Azure because the custom routes override the default system configurations.

Deploying Azure Firewall

Protecting the enemy from trying to breach your Azure infrastructure, whether a VM or managed application, is no longer a maybe. While Microsoft does provide many security defenses to thwart bad actors out of the box, it also expects you to spend money on extra defenses. If you don't put a minimum number of defenses into your Azure instance, one of the bad guys will eventually creep through a hidden door and compromise your environment. It's not a matter of *if*; it's *when*.

If your organization plans on using Azure Virtual Network resources, add the Azure Firewall to the list of requisites. Azure Firewall is a cloud-based network security service. A classic example is when an organization hosts a VM that end-users on the Internet regularly interact with such as a WordPress Powered by Bitnami VM. Implementing just-in-time virtual machine connectivity is considered the gold standard. Remember, Microsoft covers the essential security measures to thwart attackers — not all. Still, a firewall prevents your VM instance from being targeted when exposed to network volume-based attacks. Using the Azure Firewall, you can configure controlled access to VMs when needed through proper assignment of NSG and Azure Firewall rules.

REMEMBER

Azure firewalls are by no means the only security defense that you should put in place to protect your virtual network infrastructure. The firewall establishes policies that determine the ports to be protected, how long those ports should remain open, and those IP addresses that should be deemed accessible.

TIP

Further along in the book, we'll take a look at Azure Security Center. It is essential to know that Azure Security Center exposes Azure Firewall activities including approved requests, configured VMs using the firewall, and all those addresses that contain connectivity details to the Destination Network Address Translation (DNAT). The Azure Firewall DNAT enables you to translate and filter inbound internet traffic to one or more subnets. The result of configuring DNAT is that the NAT rule collection becomes set to DNAT.

Let's consider one final thing about how firewall rules operate in Azure. There is not just a one-size-fits-all rule. Instead, there are three firewall rules: NAT, Network, and Application.

>> **NAT rules:** NAT rules are used to forward traffic from a firewall to other devices on a network.

>> **Network rules:** Network rules enable traffic on specific IP address ranges to communicate using self-assigned parameters.

>> **Application rules:** Application rules are, you guessed it, application-specific that bring together enterprise applications using specific targets in the network, including domains.

Digging into Virtual Private Networks and Gateways

Suppose you want to connect your VNet to another network. It can be in Azure or another cloud solutions provider. It may be on-premises or even pointing to another cloud instance. Regardless of the scenario, you need to address the connectivity approach you will take to connect over the Internet. Because you don't want your organization's data to be vulnerable to outside threats, you want to create a virtual private network (VPN).

While we have already talked about the Azure VNet, the big difference for a VPN is the networking approach that allows an organization to connect between a private network and a public network. Again, notice the use of public versus private because this is a differentiator with a VPN. For example, suppose you are connected to a resource on your company's network from home (a shared drive). Will you simply log in to your internet connection and be able to see the entire shared drive as if it is on your computer? Likely not. Instead, you must connect via public connection (the Internet) to your organization's private network to view all the available data.

The VPN scenario is vanilla because the connection allows you to connect to a single infrastructure instance. What happens when you need to connect to multiple infrastructure instances, such as several VMs that may be deployed to a specific subnet? In this case, you utilize a virtual network *gateway*. When creating a virtual network gateway, you connect the primary subnet to the gateway subnet. Each virtual network gateway created can then be associated with a routing table. That way, the VPN gateway supports running targeted services.

TECHNICAL STUFF

You can't just create a VM and connect it to a gateway. The process is a bit more laborious because you must first configure the virtual network gateway to a targeted VNet. Once you determine the gateway type and how it will be used, you can then create the connection.

WARNING

Creating VPN gateway connections does not offer instant gratification! Depending on the compute resource associated with the instance configuration, it may take several hours to appear in the Azure portal. Don't fret; it's part of the process.

Planning and configuring a VPN gateway

Planning and configuring a VPN gateway takes a bit of time. You first need to consider the conditions in establishing your virtual network gateway. For example, you need to assess whether your gateway VM instances will be deployable to a gateway subnet. Then, you need to determine what specific settings are applicable. That's just the first step, not the last, because you also need to create different tunnel types to support your chosen connectivity options. Options might include IPsec/IKE between the VPN gateway and another VPN gateway that incorporates a VNet-to-VNet connection. Or perhaps you create

>> A cross-premises IPsec/IKE VPN tunnel between the VPN gateway and your on-premises VPN devices, mimicking a site-to-site deployment

>> A point-to-site VPN connection using Open VPN, IKEv2, or a Secure Socket Tunneling Protocol (SSTP), allowing you to create a virtual network from any remote location

No matter what the setup, planning and then configuring the architecture takes a bit of time depending on targeted Azure resources.

Among the most important considerations are security and encryption. Because a virtual network gateway sends encrypted traffic to and from Azure networks and on-premises locations over the public Internet, creating the appropriate tunnels and encryption protocols in Azure is critical. While each virtual network is initially limited to a single VPN gateway, you can create multiple connections with some planning, too. However, if you use the same gateway for multiple connections, your VPN tunnel will share the available bandwidth, and things might slow down for end-users.

ON THE WEB

Earlier in the chapter, you created the Azure Virtual Network. Creating a gateway follows the same process (for the most part) but requires a bit more confirmation given that you are creating connection points and establishing security protocols. Covering the configuration of connection points and security protocols is a complicated process, outside the scope of this book. To learn more about your configuration options, go to https://docs.microsoft.com/azure/vpn-gateway/tutorial-create-gateway-portal.

Speeding through Azure ExpressRoute

Picture this: an organization complaining about connectivity to its on-premises network and cloud service providers. Okay, to be fair, this scenario is all too common depending on traffic load and resource availability. Microsoft solved this problem in mid-2020 as many enterprise clients who support a hybrid architecture clamored that the connectivity was simply inadequate. The solution was Azure ExpressRoute.

Azure ExpressRoute allows you to extend the network connection from an on-premises network into the Microsoft cloud using a private connection in four ways: Cloud Exchange Co-Location, Point-To-Point Ethernet Connection, Any-To-Any (IPVPN) Connection, and ExpressRoute Direct.

TECHNICAL STUFF

Notice my use of the word *private connection* in describing ExpressRoute. Why is this special, you ask? An organization can connect its Microsoft Cloud Services such as Azure and Microsoft 365 to the on-premises environment using bandwidth explicitly targeted to the organization, not shared capacity. You might think this sounds like you are setting up a virtual network gateway. Not the case. With Azure ExpressRoute, it's a bit simpler, as you forego having to connect multiple IP addresses and establish encryption tunneling. (See Figure 4-8.)

Azure ExpressRoute offers several connection models; therefore, it's essential to work with your connectivity provider to pick the optimal choice for excellent streaming bandwidth. You have four connectivity options, as shown in Figure 4-9:

>> **Cloud Exchange Colocation:** If you use a facility that has a cloud exchange, you can procure virtual cross-connections to a Microsoft cloud instance. You'll need to utilize the colocation provider's Ethernet exchange. The benefit of this option is that a colocation provider may offer either a Layer 2 cross-connection or managed Layer 3 cross-connection. The connection between your on-premises infrastructure in the colocation facility and Microsoft Azure is established.

>> **Point-To-Point Ethernet Connection:** If you can connect your on-premises data center to the Microsoft cloud through point-to-point Ethernet links, the point-to-point Ethernet provider may be your best option as you can create a Layer 2 connection or managed Layer 3 connection between your site and the Microsoft cloud.

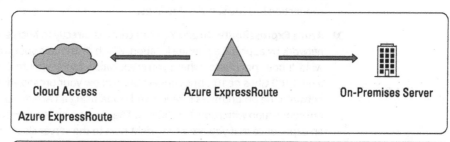

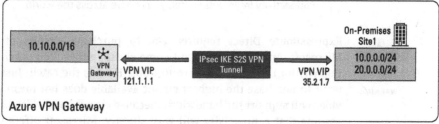

FIGURE 4-8:
Difference
between a virtual
network gateway
and Azure
ExpressRoute.

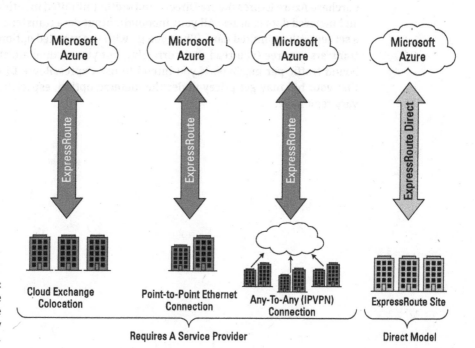

FIGURE 4-9:
Azure
ExpressRoute
connectivity
approaches.

- » **Any-to-Any Internet Protocol Virtual Private Network (IPVPN) Connection:** If you manage your WAN, a simple integration between the Microsoft cloud and your infrastructure can be created. An IPVPN provider allows you to create an any-to-any connection between one or more offices and the targeted data center. The Microsoft cloud can be interconnected to the WAN to make it appear as if it is just another branch office. Regardless of the connectivity model, ExpressRoute's capabilities make it appear that any connection has the same capabilities.

- » **Azure ExpressRoute Direct:** You can connect directly to Microsoft's global network by applying a peering location, which distributes your traffic world-wide. It does not matter where you are located; ExpressRoute Direct provides a dual 100 Gbps or 10 Gbps connection to allow your organization to connect between the on-premises location and cloud using an Active-Active (always on) connection with robust scalability. The connection is supposed to mimic an experience as if you are sitting right next to the server closet without any connectivity interruption. Yet, you can be across the world.

WARNING

ExpressRoute Direct requires you to purchase circuits of bandwidth from Microsoft. And it often doesn't come cheap, either. You purchase circuits (as of this writing) from 50 Mbps to 10 Gbps. Here is the catch: Just because you may want to purchase the highest circuit available does not mean your hosting provider will support the bandwidth. Because circuit bandwidth is fluid, you need to assume that connectivity will vary slightly. Microsoft offers users two ways to purchase Azure ExpressRoute Direct bandwidth: unlimited monthly consumption and metered data charges. All your inbound/output data transfer costs are part of a set fee with unlimited data. When you go with the metered option, inbound data transfers are free (you read that correctly), but you accumulate charges on outbound traffic per gigabyte. If you intend to use ExpressRoute Direct, be warned that your bill may get pricey under the metered option, especially because rates vary regionally.

Chapter **5**

Deploying and Configuring Azure Virtual Machines

When you are first introduced to cloud computing, it's usually because someone told you that they need to either migrate their data center workloads into the cloud or run self-contained systems to the Internet without the organization paying extra for the hardware. Sound familiar? The virtual machine (VM) is synonymous with cloud computing and remains one of Azure's top features, hands down.

But here is the reality: As you have probably already figured, the VM is not the be-all and end-all in Azure. There is a purpose for Azure VMs — when you need full-stack control of the environment you run. And there is no shortage of ways to deploy an operating system on a VM, whether it be Windows, Linux, or another platform in Azure. In this chapter, I explain the various Azure VM options and how to deploy and configure Windows Server and Linux VMs in Azure. Let's get this party started!

Planning Your VM Deployment

You may recall the carpenter's aphorism "measure twice, cut once," which stresses the importance of planning before you jump into a project. With Azure VM deployment, you need to think carefully to make the right decisions the first time; otherwise, you risk having to delete and re-create your VM.

Before you plan your deployment, however, you need to understand how VMs operate in Azure.

Understanding VMs

A VM is a software representation of a computer. Each Azure region consists of multiple data centers; each data center consists of thousands of hardware blade servers. VMs run within this massive compute fabric.

Each VM is allocated virtual hardware resources from its parent hardware host:

>> Compute (CPU [central processing unit] and RAM [random-access memory])

>> Storage

>> Network

TECHNICAL STUFF

Microsoft's data center servers run a specialized Windows Server Core version, and your VMs reside on Microsoft Hyper-V hosts. By contrast, Amazon Web Services (AWS) runs its Elastic Compute Cloud VM instances under the open-source Xen hypervisor.

As of this writing, the Microsoft Azure VMs service supports the following 64-bit versions:

>> Windows 7

>> Windows 8.1

>> Windows 10

>> Windows 11

>> Windows Server 2008 R2

>> Windows Server 2012 R2

- Windows Server 2016
- Windows Server 2019
- Windows Server 2022

TIP

Microsoft supports Windows Client VM images in Azure only for development purposes. The idea is that developers can deploy Windows Client VMs to use as test agents against cloud-based line-of-business applications.

Azure also supports the following endorsed 64-bit Linux distributions:

- CentOS
- CoreOS
- Debian
- OpenSUSE
- Oracle Linux
- Red Hat Enterprise Linux
- SUSE Enterprise Linux
- Ubuntu

Starting your VM deployment from the Azure Marketplace

Perhaps the fastest way to deploy a VM in Azure is to do so from the Azure Marketplace. Azure Marketplace is an online portal consisting of thousands of Microsoft and non-Microsoft VM images, including all the naked operating system (OS) images described earlier in this chapter. It can be a little bit confusing, too, as many Microsoft partners may offer up the same software with a few differences, even on the same operating system. Figure 5-1 shows the Azure Marketplace.

You get to the Azure Marketplace from the Azure portal by entering **marketplace** in the global search box. Alternately, you can log in with your Azure account and start seeking the VM of your dreams at www.azure.com/marketplace.

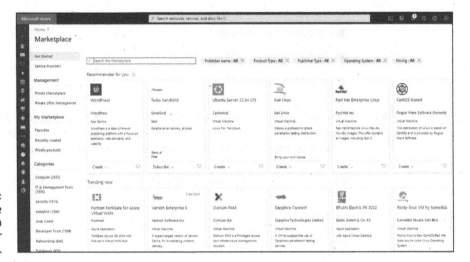

FIGURE 5-1:
Azure
Marketplace is a
one-stop shop for
several VM types.

Starting your VM deployment from your on-premises environment

Later in the book, I describe how to use Azure Migrate to migrate your on-premises physical and virtual servers to Azure. That said, you can always upload your generalized OS images to Azure. To do this, you need a fast internet connection or a private connection to the Azure Cloud; that's all.

WARNING

The instructions I provide here are illustrative not comprehensive. Consult the Azure documentation at https://docs.microsoft.com/azure/migrate for complete, step-by-step guidance on preparing your on-premises Linux and Windows Server VMs for upload to Azure.

Here's the general workflow:

1. **Prepare your VM disks for upload to Azure.**

   If your on-premises VMs aren't Hyper-V, you need to use appropriate tools to convert them. Although Azure supports Hyper-V Generation 2 virtual hard drives (VHDs), the disks need to be in .vhd format (not .vhdx) to work in Azure.

   To convert a .vhdx virtual disk to a fixed-size .vhd, you can run the Convert-VHD PowerShell cmdlet on your local Hyper-V host like so:

   ```
   Convert-VHD -Path d:\dev\vm1-gen2.vhdx -DestinationPath d:\dev\vm1-gen1.
       vhd -VHDType Fixed
   ```

TIP

By the way, PowerShell commands are commonly called cmdlets, pronounced *command-lets*.

Note also that your OS VHD must be generalized. Generalization removes all unique information from the VM disk image, including security identifiers, static IP address, host name, and so on. In Windows Server, you can use the built-in Sysprep utility.

2. **Upload your generalized OS image to the blob service of an Azure storage account.**

3. **Add the uploaded VHD to the Azure Managed Storage service with Azure PowerShell, as follows:**

   (a) Define some variables to make your code tidier:

   ```
   $vmName = "vm1"
   $rgName = "myResourceGroup"
   $location = "EastUS"
   $imageName = "myImage"
   $osVhdUri = "https://mystorageaccount.blob.core.windows.net/vhds/vm1-
       gen1.vhd"
   ```

   (b) Create what Microsoft calls a managed image:

   ```
   $imageConfig = New-AzImageConfig -Location $location
   $imageConfig = Set-AzImageOsDisk -Image $imageConfig -OsType Windows
       -OsState Generalized -BlobUri $osVhdUri
   $image = New-AzImage -ImageName $imageName -ResourceGroupName $rgName
       -Image $imageConfig
   ```

4. **Use the managed image for your VM deployments.**

Recognizing Azure VM Components

At a higher level of abstraction, an Azure virtual machine is a cloud resource that consists of the following three subsystems. Folks often scratch their head determining if they need a general cloud environment or an optimized environment. When you think optimized, there are three variables to consider:

>> Compute

>> Storage

>> Network

Before I explain how to deploy and configure a VM, I'll go over how Azure VMs implement these subsystems.

Compute

You're charged for each minute that your Azure VMs are allocated and running. *Allocated* means that Microsoft reserves hardware compute power — primarily CPU and RAM resources — for your VM.

The available VM instance sizes are divided into families. Table 5-1 lists the Windows Server VM sizes and the intended workload for each size, which will help you get a feel for the difference among the VM size families. You can find the associated Linux VM sizes in the Azure documentation (https://docs. microsoft.com/azure/virtual-machines/linux/sizes).

TABLE 5-1

Windows Server VM Sizes in Azure

Family	Sizes	Intended Workload
General-purpose	B, Dsv3, Dv3, Dasv3, Dav3, DSv2, Dv2, Av2, DC	Testing and development
Compute-optimized	Fsv2	Web servers
Memory-optimized	Esv3, Ev3, Easv3, Eav3, Mv2, M, DSv2, Dv2	Database servers
Storage-optimized	Lsv2	Big data workloads
GPU	NC, NCv2, NCv3, ND, NDv2, NV, NVv3	Heavy graphic rendering jobs
High-performance compute	HB, HC, H	High-performance computing

TIP

If you're not bound to a particular Azure region for compliance purposes, consider shopping around before deploying your VMs, because running VMs in different regions creates significantly different costs. Price differences are due to electricity costs, physical plant costs, and the like, which vary based on the regions in which Azure data centers reside.

A VM located in the eastern region of the United States can cost $1.00/hour versus $9.00/hour in an Azure data center in the Asia Pacific region of the world. Even domestically, the prices often vary slightly. So, think about who your users are and which data center is closest. That's where you want to place your cloud workloads.

Over time, you'll come to recognize which family a particular VM size comes from by inspecting its ID tag. D-series VMs, for example, are general-purpose and therefore are used most often by Azure customers. Note that these sizes are versioned; you can expect a v3 image to have features that v2 images don't, for example.

TIP

Don't worry if you deploy a VM at a size that turns out to be insufficient for your needs from a cost or performance perspective. You can resize VMs dynamically to align better with your situation.

Storage

Azure uses a feature called Managed Disks to store your OS and data VHDs. What's cool about Managed Disks is that you don't have to manage the underlying storage account infrastructure, which once was the case.

The big question about your VM disk storage relates to performance. Here are your options:

» **Standard HDD storage:** Lower-speed and lowest-price mechanical disk storage. Offers 2,000 maximum input/output operations per second (IOPS).

» **Standard SSD storage:** Balance between affordability and speed; underlying disks are solid-state. Offers 6,000 maximum IOPS.

» **Premium SSD storage:** High-speed but higher-price solid-state disk storage. Offers 20,000 maximum IOPS.

» **Premium SSD storage:** Production and performance quality storage for workloads requiring lower latency and high iOPS and throughput. Offers a maximum of 80,000 IOPS.

» **Ultra disk storage:** Super-high speed, highest-price solid-state disk storage. Offers 160,000 maximum IOPS.

Which storage tier is suitable for your VM workload depends on your need for speed and high availability. For example, a testing/development VM usually requires Standard HDD storage. On the other hand, a production database server VM may need the speed and predictable performance provided by Premium SSD storage. The best way to think scale here is: more transactions = more users = higher IOPS.

Network

The main idea to keep in mind is that your VM's networking configuration is independent of the VM resource itself. Understand that a VM's networking stack consists of the following components:

>> VM resource

>> Virtual network interface resource

>> (optional) Public IP address resource

>> (optional) Network security group resource

You configure TCP/IP protocol properties on the virtual network interface card (vNIC) rather than on the VM. This capability is fantastic for many reasons, not the least of which is that you can detach a vNIC from one VM and attach it to another. Portability!

Architectural Considerations

The process of deploying a VM in Azure has quite a few moving parts, and it's worth your while to take the most important of these parts — high availability and scalability — into account before you log into the Azure portal.

High availability

You don't want to have a single point of failure in your VM deployment. If your workload has a front-end web tier, you probably want at least two identically configured VM instances so that your service remains online if one node goes offline (expectedly or unexpectedly).

Microsoft offers a 99.99 percent high availability service-level agreement (SLA) when you place two or more matching VM nodes in separate availability zones. The SLA is 99.95 percent when you place two or more identical VM instances in an availability set. Finally, the SLA is 99.9 percent if you have a single VM instance using premium storage.

REMEMBER

You're responsible for configuring matching VM nodes. Azure doesn't automatically spawn additional identical VM nodes as it does with, say, Azure App Service. To make replica VMs, all sorts of possibilities exist: You could do so manually in the Azure portal or use Azure Resource Manager templates to automate the process.

Take a look at Figure 5-2 to get a handle on the difference between availability sets and availability zones.

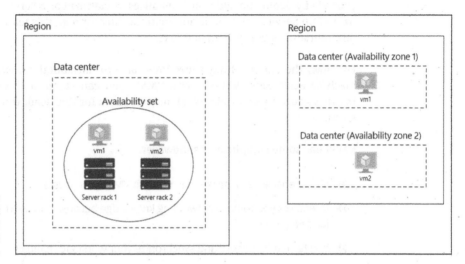

An *availability set* is a container object that you can populate with VM instances in the same region. Availability sets protect your VM tier against failures within a single data center in your home region. Your VMs are placed on separate hardware hosts on separate racks; thus, if Microsoft has a power or switch failure on a rack, or if it needs to take your hardware host offline, your service remains available because you have at least one member hosted elsewhere.

By contrast, *availability zones* protect against entire data center failures within your home region. You place your VMs in separate data centers in the region. You don't have to worry about latency, because Microsoft has redundant power, cooling, and network links among regional data center clusters.

WARNING

If you forget to place a VM in an availability zone or availability set during deployment, you need to redeploy to make this change. Yes, it's a pain, so make sure to do this task right the first time.

"Why wouldn't you always choose availability zones, then?" you may ask. The answer is simple: Microsoft hasn't enabled availability zones for all public regions yet, so that option may not be available in your region. In time, I'm sure that availability zones will be offered in all regions.

Thus, Microsoft's guidance is that if your Azure region supports availability zones, then you should use them. Otherwise, use availability sets to provide high availability for your Azure VMs.

Scalability

Scalability refers to your ability to resize your VM. It also means that you can scale your VM by deploying additional instances. A Platform as a Service (PaaS) such as Azure App Service can handle automatic scaling for you; this feature is a powerful differentiator between PaaS and IaaS.

For now, the closest thing Azure VMs have to horizontal autoscaling is Virtual Machine Scale Sets (VMSS). With VMSS, you can create a cluster of VMs and instruct Azure to autoscale based on your specs for CPU load, time schedule, and so on.

VMSS has some complications, however:

>> It's expensive because you pay for each VM in your cluster.

>> It requires you to have networking knowledge because you need an Azure load balancer.

>> You have to configure and synchronize your workload manually.

Whether you decide to use scale sets or create identical VM replicas on your own depends on how comfortable you are with conducting VM deployments and configuring VMs. Scale sets are intended to abstract away much of the underlying infrastructure complexity.

Isolation mode

Azure offers a feature that enables you and your organization to segregate applications and data from other customers. While not a private cloud, your ability to scale using public cloud resources is still enforced. Scalability and economic benefits are plentiful because you get the opportunity to build using multitenant cloud services while protecting the applications and data so that other Azure customers cannot touch your applications and data.

TIP

As you plan your architecture, you might hear terms such as identity-based isolation, zero-trust architecture, Azure Active Directory, data encryption key management, Azure Key Vault, or Managed HSM. These are complicated concepts, often associated with government, healthcare, and financial institutions apps and data sources. I can go on for chapters talking about each approach. Microsoft sums it up pretty nicely though at https://docs.microsoft.com/azure/azure-government/azure-secure-isolation-guidance.

Cost-Savings Opportunities

When organizations decide to move to the cloud, there is usually a lot of hype about how there is an abundance of cost savings. Okay, so there is some truth to this hype, but it does take planning and commitment to realize the value. You don't see the money falling from the sky immediately — quite the opposite. The value takes anywhere from 18 to 35 months to realize.

There are two approaches to cost savings: long-term using Azure Reservations, and short-term using Azure Spot Instances.

Azure Reservations

With Azure Reservations, Microsoft helps you save money so long as you are willing to commit to a one- or three-year cloud services plan across multiple Azure products. Azure Reservations enables you to significantly reduce resource costs by up to 72 percent from a pay-as-you-go plan. Assuming you are billed, this is an up-front billing discount and does not affect the runtime state of your resources. Why is that the case you ask? Well, you must purchase the reservation up front. As soon as you make the purchase, the discount is applied to all associated resources.

TIP

The nice thing about Azure Reservations is that you can pay up front or spread the cost out across the duration of the commitment. You'll never pay an extra fee unless you exceed the capacity purchased. Bear in mind that Azure Reservations are available for Azure reservation resources only, not third-party products.

Azure Spot Instances

For those individuals seeking temporary storage needs who don't care about always-on uptime and can forego stability and reliability, Azure Spot Instances can save you as much as ninety percent. Why would you use a spot instance, though? Well, if you intend to access your VM sporadically and are perfectly content with leveraging the pooled capacity available in your Azure region, then Microsoft is willing to provide you a discount. If you access the cloud midday in the middle of the week, it is more likely that your speed and reliability will not be as robust as that experienced midweek in the middle of the night. The trade-off, of course, is significant cost savings. The ideal users of Spot Instances are those who have light workloads and are not reliant on the lights always being on when they need them to be. They have some wiggle room, with the benefit of significant cost savings.

Deploying Azure VMs from the Azure Marketplace

I have a feeling that you've been waiting for this part of the chapter in which I explain how to work with the Azure technology directly. Thanks for your patience.

Deploying a Linux VM

I'll start with Linux because I never cease to get a kick out of the fact that Microsoft supports Linux natively in Azure. I've been a Microsoft specialist since 1997, and it was inconceivable up until a handful of years ago that we'd be able to run non-Windows VMs by using Microsoft technologies.

In this section, I explain how to deploy a simple Linux web server in a new virtual network using an Ubuntu Linux 20.04 Long-Term Support (LTS) VM image from the Azure Marketplace.

Deploying from the Azure portal

Follow these steps to deploy a Linux VM in the Azure portal:

1. **Choose Favorites ⇨ Create a Resource, and choose Ubuntu Server 18.04 LTS.**

Alternatively, you can browse to the Virtual Machines blade and click Add to deploy a new resource.

If Ubuntu doesn't show up in the Azure Marketplace list, type its name to find it in the VM template gallery.

2. **On the Create a Virtual Machine blade, complete the Basics tab.**

Figure 5-3 shows the Create a Virtual Machine blade. Oh, boy, it's tough not to feel overwhelmed when you see all the tabs: Basics, Disks, Networking, Management, Advanced, Tags, and Review + Create.

From now on, when I give you suggested choices on these deployment blades, I'll leave out fields you already know about, such as Subscription, Resource Group, and Region. Use the following information to complete the other fields:

- *Virtual Machine Name:* The name needs to be unique only within your resource group. Pay attention to the validation helpers that pop up when you place your cursor in a field.

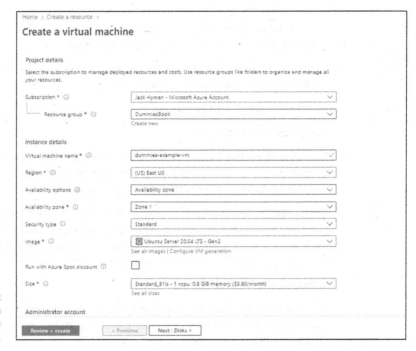

Home > Create a resource >

Create a virtual machine

Project details

Select the subscription to manage deployed resources and costs. Use resource groups like folders to organize and manage all your resources.

Subscription * ⓘ	Jack Hyman - Microsoft Azure Account ⌄
Resource group * ⓘ	DummiesBook ⌄
	Create new

Instance details

Virtual machine name * ⓘ	dummies-example-vm
Region * ⓘ	(US) East US ⌄
Availability options ⓘ	Availability zone ⌄
Availability zone * ⓘ	Zone 1 ⌄
Security type ⓘ	Standard ⌄
Image * ⓘ	🔲 Ubuntu Server 20.04 LTS - Gen2 ⌄
	See all images	Configure VM generation
Run with Azure Spot discount ⓘ	☐
Size * ⓘ	Standard_B1ls - 1 vcpu, 0.5 GiB memory ($3.80/month) ⌄
	See all sizes

Administrator account

[Review + create] [« Previous] [Next : Disks »]

FIGURE 5-3:
The Create a
Virtual Machine
blade.

- *Availability Options:* If you don't see both Availability Zone and Availability Set in the drop-down menu, choose a different region. (East US is a good choice.) Because this is a practice deployment, you can choose No Infrastructure Redundancy Required.

- *Image:* You specified the Ubuntu image in step 1, but if you're curious about other options, open the drop-down menu to see the most popular VM images. You can also click Browse All Public and Private Images to view all templates in the Azure Marketplace.

- *Run with Azure Spot Discount:* If you don't need your VM image 24/7 and want to save money, consider selecting the check box. An Azure Spot Instance enables customers to purchase VMs from a pool of unused spare capacity at a significantly lower price. You can save as much as 90 percent (you read that correctly) versus the pay-as-you-go pricing.

- *Size:* For now, accept the Microsoft-recommended default VM size.

- *Authentication Type:* Linux VMs are different from Windows because you can use Secure Shell (SSH) key-based authentication or password-based authentication. For this exercise, choose a password.

  You should choose a creative default administrator account name. ARM won't let you use commonly guessed administrator account names such as root or admin.

REMEMBER

- *Public Inbound Ports:* For testing purposes, associate a public IP address with this VM, and connect to the instance via SSH.

  You'll tighten network security group security later to prevent unauthorized access attempts by internet-based bad actors.

- *Select Inbound Ports:* Choose SSH.

3. **Complete the Disks tab.**

   This tab is where you make an initial choice about the VM's OS and data disks. Choose Standard HDD to save money. (Refer to the section "Storage" earlier in this chapter for more information about the various options.)

   The number of data disks you can create depends on your chosen VM instance size. You can always add data disks later, so for now, proceed to the next blade. Note that the default number of data disks Azure provides the new VM is zero; it's up to you as administrator to decide whether you want to use them.

4. **Complete the Networking tab.**

   You have some crucially important decisions to make in terms of where you want to place your VM and how you want to configure its connectivity. Here are the configuration options:

   - *Virtual Network:* The template deploys a new virtual network by default. That's what you want here, so leave this setting alone.

   If you place your VM on the wrong virtual network, you'll need to redeploy it to move it, which is a pain, so try to make the right choice the first time around.

   - *Subnet:* Leave this setting at its default.

   - *Public IP:* Leave this setting at its default. You do in fact want a public IP address, at least initially.

   - *NIC Network Security Group:* Select Basic.

   - *Public Inbound Ports:* Allow Selected Ports.

   - *Select Inbound Ports:* Select SSH.

   - *Accelerated Networking:* Not all VM templates support this option. For VM templates that support this feature, accelerated networking gives the VMs a network speed boost by allowing the VM to use the Azure networking backbone more directly.

   - *Load Balancing:* Select No.

5. **Complete the Management tab.**

Ensure that Boot Diagnostics is enabled and all other options are off. Boot Diagnostics is required to use the VM serial console, so it's always a good idea to enable it sooner rather than later.

6. **Review the Advanced and Tags tabs.**

You don't need any of these options right now, but they're worth examining. Extensions allow you to inject agent software or management scripts into the VM. You can handle configuration after deployment, however.

Taxonomic tags are a way to track resources across subscriptions for accounting purposes.

7. **Submit the deployment, and monitor progress.**

Click the Review + Create tab; then click Create after ARM informs you that your selections passed validation. If an error occurs, ARM places a red dot next to the configuration blade(s) where it detects invalid settings.

Connecting to the VM

Use Azure Cloud Shell to make an SSH connection to your VM. Follow these steps:

1. **In Azure portal, browse to the Overview blade of your newly created VM, and note the public IP address.**

You can see my VM's configuration in Figure 5-4.

FIGURE 5-4:
The Overview blade with IP address.

2. **Open Cloud Shell, and connect to your Linux VM by specifying your default administrator account name and the VM's public IP address.**

   To connect to my Linux VM at 20.84.118.159 using my jack admin account, I type

   ```
   ssh jack@ 20.84.118.159
   ```

   Type **yes** to accept the VM's public key and then type your password to enter the SSH session. At this point, you're working directly on the Linux VM.

TIP

You can get help for any Linux command by typing **man <command-name>**. Scroll through the Help document with your arrow keys, and press Q to quit.

WARNING

When you initially set up a VM, you may need to configure the extensions prior to connecting to the SSH instance. That is evident in Figure 5-4. You'll be told to install the extensions on VM instance if they are missing. Once set up, it's smooth sailing.

Deploying the VM

Assuming you have Visual Studio open and you're logged in to your Azure subscription, you're ready to rock. In this section, you're deploying a Windows Server VM from the Azure Quickstart Templates gallery, which you can find at https://azure.microsoft.com/resources/templates. I'm using a template definition that includes Managed Disks. Follow these steps:

1. **In Visual Studio, choose File ⇨ New ⇨ Project.**

   The Create a New Project dialog box opens.

2. **Search the Visual Studio template gallery for Azure Resource Group, select it, and click Next.**

   I entered **Azure Resource Group** and quickly found multiple instances. Select the one that includes Visual Basic, Cloud, and Azure.

3. **Name and save your project.**

   Choose a meaningful project name such as Simple Windows VM, choose your favorite directory location, and click Create.

4. **Select the 100-Blank-Template (BMOORE-MSFT) in the Azure Quickstart Templates gallery and click OK, as shown in Figure 5-5.**

5. **Double-click the azuredeploy.json template file.**

   This action loads the JavaScript Object Notation (JSON) file into your code editor. Pay particular attention to the JSON Outline pane, as shown in Figure 5-6.

FIGURE 5-5:
Creating a
resource group
deployment
project in Visual
Studio 2022.

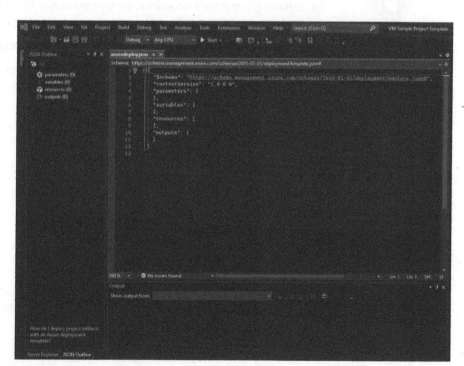

FIGURE 5-6:
The ARM
template in the
code editor.

6. **Browse the ARM template's contents.**

   The three elements shown in JSON Outline view are

   - *parameters:* You supply these values to the template at deployment time.

   - *variables:* These values represent fixed or dynamic data that is referenced internally within the template.

   - *resources:* In this deployment, you create four resource types: virtual machine, virtual NIC, virtual network, and public IP address.

7. **In Solution Explorer, right-click the project and choose Validate from the shortcut menu.**

   The Validate to Resource Group dialog box opens, as shown in Figure 5-7.

8. **Fill in the fields of the dialog box and then click Edit Parameters to supply parameter values.**

   Your variables will vary from environment to environment. In my environment, it is limited to credentials and storage type.

REMEMBER

   Visual Studio allows you to validate your template before deploying it to Azure. The resource group is the fundamental deployment unit in Azure. Therefore, your deployments must specify a new or existing resource group.

9. **Click Validate, and watch the Output window for status messages.**

   Make sure to look behind your Visual Studio application; Azure spawns a PowerShell console session to prompt you to confirm the admin password.

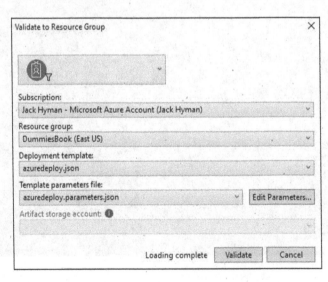

FIGURE 5-7:
Validating our
ARM template.

The feedback you're looking for in the Output window is

```
Template is valid.
```

If the template fails validation, Visual Studio is pretty good about telling you the template code line(s) on which it found an issue. You can debug and retry validation as many times as you need to until the template passes.

10. **Deploy the VM by right-clicking the project in Solution Explorer and choosing Deploy from the shortcut menu.**

TIP

The shortcut menu contains a reference to your validation configuration.

11. **Monitor progress, and verify that the VM exists in the Azure portal.**

You'll know that the deployment completed successfully when you see the following status line in the Output window:

```
Successfully deployed template 'azuredeploy.json' to resource group
    'your-resource-group'.
```

TECHNICAL STUFF

IDEM WHAT?

Azure Resource Manager templates use a declarative syntax that is described as idempotent. In ARM, *idempotency* allows you to run the same deployment multiple times without fear of deleting existing resources.

First, declarative code describes how you want the end state to look. The template code leaves the how of the deployment to the ARM platform. Declarative code is fundamentally different from imperative code such as C#, in which the programmer must instruct the .NET framework precisely what to do and when (and how) to do it.

By default, ARM deployments run in incremental mode, in which ARM operates under this assumption: "Make sure that the resource group contains all the template resources, but don't remove any existing resources that don't exist in the template definition."

You can also run deployments in Complete mode. In this mode, ARM operates under this assumption: "The only resources that this resource group should contain are those defined in the template." Any nonreferenced existing resources are deleted in this case.

Connecting to the VM

You usually use Remote Desktop Protocol to manage Windows Servers remotely on-premises, and Azure is no different. Browse to your new VM's Overview blade and click Connect. The Remote Desktop Connection dialog box opens (see Figure 5-8). You can download the .rdp connection file and open it from here.

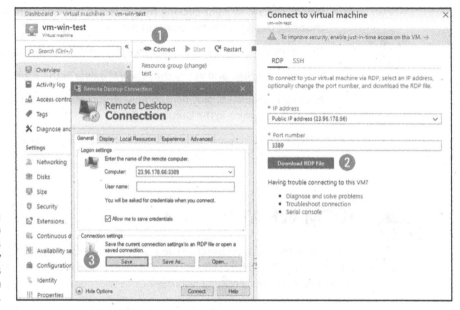

FIGURE 5-8:
Remote Desktop
Connection works
the same way
with Azure VMs
as it does with
on-premises VMs.

As shown in Figure 5-8, the steps to make an RDP connection are

1. Click Connect from the Overview blade toolbar.

2. Download the RDP connection file to your local computer.

3. Open the connection using your preferred RDP client software.

Microsoft makes a native Remote Desktop Protocol client for macOS; it's available in the Mac App Store.

TIP

Configuring Your VMs

Configuration management in the Azure Cloud is essentially the same as it is on-premises. You want to get your configuration right as early in the VM's life-cycle as possible.

First, I explain how to tweak networking, a VM's crucially essential and potentially vulnerable subsystem.

WARNING

Don't attempt to configure your Azure VM's networking settings from within the VM. If you do, you'll lock yourself out of the VM. Instead, you need to perform all your TCP/IP configurations in ARM.

It's not the VM resource but vNIC that contains the machine's IP configuration. Follow these steps to configure TCP/IP for a Windows Server VM:

1. Open the Windows Server VM's settings blade, and select Networking.

The Networking blade gives you at-a-glance TCP/IP configuration with direct hyperlinks to associated network resources:

- vNIC
- Virtual network
- Public IP address
- Network security group

I show you this interface in Figure 5-9. If you deployed the Windows Server VM from the VM template you used in the previous exercise, you'll be unpleasantly surprised to see that you don't have a NSG protecting the VM. You can fix that situation.

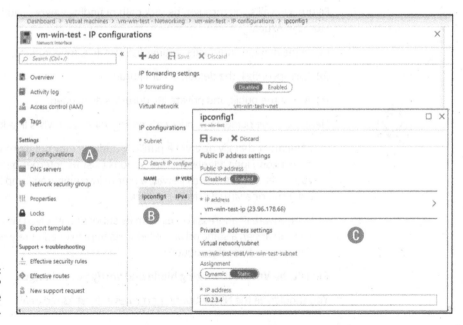

FIGURE 5-9: Azure VM TCP/IP settings in the Azure portal.

2. In the Azure search box, browse to the Network Security Groups blade, and click Add.

WARNING

Make sure to place any additional NSGs in the same Azure region as your NSG. Otherwise, neither your VMs nor your VNet will be able to use them.

If you've been reading this book sequentially (and for this situation, I hope you really have), you already know how to create NSGs.

3. Add a single inbound rule to allow inbound Remote Desktop Protocol traffic.

4. Browse to your VM's Networking blade, and select its vNIC.

You want to associate your new NSG with the VM's vNIC to protect it against internet-based access.

5. From the Network Interface settings menu, choose Network Security Group, click Edit, select your new NSG, and click OK.

Now we're talking! With this simple step, you've dramatically reduced the attack surface of this new VM.

6. In the Network Interface settings, select the IP Configurations setting and then click ipconfig1.

A vNIC always has a single IP configuration called (unimaginatively enough) ipconfig1. You specify your private and public IP addresses in the IP configuration.

Figure 5-9 walks you through the click path of finding where IP addresses are stored in Azure:

(a) In the network interface's settings list, click IP Configurations.

(b) Click ipconfig1, the default IP configuration.

(c) Adjust the public and private IP addresses as needed.

TIP

Here are some points to ponder concerning your Azure VM's IP addresses:

- Remember that giving a VM a public IP address may not be required or even a good idea. Plenty of other options exist for internet-based access to your VMs, such as Azure Firewall, a manually configured jump box, a load balancer, or a virtual private network.

- Your private IP address comes from its subnet on its given virtual network. You can assign a static private IP address here instead of relying on Azure dynamic address distribution.

7. Revisit the VM's Networking blade and verify your changes.

You should see the NSG inbound port rules at least. Good deal!

Starting, Stopping, and Resizing VMs

REMEMBER

Before I teach you how to start and stop VMs, I want to remind you that Microsoft charges you for each minute the VM is running or stopped but in an allocated state. A rule I stated earlier applies here too: Perform as much Azure-related VM management as possible from outside the VM.

If you shut down the VM by using the Azure portal, PowerShell, or the Azure command-line interface, depending on what parameters you add, you shut down and deallocate the VM, which stops billing.

Just know that deallocating a VM releases any dynamic resources it has been assigned, such as public/private IP addresses and temporary storage.

Starting and stopping a VM

You may have noticed the Start, Restart, and Stop buttons on the VM's Overview blade in the Azure portal. You can use those buttons to control your VM's allocation state (and, therefore, billing), but I'm going to teach you how to stop and start a VM by using PowerShell. Figure 5-10 shows the interface.

FIGURE 5-10:
Use the toolbar to start, stop, or restart a VM in the Azure portal.

When you use Cloud Shell, Azure automatically authenticates your user account to Azure Active Directory. By contrast, you need to authenticate manually before you can use Azure PowerShell on your local computer.

Follow these steps to use PowerShell on your Windows workstation to stop and then start a given VM:

1. **Open an administrative PowerShell console, and log into Azure.**

   To do so, run Connect-AzAccount, and authenticate to Azure.

TIP

   If you have more than one subscription, and Azure associates your session with the incorrect one, use the following command to make the switch:

   ```
   Set-AzContext -SubscriptionName 'MySubscription'
   ```

2. **List the VMs in a resource group.**

   You may not remember your VM's name, but if you remember the resource group name, try this:

   ```
   Get-AzVM -ResourceGroupName 'DummiesBook'
   ```

TIP

   You can enclose string (character) data in either single or double quotes in PowerShell. PowerShell was designed not to be fussy about such things.

3. **Stop the target VM with this command:**

   ```
   Stop-AzVM -Name dummies-example-vm' -ResourceGroupName 'DummiesBook'
      -Force
   ```

   Make sure to include the -Force switch parameter to ensure that you both stop and deallocate the VM.

4. **Start the VM.**

   Whoa — whiplash! But this step is a good learning opportunity. Check out this technique:

   ```
   Get-AzVM -Name 'dummies-example-vm' -ResourceGroupName 'DummiesBook' |
      Start-AzVM
   ```

   The pipe (|) character passes the results of the first segment (getting a reference to the target VM) to the second segment. This technique is called *pipelining*.

Resizing a VM

As I mention earlier, the ability to resize your VM dynamically is a massive paradigm shift from maintaining on-premises hardware.

WARNING

VM resizes in Azure have one drawback: They restart your VM. Be sure to perform this operation only during a predefined maintenance window.

To resize a VM, follow these steps:

1. **In your VM settings, select Size.**

   The Size blade contains a table of all VM sizes that are available in your region. Not all VM sizes are available in every region.

2. **Edit the filters to filter available VM sizes.**

   You can filter the VM size by using any combination of the following properties:

   - *Size:* Choices are Small, Medium, and Large.

- *Generation:* Choices are Current, Previous, and Older.

- *Family:* Choices are General Purpose, GPU, High Performance Compute, Compute Optimized, Memory Optimized, and Storage Optimized.

- *Premium Disk:* Choices are Supported and Not Supported.

- *vCPUs:* Choices range from 1 to 64 vCPU cores.

- *RAM:* Choices range from 2GB to 432GB.

3. **Select your desired VM size, and click Resize.**

   Your VM restarts with the new virtual hardware resources. Isn't that a world easier than requesting, ordering, and installing hardware in your on-premises data center?

Using Azure Virtual Desktop

Suppose your organization decided it no longer wants employees to directly work off a laptop or desktop to complete their work. Everything — and I mean everything — will be completed using a virtualized desktop in the cloud. You may know this as thin client computing, but in Azure-speak, this is known as a *Azure Virtual Desktop*. What makes Azure Virtual Desktop so different is the ability to consistently deploy and scale the VM to many users, possibly tens of thousands of users, in a repeatable fashion.

Once upon a time, an organization would need to log in to a computer, install each software piece using a license key, and sit there. And wait. And wait some more. Sounds inefficient, right? Many folks thought it was how business was done. We know better now, as it creates chaos and a highly insecure and error-prone environment. A business often dealt with data sprawl, given that no two systems were configured consistently. Now, with Windows Virtual Desktop, using a VM infrastructure as the baseline, a business can install a consistent operating system and software baseline for all employees without much deviation. You want to use a Windows Virtual Desktop because you no longer download a single application to the desktop other than the Remote Desktop Client client file. The user accesses everything, and I mean everything, using a Web browser.

WARNING

You should not confuse the Windows Remote Desktop feature discussed earlier with Azure Virtual Desktop. Logging into a VM is not the same as accessing a repeatable virtualized infrastructure. Remote Desktop enables a user to connect to an end-user's computer using a single-point secure connection, assuming that a trusted relationship exists. The Azure Virtual Desktop completely replaces the fat client (desktop), putting all compute resources in Azure.

Configuring an Azure Virtual Desktop takes a bit of time. Here, I'll explain the architectural principles only. An Azure Virtual Desktop is a PaaS-based solution. You'll be required to create an Azure Virtual Desktop tenant to operate your applications within your organization. So what does the tenant include?

First, the tenant incorporates one or more host pools. A *host pool* is comprised of one or more identical VMs. You read that correctly: It's comprised of identical VMs so that as users access the environment, they gain access to the same desktop environment from one user to another. Bear in mind, that each time a user accesses the VM, they are being allocated a dedicated Azure Virtual Machine instance against the configured Azure Virtual Desktop

Once the tenant is configured, you'll add users from your Azure Active Directory (those individuals who gain access to the repeatable VM instances). Those users can then access the Azure Virtual Desktop and run different client apps on the hosting operating system, including Windows or even Mac OS, via an icon to their web browser whether it is Microsoft Edge, Apple Safari, or Google Chrome.

ON THE WEB

The configuration process varies wildly depending on the operating system and number of host pools you intend to use. Because operating system configurations are all over the map, I find it much easier to point you to the instructions on the Microsoft site. You can find these details at https://docs.microsoft.com/azure/virtual-desktop.

Extending Your VM's Capabilities

As you enter this chapter's home stretch, I want to show you how to configure automated VM updates and basic diagnostics logging for Windows Server and Linux VMs in Azure.

Maintaining your VM environments

Keeping up with the updates on your operating system can be a real bear, especially when some vendors release patches weekly. If you had a way to automate the maintenance of your virtual machine environment would you jump at it? Of course you would!

Similar to the inner workings of the PaaS option, Azure allows for automated VM maintenance if you apply a few tactics along the way when initially configuring your virtual machines.

To start, you need to have VM images available as VM scale sets. This allows you to enable automatic OS images upgrades across all disks assuming the following:

>> The image publisher must publish an image generally available before the latest OS image can be consumed.

>> Upgrades should occur in batch instances once a new image is published by the publisher, not as a one-off.

>> Integration with health probes and application health extensions are enabled to ensure constant reliability.

>> Images are made available for all VM sizes and operating system types.

>> Ability to opt-out of automatic upgrades is possible at any time, including if you decide to use manual versus automatic upgrades.

>> Extension sequencing and automatic OS image upgrade support are enabled across any scale set size.

>> Replacing an OS disk with a new OS disk using the latest image is possible, including configurable extensions and custom data scripts while ensuring data persistency.

TECHNICAL STUFF

Automating VM upgrades requires some overhead planning as you can tell. Even if you are supporting guest patching for safety and security, there are things you need to plan for as part of the process. One-off guest patching should be a sched-uled event when the need is for critical or security purposes only. You should time the patch updates for off-peak hours in the VM's native time zone. But, most important, ensure that Azure manages patch orchestration by following the availability-first principle. In other words, the known patches should first be applied with any associated health data. Also, the patches should work on any VM sizes, not just a specific type of VM.

ON THE WEB

Automation takes on many forms in Azure. And believe me when I say this, Microsoft is constantly updating how updates can be deployed. I can guarantee you if I wrote about Azure Automatic Updates here, by the time you read this book, this section would be outdated. Instead, you should know the overarching architectural principles here. Head over to https://docs.microsoft.com/azure/automation/ to read up on how you can automate updates for your virtual machines (and then some).

Enabling diagnostic logging

Microsoft offers three increasingly granular monitoring options for Linux and Windows Server VMs:

>> **Host-level metrics:** Basic CPU, disk, and network utilization data pulled by the Azure platform that requires no agent software

>> **Guest-level monitoring:** More detailed monitoring; requires the Azure Diagnostics agent

>> **Azure Monitor Log Analytics:** Most robust monitoring; requires the Log Analytics agent and an associated Azure Monitor Log Analytics workspace

Here, we'll dabble in guest-level monitoring. To access it, open the Diagnostic Settings blade, and select Enable Guest-Level Monitoring.

Guest-level monitoring picks up the following data from your Windows Server VMs:

>> **Selected performance monitor counters:** CPU, memory, disk, and network.

>> **Event log messages:** Application, Security, and System.

>> **CPU kernel crash dump data:** This data can be helpful to Microsoft support representatives to diagnose problems with your VM.

Guest-level monitoring includes the following metrics and logs from your Linux VMs:

>> CPU, memory, network, file system, and disk metrics

>> Syslog log data for authentication, task scheduling, CPU, and other facilities

TECHNICAL STUFF

In Azure monitoring nomenclature, a *metric* is a time series of measured values that are stored for later analysis.

Viewing diagnostics data in Azure Monitor

Suppose that you need to plot CPU utilization data for the Linux and Windows Server VMs you've created to generate baseline data for your manager.

Follow these steps to create a monitoring chart in Azure Monitor:

1. **In the Azure portal, open Monitor, and navigate to the Metrics blade.**

   I show you Azure Monitor in Figure 5-11.

2. **In the Chart Title field, give the new chart a descriptive name.**

   For this exercise, I called mine "Avg CPU Credits Consumed for Jack Hyman – Microsoft Azure Account in East US Region by ResourceId."

3. **Configure the initial metric row to plot CPU data for one of your VMs.**

   Here are the properties I specified for my Windows Server VM:

   - *Resource:* dummiesbook
   - *Metric Namespace:* Virtual Machine Host
   - *Metric:* CPU Credits Consumed
   - *Aggregation:* Avg

4. **While I do not add a secondary metric, you can click Add Metric and configure the metric row to plot a secondary metric.**

   Being able to plot metrics from multiple Azure resources can be enormously helpful in your monitoring.

5. **Experiment with the other metrics controls in Azure Monitor.**

   Check out these controls:

   - *New Chart:* You can create a chart showing something such as Azure storage account read transactions.

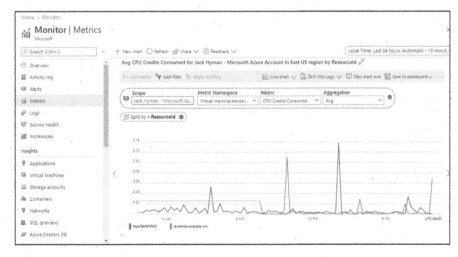

FIGURE 5-11:
Azure Monitor is a method to monitor infrastructure and application performance.

- *Line Chart:* Try changing the plot type to observe how the view changes your data's visibility.

- *New Alert Rule:* You can generate alerts, notifications, and remediation actions based on defined metric thresholds (such as triggering an alert when your Linux VM exceeds your predefined CPU utilization threshold).

- *Pin to Dashboard:* You can use the Azure dashboard as a business intelligence dashboard.

Chapter **6**

Shipping Docker Containers in Azure

D ocker containers are taking over the world! Okay, so maybe not the world, but they are surely becoming a significant part of the Azure Cloud land-scape. Many businesses are realizing the financial benefits of using Docker containers in their development and production environments. Quite simply, Docker containers make it a lot faster and easier for developers to build repeat-able, affordable software products.

Microsoft supports Docker containers in its cloud in a variety of ways. Docker can get a bit complicated, so don't assume you'll be the world-renowned expert in Docker by the time you finish this chapter, but you'll grasp the use of containers and the possibilities of using Docker as part of your Azure solution.

Understanding Docker

If you've read Chapter 5, you probably have a pretty good idea of what virtual machines (VMs) are and how they work. To me, Docker containers represent a more agile degree of virtualization. Containers allow developers or administrators to package an application and all its dependencies into a single, modular unit that can be deployed quickly.

REMEMBER

A Docker container is a virtualized application, not an entire VM. Think small picture here as it is intended only for a specific activity, not the whole system. You might create and run Docker containers running different databases and database versions against which to test your application. These containers contain specific functionality such as the database engine binaries and their dependencies — nothing more, nothing less.

Whereas each VM may weigh hundreds of gigabytes and need to be updated, backed up, monitored, and maintained (remember VMs are Infrastructure as a Service [IaaS]), containers can range from less than 100MB to a few gigabytes. The footprint is entirely dependent on the resources deployed and the infrastructure required, which is minimized for operations.

TECHNICAL STUFF

People often wonder, are containers an IaaS or a Platform as a Service (PaaS)? The answer is, it depends! Because most containers do not require configuration of infrastructure services for containers or Kubernetes, you are likely to find that many organizations put the applications in a managed setting (PaaS). That doesn't mean that configuration is out of the question. If infrastructure configurations are necessary, especially at the operating system (OS) level, the container is in effect IaaS.

Like VMs, containers share hardware resources with their container host server. Unlike VMs, containers are defined fundamentally in plain-text Dockerfiles, which contain the instructions for building a container.

The idea is to put all the assets that will comprise your container in a single directory and create a Dockerfile that orchestrates the container's composition. Then you compile the Dockerfile into a binary image, which serves as your deployment unit. Finally, you create as many containers as you need by deploying instances of your image template. Figure 6-1 illustrates the Docker deployment process.

TIP

Docker is an enormous topic that could fill a separate book. If you want to know more about creating container images, check out the Docker documentation at https://docs.docker.com.

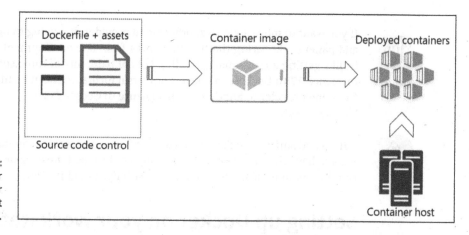

FIGURE 6-1:
The Docker
container
deployment
process.

TECHNICAL
STUFF

Application virtualization existed in Linux long before Docker. Docker is a business that simply standardized and extended these preexisting technologies. Microsoft and Docker partnered primarily to bring Docker containers to Windows Server, and this chapter deals almost exclusively with Windows Server containers.

Using Docker containers

Developers love Docker containers because containers are agile. Dockerfiles are plain-text documents, which means that development teams can store them in source-code control and track their changes over time.

Suppose you need to test your business's line-of-business application against three MySQL database versions. Starting three separate VMs is ordinarily a slow, labor-intensive process (and quite expensive, too). This pain becomes greater when you need to spin up and work with multiple instances of each VM-based MySQL installation. If the VM's guest operating system needs an update or if MySQL requires an update, the process is even slower.

By contrast, you can use the Docker command-line interface or a hosted container platform to start up any number of MySQL containers running different software versions. When you finish testing, it's pretty easy to disposes of the containers with a single command. If MySQL needs an update, you or one of your teammates can simply edit the Dockerfile and recompile an image.

Portability is another huge advantage of containers. Microsoft Azure is a Hyper-V ecosystem. What if you need to migrate your VMs to, say, Google Cloud Platform where they use another hypervisor?

If you want to move a VM to another cloud provider, it's going to take a lot of time and patience. Ensuring that the VM works from one environment to another can be like getting a root canal (literally). Lots of pain, lots of time, sub-optimal performance. With Docker, you have a universal format that can be lifted and shifted from one provider to another (such as Azure to Google Cloud or Azure to Amazon Web Services).

Lifting and shifting Docker does require a few server service components. Assuming you have the components (depending on the cloud-hosting provider), you can run the container just about anywhere with light modifications.

Setting up Docker on your workstation

The Docker run-time environment is relatively lightweight and portable. In this section, I show you how to install Docker Desktop on your Windows 10 or 11 workstation.

For purposes of this book, I assume that you're working on a Windows 10– or 11–based computer. Docker Desktop and its associated tools are also available for macOS and Linux, however. Docker does a good job of standardizing the user interface, so you should find that the following steps work for you if you are on macOS or Linux.

Installing Docker Desktop

Follow these steps to set up Docker on your Windows 10 system:

1. **Register for a free user account at Docker Hub.**

   Docker Hub (https://hub.docker.com) is the main public repository for Docker containers.

2. **Download and install Docker Desktop from www.docker.com/products/docker-desktop.**

   The website encourages you to work through an interactive tutorial; do so at your leisure.

3. **Accept the default settings during installation.**

   The exception to this rule occurs when the installer asks whether you want to use Windows containers instead of Linux containers. Select Windows containers. You won't see this option on macOS or Linux computers.

4. **Restart your computer.**

   The installer requires you to log out and restart to install the Hyper-V and Containers Windows features.

5. **Verify that the Docker service is running.**

Docker Desktop appears as an icon in the Windows notification area (see Figure 6-2).

Right-click the Docker icon and you'll see all sorts of options on the shortcut menu (including to Switch to Windows Containers if you forgot to enable that feature during installation). Figure 6-2 shows Switch to Linux Containers, which Docker displays if you're currently configured for Windows containers.

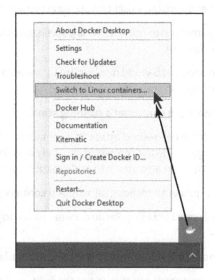

FIGURE 6-2:
Docker Desktop is easily accessible from the Windows notification area.

REMEMBER

The Docker service needs to run with elevated permissions. If you find that Docker Desktop doesn't put its icon in your notification area, run the app from the Desktop or Start-menu shortcut as an administrator.

Running the hello-world container

Docker's hello-world reference image can give you a feel for how to use Docker from the client's perspective. Follow these steps:

1. **Open an elevated PowerShell or Command Prompt console.**

To do so, find the PowerShell or Command Prompt icon on your Start menu or taskbar, right-click it, and choose Run as Administrator from the shortcut menu.

2. **Check your Docker version by running** `docker — version`.

This step is a sanity check to make sure that the Docker command-line interface and server components are functional.

3. **Check for any locally available container images by running** `docker images.`

    You should see only the Repository, Tag, Image ID, Created, and Size properties with no images. (You correct that situation in Step 4.) You can also use `Docker info` to see more condensed metadata.

4. **Pull and run the hello-world image from Docker Hub.**

    Issue the command `docker run hello-world` and watch what Docker does:

    (a) Docker checks whether the image exists on your local system. It doesn't.

    (b) Docker issues a pull command to retrieve the latest version of the hello-world image from Docker Hub.

    (c) Docker runs the container. hello-world displays `Hello from Docker!`, confirming that the image ran correctly.

5. **Run** `docker ps -a` **to view the container's running state.**

    Docker is telling you it ran the hello-world image as a container and that it exited as soon as the image ran. In the real world, you may want Docker containers to run longer. You can also attach to and detach from containers.

6. **Run** `docker container prune` **to remove all stopped containers.**

    In this case, you have only one container. Rerun `docker ps -a` to verify that the container is gone.

7. **Verify that the hello-world container image is locally available.**

    Use the `docker images` command; you should see the hello-world image listed.

Using this test run of Docker, you've seen that the ordinary user's workflow with containers is the following:

1. Pull container images as needed from a central repository.

2. Run new containers based on those images.

3. Dispose of containers when they're no longer needed.

TECHNICAL STUFF

When you install Docker Desktop on your Windows system, you're installing both the Docker daemon and the Docker CLI (client). If you right-click the Docker icon in your notification area, you can open Kitematic (a graphical Docker front end) from the shortcut menu. Kitematic can be helpful to Docker beginners who aren't yet comfortable running Docker commands from the command line.

THE WINDOWS HELLO-WORLD CONTAINER

If you're wondering exactly what the Windows hello-world container does, let me enlighten you. This container derives from a Windows Nano Server image. (Nano is a super-stripped-down Windows Server version.) The container starts a cmd.exe console process, which in turn displays the contents of a file called hello.txt. These file contents represent the output you see in your Docker CLI session, after which the container terminates automatically.

Running containers in Azure

"All this Docker Desktop stuff is well and good," you may be saying, "but when will I get to Azure?" You're there now.

In the Azure ecosystem, the following resources support Docker containers natively:

» VM-based container hosts

» Azure Container Instances

» Azure Container Registry

» Azure Kubernetes Service

» Azure App Service Web App for Containers

I'll discuss each option briefly before you get your hands dirty with the technologies.

VM-based container hosts

You will be starting a Linux or Windows Server VM in an Azure virtual network, installing the Docker daemon and launching Docker containers from there. Although this strategy works, it makes little sense to me under most circumstances, given the PaaS resources that are already available and ready for your consumption.

Azure Container Instances

Azure Container Instances (ACI) is for Azure professionals who need to run Docker containers quickly without worrying about the overhead of installing and maintaining the Docker daemon and client. ACI is excellent for one-off container work, in which centralized management and orchestration are unnecessary.

Azure Container Registry

By now, you know about Docker Hub, the public image repository hosted by Docker. Microsoft publishes the bulk of its publicly accessible container images to Docker Hub. This of course is with exception. Azure Container Registry (ACR) is designed for businesses whose teams need a private, central image registry from which they can work with their own internal Docker images.

Azure Kubernetes Service (AKS)

Azure Kubernetes (pronounced *koo-burr-NET-eez*) Service, or AKS, is a container orchestration platform for Docker containers that was developed by Google. It allows you to create a compute cluster that provides powerful centralized management for your container workloads.

AKS is popular because many businesses use Dockers to host multitiered applications consisting of multiple containers that need to be managed as a group. It also provides high availability, scheduled application upgrades, and massively parallel scaling. AKS is also popular as it allows for optimizing resources when utilizing a hybrid cloud environment.

In a nutshell, AKS is Azure's hosted Kubernetes cluster service. You still get to work with the native Kubernetes client tools, such as the web UI and the kubectl command-line client, but you can take advantage of seamless integration with other Azure services and features.

Azure App Service Web App for Containers

Azure App Service is a hosted web application service in Azure that can integrate with Docker container-based apps. App Service, which I discuss in Chapter 7, allows you to easily

>> Integrate your application in a build/release pipeline.

>> Autoscale your application to meet usage spikes.

>> Let Microsoft take care of patching, backing up, and maintaining the underlying host environment.

Therefore, Web App for Containers combines the agility of containers with the powerful App Service PaaS platform.

TECHNICAL STUFF

Because Microsoft is handling the infrastructure and underlying applications but you are responsible for the code-wrapper, any product that is containerized or built using Kubernetes is by default a PaaS resource, not an IaaS resource.

Implementing Azure Container Instances

It's time to log in to the Azure portal and drill down into each of these Docker-related Azure resources. This section covers the following tasks:

>> Defining a new container instance with Microsoft's publicly available Internet Information Services (IIS) web server container from Docker Hub

>> Associating a public IP address resource with the container so that you can reach it from your workstation

>> Testing connectivity with your browser

>> Removing the container

To complete any of these jobs, you need to log in to the Azure portal with your administrative account.

Deploying an Azure container instance

Follow these steps to deploy an IIS-based Windows Server container with a public IP address:

1. **Navigate to the Container Instances blade, and click Add.**

To get to the Container instances blade, type **azure container** in the global search box.

2. **Fill out the Basics tab, which appears by default and is shown in Figure 6-3. Click Next to continue.**

You need to complete the following items:

- *Subscription & Resource Group:* Choose the option that meets your requirements.

- *Container Name and Region:* The name needs to be unique within your resource group. Select the Azure region closest to you.

- *Image Type:* Public is the appropriate option when you're pulling the IIS image from the Docker Hub, as in this example. You'd choose Private to authenticate to a private image repository.

- *Image Source:* Quickstart images are the use of pre-existing container images already created. Azure Container Registry enables you to apply the use of an existing ACR within a container instance.

- *Image Name:* Type the name of the image — in this case, **microsoft/iis**, which is an extremely popular container image.

- *OS Type:* Select the OS you're using.

- *Size:* Accept the default setting. Your container will run on a host VM under the hood, even though you'll never interact with the host directly.

3. **Fill out the Networking tab.**

   Complete these items:

   - *Include Public IP Address:* Select Yes. You need a public IP address to connect to the container from over the public Internet.

   - *Ports:* Because you're deploying a web server container, you need to access TCP port 80 (HTTP) on the container.

   - *DNS Name Label:* This field is optional, but it's a good idea to supply a name label that you'll recognize in case your public IP address changes for some reason. Note that this host name needs to be globally unique, so you may need to apply some creativity in coming up with a name.

4. **Submit the deployment.**

   To do so, click Review + Create and then click Create.

5. **Monitor deployment progress.**

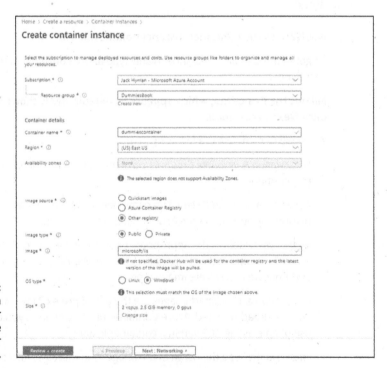

FIGURE 6-3:
Deploying a
Docker container
using the Azure
Container
Instance service.

Verifying and disposing of the container instance

Follow these steps to get familiar with the ACI Azure portal experience and verify connectivity to your new IIS container:

1. **On the Container Instances blade, select a container instance.**

   You can select the IIS container you created in the previous procedure. Selecting the container instance takes you to its Overview blade.

2. **On the Essentials pane of the Overview blade, verify the Status and IP Address fields.**

   The container status should be Running. Make a note of the public IP address, because you'll need it in Step 3.

3. **Copy the container's IP address, paste it into the Address field of a new web browser tab, and press Enter.**

   If all goes well, you should see the blue Windows Server IIS test page. If so, you've launched an internet-accessible container.

4. **Back in the Azure portal, click the Containers setting.**

5. **On the Containers blade, click Connect.**

   You're making a terminal connection to this container.

6. **In the Choose Start Up Command window, type /bin/bash, and then click Connect.**

   When you reach a command prompt, you can use command-line tools to perform tasks such as copying files to the container and downloading configuration files.

TIP

   It's convenient to attach to your container through the Azure portal. Be aware, though, that other methods exist, some through the Docker command-line interface on your workstation or Azure PowerShell.

7. **Browse to the container instance's Overview page, click Delete, and confirm your choice.**

   The Overview toolbar has Stop, Restart, and Delete controls. Although Docker containers are ordinarily considered to be ephemeral and disposal, you may want to stop and restart the same container in the future. In this case, you no longer need the container, so you can delete it from your subscription.

CHECKING YOUR UNDERSTANDING

As your guide through Azure, its essential that you understand why you're taking these steps and why you should care. If you're a web developer, you'll want to test your site code against a running web server. In the demo in this section, you used an existing IIS container image at Docker Hub.

What I want you to think about next is what happens if your team wants to use its own customized Docker images rather than the public Docker Hub.

Great question! You can do that with the ACR, which is the next stop on this Docker-in-Azure trolley ride.

Storing Images in Azure Container Registry

I want to be respectful of your network bandwidth, so in this section you'll push the (relatively) small hello-world container you pulled from Docker Hub in an earlier section to your new container registry.

Azure Container Registry (ACR) is a cloud-hosted repository for Docker images. ACR provides a centralized storage/management location for your team's images; these images are accessible only to Azure users to whom you give proper permissions.

Deploying a container registry

Before you push a container to ACR, you need to deploy the registry. Follow these steps:

1. **In the Azure portal, browse to the Container Registries blade, and click Add. The Create Container Registry form appears.**

2. **Complete the Create Container Registry form.**

   Following are the settings you need to address:

   - *Registry Name:* You can choose any name for your registry as long as it's globally unique. Azure will not let you proceed if you happen to choose a name that's already in use.

   - *Subscription, Resource Group, and Location:* Choose your subscription and desired resource group and Azure region.

- *Admin User:* Enable this option. Doing so will make authenticating to your registry easier.

- *SKU:* Choose Basic. SKU is short for *stock-keeping unit*, and Basic is the lowest-cost ACR pricing tier. The Standard and Premium SKUs offer higher performance and scale.

3. **Click Create to submit the deployment.**

   In most cases, Azure completes the deployment in less than one minute.

4. **When deployment is complete, open your new registry in the Azure portal and note the content of the Login Server field.**

   You'll need this DNS name in the next section, when you push a container image to the registry. The registry takes the name *<your-registry-name>.azurecr.io*.

Pushing an image to a new container registry

To show you how to push an image to a container registry, I'm using the hello-world image you worked with in "Setting up Docker on your workstation" earlier in this chapter. To push an image to a container registry, follow these steps:

1. **Obtain your admin credentials from your registry's Access Keys settings blade.**

   I show you this blade in Figure 6-4. Specifically, you'll need to note the Username field, which should be your registry name, and one of the two passwords. It doesn't matter which password you copy; you need one to complete Step 2.

2. **Open a command prompt session and log in to your container registry using the docker login command.**

   Supply the registry short name as the username and the previously copied password as the password. Here's the command:

   docker login dummiesregistry .azurecr.io

   If all goes well, you see a Login succeeded status message.

3. **Define a tag for the hello-world image.**

   A tag looks like <owner–name>/<image–name>, but in this case, the owner is the registry. Here's the command I use for my dummiesregisry registry:

   docker tag hello-world dummiesregistry.azurecr.io/hello-world

4. **Push the hello-world image to your registry.**

   To do this, use this command:

   docker push dummiesregistry.azurecr.io/hello-world

   The amount of time that this process takes depends upon your upstream network bandwidth to Azure.

5. **Verify that the hello-world image appears in your container registry.**

   To do so, navigate to the registry's Repositories blade. You'll find that the Azure portal doesn't give you too many options for what you can do with this container image. The implication is that you'll interact with the image by using the Docker CLI, an automation tool, or a tool chain.

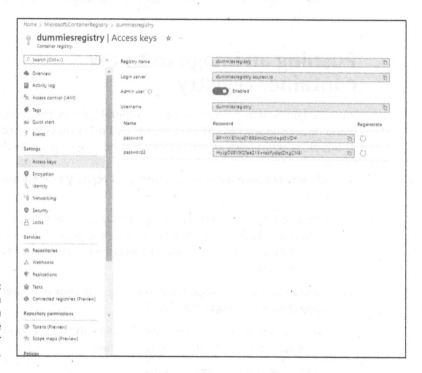

FIGURE 6-4:
Retrieving admin credentials from our Azure Container Registry.

Pulling the repository image via ACI

Once you've placed a Docker image into a registry, you can use the docker pull command to download the image and spawn containers on your local system based on the image.

HOW THIS STUFF WORKS IN THE REAL WORLD

Consider how a development team might stitch together solutions by using ACIs and ACRs. The developer team, working in conjunction with the operations team (DevOps), might place all assets and associated Dockerfiles in a central source-code repository.

Automatically, on a schedule, or manually, the team can push new and/or updated Docker container image builds to their registry. Then, when developers need to start a new container, they can do so from ACI, either automatically, on schedule, or as needed. For now, you should know that Azure DevOps is a platform from which you can orchestrate the entire container lifecycle in an almost completely automated process.

In this section, you'll run the registry-housed hello-world container image from the ACI service. To do so, follow these steps:

1. **Navigate to the Container Instances blade, and add a new container instance.**

2. **Specify the image type, image name, and OS type.**

   Here's the info:

   - *Image Type:* Choose Private when you're pulling the image from a private, Azure-based container registry; otherwise, choose Public.

   - *Image Name:* For my registry, I use twwiley.azurecr.io/hello-world. Substitute your own registry name.

   - *Image Registry:* Add your login server, username, and password.

   - *OS Type:* Select the OS you're using.

3. **Submit the deployment by clicking Review + Create and then clicking Create.**

   You don't need to worry about networking, tagging, and the like.

4. **If the deployment fails, read the operation details.**

   ARM may validate yet still fail the deployment. If this happens, as in the case of any failed deployment, read all the operational details that Azure offers.

A failed deployment is no big deal, though. You can rerun deployment templates as many times as you need to until you get it right. Just click the Redeploy button, as shown in Figure 6-5. By default, deployments don't delete existing resources. Instead, the template picks up where it left off, so to speak, until your deployment matches the underlying template definition.

FIGURE 6-5: Redeploy options for a Container.

TECHNICAL STUFF

Another place to research deployment details (successful or failed) is the Resource Groups blade in the Azure portal. Open a resource group and navigate to the Deployments blade. Every deployment in Azure is recorded for your reference and/or troubleshooting pleasure.

Everything I've explained about container support in Azure is well and good, but frankly, ACI suffers because it offers basic orchestration, unlike some of its competitors such as Google Cloud and Amazon Web Services. The chances are good that your developers may deploy multiple containers simultaneously and manage them as a group. Your business may also require your containers to be capable of horizontal scaling to adapt to user load and to be highly available. For small deployments, Azure fits the bill. Otherwise, you will need a container orchestration platform for anything beyond the most basic of container use cases in business, which at this point in time can be best completed using AKS.

Introducing Azure Kubernetes Service

AKS began life as Azure Container Service (ACS), which supported multiple container orchestration platforms, including Kubernetes, Swarm, and DC/OS. The downsides of ACS were its complexity and the fact that most customers wanted first-class support for Kubernetes only. Therefore, although you may see an occasional reference to ACS in the Azure portal or elsewhere, you are better served using AKS.

ON THE WEB

Walking you through the deployment and management process of an AKS is fairly complicated, and it's best to learn from the source, Microsoft. The documentation changes frequently for this topic as the technology constantly evolves. To find the most recent details on the Azure Kubernetes Service, go to `https://docs.microsoft.com/azure/aks`.

REMEMBER

Developers don't necessarily start containers because they're fun to use; developers start containers because they're practical. Containers host application components such as web servers or database servers and then form application solutions. Therefore, I want you to relate the words *container* and *application* from now on.

AKS architecture

The following are the basic elements of AKS (see Figure 6-6):

>> **Master node:** Microsoft abstracts the control plane (called the *master node* in Kubernetes nomenclature) so that you can focus on your worker nodes and pods. This hosted PaaS platform is one reason why many businesses love AKS. The master node is responsible for scheduling all the communications between Kubernetes and your underlying cluster.

>> **Worker node:** In AKS, the worker nodes are the VMs that make up your cluster. The cluster gives you lots of parallel computing, the ability to move pods between nodes easily, to perform rolling updates of nodes without taking down the entire cluster, and so on. One option is using ACI to serve as worker nodes.

Figure 6-6 also shows ACR, from which AKS can pull stored images. Isn't all this Azure integration compelling?

>> **Pod:** The pod is the smallest deployable unit in the AKS ecosystem. A pod may contain one Docker container, or it might contain a bunch of containers that you need to stay together, communicate with one another, and behave as a cohesive unit.

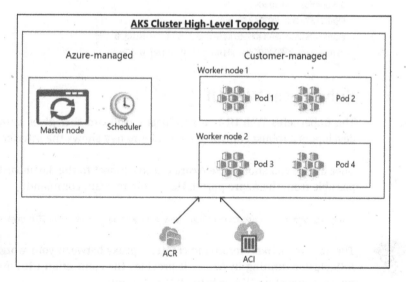

FIGURE 6-6:
AKS high-level
architecture.

AKS administration notes

Before I move on, I review how developers and administrators interact with AKS. From a control-plane perspective, you have AZR, with which you can protect your AKS cluster with role-based access control, upgrade your Kubernetes version, scale out the cluster, add or remove worker nodes, and so on.

From the application-plane perspective, Microsoft wants to ensure that customers don't have to learn a new tool set to work with containers in AKS.

kubectl command-line tool

Most Kubernetes professionals use the kubectl (generally pronounced *KOOB-see-tee-el*, *KOOB-control*, or *KOOB-cuttle*) to interact with their Kubernetes cluster and its pods programmatically. If you have Azure CLI installed on your workstation, you can install kubectl easily by issuing the following command:

```
az aks install-cli
```

In fact, Azure CLI seems to borrow quite a bit from kubectl syntax in terms of the app context command workflow. To list your running pods (containers) with kubectl, for example, run

```
$ kubectl get pods
READY STATUS RESTARTS AGE
azure-database-3406967446-nmpcf 1/1 Running 0 25m
azure-web-3309479140-3dfh0 1/1 Running 0 13m
```

Kubernetes Web UI

The Kubernetes Web UI is a graphical dashboard that gives administrators and developers a robust control surface. Figure 6-7 shows the interface.

Once again, you should use Azure CLI to connect to the dashboard; doing so isn't possible from the Azure portal. Here's the relevant command:

```
az aks browse --resource-group myResourceGroup --name myAKSCluster
```

TECHNICAL STUFF

The az aks browse command creates a proxy between your workstation and the AKS cluster running in Azure; it provides the connection URL in its output. The typical connection URL is http://127.0.0.1:8001.

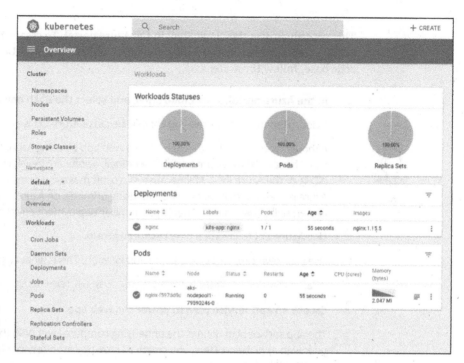

FIGURE 6-7:
The Kubernetes
Web UI
Dashboard.

Using Containers with Azure App Service

Azure Web App for Containers allows you to plug your existing container-based apps into an Azure App Service app. For businesses that aren't using an orchestration/scaling platform like AKS, this feature is a great way to autoscale an app without additional investment and complexity.

"But you can't host non-.NET apps in App Service, right?" you ask. That's incorrect, you can in fact use any supported run-time environment, including the following:

- » .NET Core
- » Node.js
- » PHP
- » Java
- » Python
- » Ruby

This procedure uses the Cloud Shell in the Azure portal. To create a new Azure App Service web app that uses a Linux container pulled from the Docker Hub as its code base, follow these steps:

1. **In the Azure portal, start Cloud Shell, and select the Bash environment.**

   It doesn't matter which shell you choose, because Azure CLI is available in both.

TIP

   Although you're creating this App Service web app by using Azure CLI, you could have used the Azure portal, PowerShell, a software development kit (SDK), or the Azure REST API. Because Microsoft makes so many updates to the Azure portal, you may be better off focusing primarily on Azure CLI or PowerShell to have a more stable and familiar deployment environment.

2. **Use Azure CLI to create a new resource group.**

   Use your own resource group name and location. This is what I used:

   ```
   az group create --name containerApp --location "East US 2"
   ```

3. **Create an app service plan to power the web app.**

   The app service plan defines the underlying compute layer (VM) that hosts your web application. Here, you create a Linux-powered service plan by using the B1 VM instance size:

   ```
   az appservice plan create --name myAppServicePlan
       --resource-group containerApp --sku B1
       --is-linux
   ```

4. **Define the web app.**

   I named my app go-container-704 to make the name globally unique and pulled the microsoft/azure-cosmosdb-emulator container image from Docker Hub. You can examine the container options by visiting https://hub.docker.com/u/microsoft.

   ```
   az webapp create --resource-group containerApp
       --plan myAppServicePlan --name go-container-704
       --deployment-container-image-name microsoft/azure-cosmosdb-emulator
   ```

5. **Browse to the app.**

   The format of the URL for projects is http:// http://<app_name>.azurewebsites.net/hello. Use that address (substituting your own app name).

6. **Verify that you see the simple Hello, world! message shown in Figure 6-8.**

   Your new container-backed app appears on the App Services blade in the Azure portal.

7. Clean up the environment.

Because you stored this test web app in its own resource group, cleaning up is a breeze. Run one final Azure CLI command, and confirm your choice:

```
az group delete --name containerApp
```

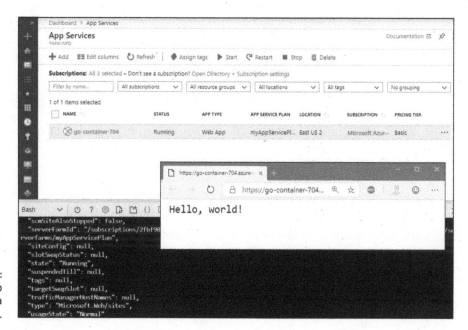

FIGURE 6-8:
A new Azure web app powered by a Docker container.

3

Deploying Platform Resources to Microsoft Azure

Chapter **7**

Deploying and Configuring Azure App Service Apps

One of the most fascinating parts of Microsoft Azure is when folks like you and me discover the constant power and agility of Azure Platform as a Service (PaaS) resources; Azure App Service is chief among them. And make no mistake about it, Microsoft is constantly improving Azure PaaS and App Service. Azure App Service frees you up to focus on your line-of-business applications instead of managing your virtual machine (VM) infrastructure. App Service provides hyperscale and seamlessly integrates with other Azure products like storage accounts and Azure SQL Database.

In this chapter, you discover App Service's place in the Azure product portfolio and how to create and configure App Service web apps. Learning how to program is beyond the scope of this book, of course, so instead I focus on answering the questions of how and why App Services are built a specific way. The coding part, which is surely organizational-centric in nature, is left for your team to decide what is best.

Introducing Azure App Service

In a nutshell, App Service is a Hypertext Transfer Protocol (HTTP)-based web application hosting service. Think of GoDaddy but with much more power. The idea is that if you're willing to surrender full control to the app's underlying infrastructure (which is what Azure Virtual Machines is for), you'll receive in exchange

» Global replication and geoavailability

» Dynamic autoscaling

» Native integration into continuous integration/continuous deployment pipelines

Yes, App Service uses VMs under the hood, but you never have to worry about maintaining them; Microsoft does that for you. Instead, you focus nearly exclusively on your source code and your application. This chapter focuses almost exclusively on web apps, but in Chapter 8 you meet other App Service family members.

Web apps

The static or dynamic *web application* is the most commonly used option in App Service. Your hosted web apps can be linked to cloud- or on-premises databases, API web services, and content delivery networks.

API apps

An *application programming interface* (API) is a mechanism that offers programmatic (noninteractive) access to your application by using HTTP requests and responses — a programming paradigm known as Representational State Transfer (REST). Nowadays, Microsoft supports API apps from App Service and the API Management service.

Mobile apps

A *mobile app* provides the back end to an iOS or Android application. Azure mobile apps provide features most smartphone consumers have grown to expect as part of the mobile apps they use, such as social media sign-in, push notifications, and offline data synchronization.

Logic apps

A *logic app* provides a way for developers to build business workflows without having to know all the underlying APIs in different services. You might create a logic app that triggers whenever someone mentions your company's name on Twitter, for example. Then this app may perform several actions, such as posting a notification message in your sales department's Slack channel or creating a record in your customer relationship management database.

Function apps

A *function app* enables developers to run specific code at specific times without worrying about the underlying infrastructure. That's why function apps are called *serverless* applications, or *Code as a Service (CaaS)* solutions. One of my consulting clients has a function app that sends a confirmation email message to a prospective customer whenever that user creates a new account on his website.

Function apps support the C#, F#, and Java programming languages.

Both logic apps and function apps operate on the basis of a trigger. This trigger could be a manual execution command, a time schedule, or a discrete operation that occurs inside or outside Azure.

App Service logical components

Figure 7-1 shows the components that make up App Service. An App Service web app is powered by an associated App Service plan. This plan is an abstraction layer; you control how much virtual compute you need to power your application or applications, and you dynamically scale vertically to suit your performance requirements and budgetary needs.

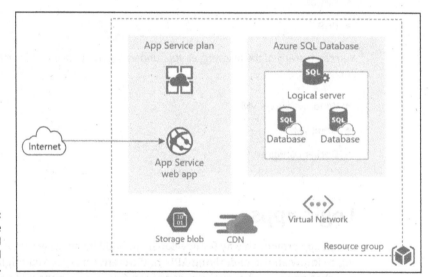

FIGURE 7-1:
App Service
required and
optional
components.

In Figure 7-1, the App Service plan is the only required component. You can extend the app's capabilities by integrating it with any of the following:

>> **Storage account:** An App Service plan has persistent storage, but many developers like to use a flexible storage account for additional space.

>> **Virtual network:** You can link an App Service app to a virtual network — perhaps to connect your web app to a database running on a VM.

>> **Databases:** Most web apps nowadays use relational, nonrelational, and/or in-memory databases to store temporary or persistent data.

» **Content delivery network:** You can place static website assets in a storage account and let Azure distribute the assets globally. This way, your users get a much faster experience because their browsers pull your site content from a low-latency, geographically close source.

App Service plans are organized in three increasingly powerful (and expensive) tiers:

» **Dev/Test:** F- and B-series VMs with minimal compute and no extra features. This compute level is the least expensive but offers few features and shouldn't be used for production apps.

» **Production:** S- and P-series VMs with a good balance of compute power and features. This tier should be your App Service starting point.

» **Isolated:** Called the App Service Environment and very expensive; Microsoft allocates hardware so that your web app is screened from the public Internet.

You can move within or between tiers as necessary. This capability is one of the greatest attributes of public cloud services. Figure 7-2 shows an App Service plan.

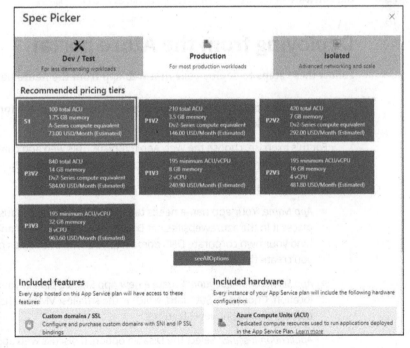

FIGURE 7-2:
An App Service plan provides raw compute power as well as potentially useful website features such as autoscale and deployment slots.

TECHNICAL
STUFF

Azure uses the Azure Compute Unit (ACU) as a standardized method to classify compute power. You see it referenced in Azure VMs, App Service, and any other Azure resource that uses VMs. Having a standardized performance metric is crucial, because Microsoft uses several types of hardware in its data centers.

WARNING

Just because you can associate more than one web app into a single App Service plan doesn't mean that you should. Sure, you can save money (the App Service plan incurs run-time costs based on instance size), but the more apps you pack into a single plan, the greater the burden on the underlying VM.

Deploying Your First Web App

In this section, you get down to business by deploying two simple web applications, the first from the Azure portal via Azure Marketplace and the second from Visual Studio via a built-in project template. You need to have both Visual Studio 2022 and the Azure workload installed.

TIP

You can download and use Visual Studio 2022 Community Edition for free; grab the software at https://visualstudio.microsoft.com/vs.

Deploying from the Azure portal

Follow these steps to deploy your first web app from the Azure portal:

1. **In the Azure portal menu, select Create a Resource, search for "Web App," and then click Create.**

   For this exercise, choose the Web App template. This web app contains example code to give you something to look at and interact with.

2. **Complete the Create Web App form as follows:**

   - *App Name:* Your app name needs to be globally unique, because Microsoft places it in the azurewebsites.net DNS domain. But you can and should bind your own corporate DNS domain to your site as soon as possible after you create the web app.

   - *App Service Plan/Location:* Create a new App Service plan in your home location. Choose S1 Standard, which is the smallest VM instance size that unlocks production-level features.

   - *Application Insights:* Select the Disable option. (I discuss web app monitoring later in this chapter in "Monitoring a Web App.")

3. **Click Create to submit the deployment.**

4. **Open the web app.**

   To do this, browse to the new web app's Overview blade, and select the contents of the URL property. The web app should display boilerplate content provided by Microsoft.

Configuring Git

TECHNICAL STUFF

Git is a free, open-source, cross-platform version-control system invented by Linux originator Linus Torvalds. It's a distributed system in which each developer has a full copy of the repository; optionally, developers push their changes to an upstream origin repository.

The idea of source-code control is simple: Multiple developers commit changes to a single shared code base. How do you preserve code history, know which developer made which change, and prevent developers from stepping on one another's work? Git solves these problems.

Even if your job role isn't development, you should get familiar with Git because it touches just about every kind of Azure work. You can find plenty of hands-on, interactive Git tutorials online; check them out to see which resonates best with your learning style. You can also read *GitHub For Dummies*, by Sarah Guthals and Phil Haack (Wiley).

Git fits in perfectly with Azure App Service; in fact, App Service apps can host their own Git repository, as shown in Figure 7-3.

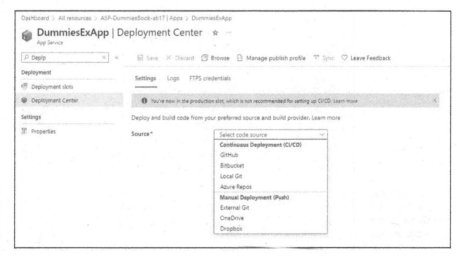

FIGURE 7-3: Deployment integration options, including GitHub.

I want to show you how you can combine Git with App Service. Visual Studio 2022 Community Edition includes a Git client. To use it to set up Git for use with App Service, follow these steps:

1. **Open Visual Studio, and click the Continue Without Code button in the Startup window.**

2. **Choose View ⇨ Team Explorer to open the Team Explorer Visual Studio extension.**

3. **From the Project list at the top of the extension, choose Settings.**

4. **In the Settings pane, Click Global Settings.**

5. **In the Git Settings pane, fill out the User Name and Email Address fields. Click Update to commit your changes.**

6. **(Optional) Change the location where Visual Studio saves your Git repositories.**

7. **Leave the other Git options at their default settings, and click the Home button to see Git project settings.**

TIP

If you don't see the elements that I describe in this procedure, you may need to choose Git as Visual Studio's source-control provider. To do so, choose Tools ⇨ Options, and find the Source Control ⇨ Plug-in Selection option. Choose Git as your source-control plug-in, and click OK to confirm. Figure 7-4 shows the interface.

REMEMBER

For you to complete the steps listed, you'll need to have an Azure DevOps environment in place. Otherwise, you won't be able to connect your project to Git. See Chapter 14 for more about the DevOps tools in Azure.

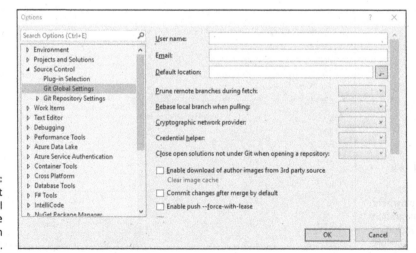

FIGURE 7-4:
Ensuring that Visual Studio will use Git for source code version control.

Connecting to a web app from Visual Studio

You use Visual Studio to connect and work with your new Azure-based web app. This is the workflow:

1. **Create a local Git repository for the app in Azure.**

2. **Clone the Azure-based repository to your local workstation.**

3. **Work with the app locally, and periodically push changes up to Azure.**

It's outside the scope of this book to go into Git in depth, but I'll do my best to ensure that you don't get lost.

Creating a Git repository for a web app

Follow these steps to create a local Git repository for your web app's sample source code:

1. **In your web app settings in the Azure portal, select Deployment Center.**

   If you followed the steps in "Deploying from the Azure portal" earlier in this chapter, the Azure Marketplace template you chose has already created a Git repository. Handy! But click Disconnect so that you can create a local Git repository.

2. **In Deployment Center, choose Local Git as your source-code provider.**

3. **For Build Provider, choose the App Service build service and then click Save.**

   The K stands for *Kudu*, which is the engine that handles building your code and performing publish actions.

4. **On the Deployment Center blade, copy the clone URL in the Repository field.**

   Typically, Git clone URLs end with the .git file extension. My DummiesExApp Git clone URL, for example, is

   ```
   https://dummiesexapp.scm.azurewebsites.net:443/DummiesExApp.git
   ```

5. **Open Azure Cloud Shell and create a Git deployment credential.**

   This credential is the identity you'll use to authenticate to the Azure-based Git repository. I recommend using Azure Cloud Shell for this purpose. When you're in the session, run the following command from the command line by entering your own username and (strong) password such as:

```
az webapp deployment user set --password <your password> --user-name <your
    username>
```

Make a note of both the username and password, because you'll need them for the next step.

6. **Go to the menu bar and locate Git.**

7. **Select Clone in the Local Git Repositories section.**

   Paste in your App Service clone URL (Step 4), and verify the local directory path and folder name.

8. **Click Clone.**

   A clone operation is simply a file copy; in this case, you're copying the Azure-based code to your local computer.

REMEMBER

9. **Enter your Git deployment credentials when Visual Studio prompts you for them.**

   You see the cloned repository on the Solution Explorer pane.

10. **On the menu bar, choose File ⇨ New ⇨ Project from Existing Code.**

    The Create a New Project dialog box opens.

11. **Locate the closest match to your existing web app.**

    You deployed an ASP.NET web application in App Service, so the logical choice is ASP.NET Web Application (.NET Framework).

12. **Give the local version a name, such as 1.0, and a save location.**

13. **Select the Empty template.**

14. **Leave all the other settings at their default values and click OK.**

As shown in Figure 7-5, clicking the Switch Views button in Solution Explorer (circled in the figure) toggles between Git repository view and Visual Studio view.

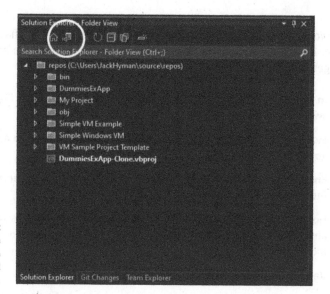

FIGURE 7-5:
Working with an
App Service web
app in Visual
Studio.

Pushing a code change to Azure

Without writing a single character of C#, you substantially changed the structure of the ASP.NET Starter Web App when you turned it into a Visual Studio solution. Verify this by switching to the Team Explorer pane's home page and clicking Changes. You'll see a detailed list of any files containing changes.

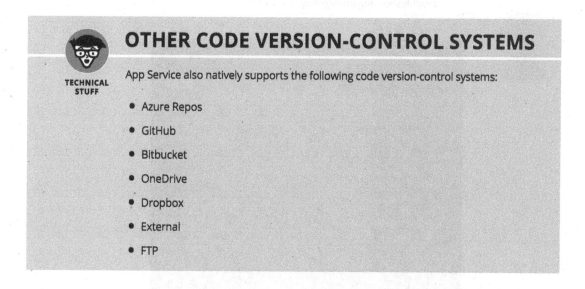

TECHNICAL STUFF

OTHER CODE VERSION-CONTROL SYSTEMS

App Service also natively supports the following code version-control systems:

- Azure Repos
- GitHub
- Bitbucket
- OneDrive
- Dropbox
- External
- FTP

After you've made a change in Visual Studio, you need to push that code change to Azure. Follow these steps to change the web app's home page and push all the changes to Azure:

1. **In Solution Explorer, click the Switch Views button (refer to Figure 7-5) to switch to Folder view.**

2. **Evaluate the files that have changed since your last push to Azure by going to Git Changes.**

3. **Enter a meaningful commit message, and then choose Commit All and Push from the menu bar (see Figure 7-6).**

How to compose a quality code-commit message is a fervent discussion among developers. What's most important, in my opinion, is that your message concisely describes the effect of your change.

4. **Verify that the Azure web app is current.**

When you load the page in your web browser (do a hard refresh if you see a cached page copy), you should see Production Slot Home Page instead of Home Page.

Alternatively, you can inspect the source code by using the App Service Editor. Select App Service Editor in your web app's Settings list and then click Go to view your source files in App Service Editor. The ability to edit your app's source code directly in the browser is convenient and potentially job-saving during a troubleshooting emergency.

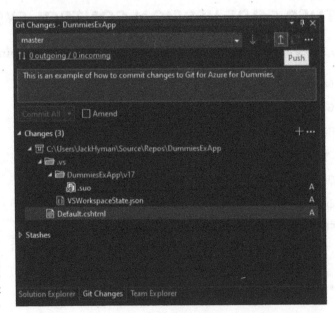

FIGURE 7-6: Committing code changes using Git and Visual Studio.

Deploying from Visual Studio

I'd be remiss if I didn't show you how to start your web app from your local computer and Visual Studio and then publish it directly to App Service. This section explains how to create another simple ASP.NET web app, publish it to Azure, and publish it again to a second deployment slot.

Creating a new web app project in Visual Studio

Follow these steps to create a solution in Visual Studio:

1. **Close any existing folders or solutions.**

   You can close recent files and solutions from the File menu. Close the Start window if it appears automatically.

2. **Choose File⇨New⇨Project.**

3. **Choose ASP.NET Core Web Application.**

   In the previous exercise, you used a .NET Framework web app. Target .NET Core this time around in the name of forward thinking and cross-platform compatibility.

4. **Give your project/solution a short name and a save location.**

   Make sure to keep Azure global uniqueness in mind. The project name has little or nothing to do with the ultimate DNS name under which users will reach the app.

5. **Click Create to move to the template selection process.**

6. **Select the Web Application template, and click Create.**

7. **Deselect the Configure for HTTPS option, and ensure that Authentication is set to No Authentication.**

8. **Run the web application by choosing Debug⇨Start Debugging.**

   Visual Studio includes a built-in web server called IIS Express. Debugging is the process of running your app in a local environment and resolving any errors or performance issues that arise. In this example, you simply start and stop debugging so you can see what the process looks like.

   If you're prompted to accept the application's self-signed digital certificate, do so.

9. **To end the debugging session, close the browser tab that hosts the app.**

Publishing to App Service

The Git publishing workflow is one of many ways to publish a web app to App Service. You can also publish to Azure directly from Visual Studio. To do so, follow these steps:

1. **In Solution Explorer, right-click your project, and choose Publish from the shortcut menu.**

   A wizard opens, allowing you to choose among the following publishing targets:

   - App Service (Windows VM)
   - App Service (Linux VM)
   - Azure IaaS VM
   - IIS, FTP
   - Folder

2. **Select App Service as your publishing target, select Create New, and then click Publish (see Figure 7-7).**

   You'll be prompted to authenticate to Azure if you aren't already signed in.

3. **Complete the App Service - Create New form.**

   I want to draw your attention to two deployment properties:

   - *Hosting Plan:* This means App Service plan.
   - *Application Insights:* Select None.

     Application Insights is a robust web app monitoring platform that I talk about in "Monitoring a Web App" later in this chapter.

TIP

Understanding deployment slots

Your development team may want to maintain your App Service app throughout its lifecycle directly in Azure. In other words, they may want to perform development and testing in one app instance while simultaneously keeping the production instance online.

Deployment slots give you this capability. As long as your App Service plan runs in at least the S tier, you can create one or more additional deployment slots to suit your app-staging needs.

Every App Service app starts with a deployment slot called (appropriately enough) Production. On the Deployment Slots blade, you can create another slot and clone the app settings from the production slot, as shown in Figure 7-8.

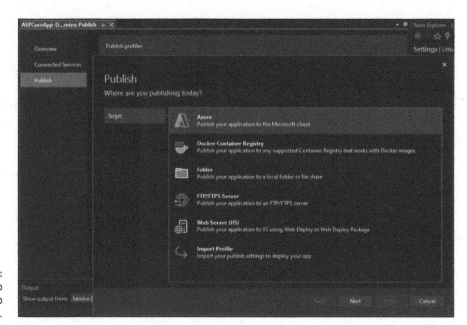

FIGURE 7-7:
Publishing a web
app to Azure App
Service.

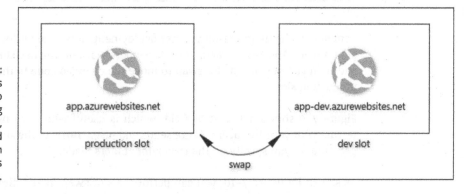

FIGURE 7-8:
Deployment slots
allow you to
move among
development,
staging, and
production
environments
seamlessly.

app.azurewebsites.net

production slot

app-dev.azurewebsites.net

dev slot

swap

REMEMBER

It's crucial to understand that each deployment slot contains a full instance of the application. Keep this fact in mind with regard to your App Service plan; the more slots you have, the heavier the burden on the plan.

Compare the URLs shown in Figure 7-9. Notice that Azure creates a slightly different host name for the named deployment slots. Specifically, Azure appends a hyphen and the slot name to the original web app's host name.

When I'm working with the web app's production slot, the URL I use is

```
https://app.azurewebsites.net
```

When I'm working with my dev slot instance, the URL is

```
https://app-dev.azurewebsites.net
```

You can see this behavior in the Azure portal by inspecting Figure 7-9. Azure puts a strong emphasis on PRODUCTION — the default deployment slot. This is your default slot, and it cannot be deleted.

FIGURE 7-9:
Each deployment
slot is a separate
instance of your
web app.

Remember, the main reason you use deployment slots is to perform phased roll-outs of your App Service app. Your developers work on the dev slot, for example, and then you perform a slot swap to move the changed code to the public-facing production slot.

Figure 7-9 shows a Traffic % field, which is useful when you need to perform testing with your live users. Azure sends end-user traffic to the slots based on the percentages you specify on the Deployment Slots blade.

As shown in Figure 7-10, you can perform a slot swap in any direction from the Deployment Slots blade of your web application. What's cool about this process is that the Azure portal shows you which settings will change after the swap. You may have different database connection strings stored in each slot, for example; in that case, you wouldn't want the swap to affect slot-specific settings.

Speaking of which, the Perform Swap with Preview option makes the swap a two-phase operation. In the first phase, you see which slot-specific settings will change if you complete the swap operation. In the second phase, you can cancel or proceed with the slot swap.

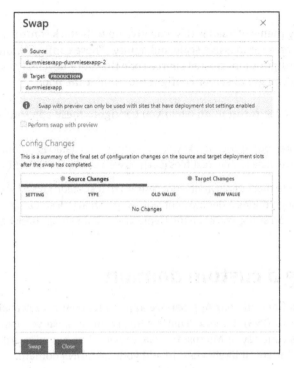

FIGURE 7-10:
The Azure portal gives you visibility into the ramifications of a deployment-slot swap.

Configuring a Web App

In this section, I cover key configuration choices for App Service web apps.

Customizing app settings

If you visit the Configuration blade of your App Service app, you'll see four application settings tabs:

>> **Application Settings:** Application-related key/value pairs; data source connection strings

>> **General Settings:** The application run-time environment(s); whether FTP is allowed; HTTP version

>> **Default Documents:** Which file types Azure should look for when determining default web app display document(s)

>> **Path Mappings:** Mapping handlers (script processors) for different file types

The primary theme of PaaS is that you give up full-stack control of the underlying VM in exchange for massive scale and agility. These configuration settings, along with any configuration-related source code that your developers add, are about as close as you can get to server configuration under the hood.

Keep two key factors in mind when you configure these app settings:

» You store your application key/value settings and database connection string data here instead of in text files (such as web.config for ASP.NET applications).

» Be sure to mark deployment-slot settings that shouldn't travel with the application during a deployment-slot swap. When you edit a setting or connection string, you'll see the Deployment Slot Setting check box.

Adding a custom domain

Microsoft defines all your App Service apps in its own azurewebsites.net Domain Name System (DNS) domain. That's convenient because you can leverage HTTP connections courtesy of Microsoft's *.azurewebsites.net wildcard TLS/SSL digital certificate. But you'll likely want to add your own DNS domain.

TIP

Don't even think about attempting to unbind your web app from the azurewebsites.net domain. Because this domain is how Azure recognizes your web app, you're stuck with that DNS name unless and until you delete the web app. Sorry!

Follow these steps to add your own DNS domain to your web app:

1. **In your web app settings, browse to the Custom Domains blade, and set the HTTPS Only setting to Off.**

   To get to your web app settings, open the web app's settings in Azure portal and select Configuration.

   Unless or until you're using your own Secure Sockets Layer (SSL) certificate that matches your custom domain, you don't want to enforce HTTPS.

2. **Click Add Custom domain, add your domain name, and click Validate. The Add Custom Domain blade appears.**

   I'm stating the obvious, I think, but this domain needs to be a DNS domain that you own, or at least one for which you have access to the zone file.

3. Edit your DNS zone file to add a verification/mapping resource record.

What you're doing is proving to Microsoft that you own the domain in question. This process requires you to log in to your domain registrar's website and add a resource record to your zone. You can also purchase a domain name from Microsoft within Azure, if you prefer.

To prove domain ownership, you need to create a temporary DNS resource record. Azure checks your domain to see whether the record exists. If it does, then Azure "knows" that you must own the domain because only owners can add resource records to their own domain.

- *Host (A) Record:* I advise against selecting this option, which maps your custom domain to your web app's public Internet Protocol (IP). The issue is that your name resolution will break if Microsoft hands your app a new public IP address.

- *CNAME Record:* I recommend selecting this option because you're mapping your custom domain's DNS to point to your web app's DNS host name under azurewebsites.net. The mapping remains valid even if Microsoft changes your app's public IP address.

4. When validation completes, click Add Custom Domain to complete the process.

Figure 7-11 shows a completed domain configuration. Take note of the following important elements:

» The domain is ready for use, but it's not usable with SSL until you bind a matching SSL certificate. Azure portal throws all sorts of scary warnings, as you see.

» The site remains accessible with HTTP or HTTPS when you use the original DNS name (such as twlocalwebapp12.azurewebsites.net).

Binding a TLS/SSL certificate

A publicly trusted Transport Layer Security/Secure Sockets Layer (TLS/SSL; I'll use just SSL from now) digital certificate provides your web app confidentiality, data integrity, and authentication. I almost always recommend that my customers bind their website certificate to their App Service app as soon as they've added their custom DNS domain.

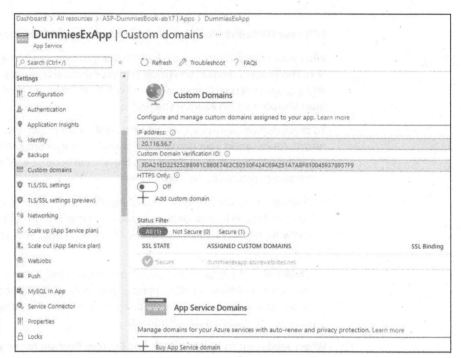

DummiesExApp | Custom domains
App Service

🔎 Search (Ctrl+/) «

Settings

- ⚙ Configuration
- 🔑 Authentication
- 📍 Application Insights
- 🔑 Identity
- 💾 Backups
- ▦ Custom domains
- 🛡 TLS/SSL settings
- 🛡 TLS/SSL settings (preview)
- 🔗 Networking
- ✎ Scale up (App Service plan)
- ⚡ Scale out (App Service plan)
- 🔲 WebJobs
- 📣 Push
- 🗄 MySQL In App
- 🔌 Service Connector
- ⚙ Properties
- 🔒 Locks

🔄 Refresh   🔧 Troubleshoot   ❓ FAQs

🌐 **Custom Domains**

Configure and manage custom domains assigned to your app. Learn more

IP address: ⓘ
20.118.56.7

Custom Domain Verification ID: ⓘ
3DA21ED2252528B981C8B0E74E2C50530F424C694251A7A8F8100459378957F9

HTTPS Only: ⓘ
⬤ Off
➕ Add custom domain

Status Filter
(All (1)) Not Secure (0) Secure (1)

SSL STATE	ASSIGNED CUSTOM DOMAINS	SSL Binding
✓ Secure	dummiesexapp.azurewebsites.net	

🌐 **App Service Domains**

Manage domains for your Azure services with auto-renew and privacy protection. Learn more

➕ Buy App Service domain

FIGURE 7-11:
Adding a custom domain to your App Service.

To bind your certificate to your App Service app, follow these steps:

1. **In your web app settings, navigate to the TLS/SSL Settings blade, and click Add TLS/SSL Binding.**

   The TLS/SSL bindings blade appears.

2. **On the TLS/SSL Binding blade, select your custom domain.**

   You should see the message No certificates match the selected custom domain.

3. **On the TLS/SSL Bindings blade, select Upload PFX Certificate.**

4. **Browse to your exported PFX certificate, which contains both the public and private key components.**

5. **Decrypt the archive with your password, and click Upload.**

TECHNICAL STUFF

For dev/testing purposes, you can create your own self-signed certificate by using the New-SelfSignedCertificate PowerShell cmdlet. You can also use free, publicly trusted certificates by using Let's Encrypt. Microsoft employee Scott Hanselman wrote an excellent document on using those certificates with App Services; you can read it at https://timw.info/ssl.

6. **On the TLS/SSL Binding blade, select the private certificate thumbprint and TLS/SSL type, and click Add Binding to complete the configuration.**

   In most cases, you'll choose IP-based SSL as your TLS/SSL type. You'll use the Server Name Indication SSL when your digital certificate protects more than one explicitly defined DNS name.

7. **Test connectivity to the web app by using HTTPS and your custom domain name.**

Configuring autoscaling

Back in the bad old days, if you wanted your on-premises public web servers to handle a predicted usage spike, you normally purchased new hardware. This kind of capital expenditure is a giant waste if the hardware isn't necessary when the spike subsides.

Instead of purchasing new hardware, you can configure manual or autoscaling for App Service apps.

REMEMBER

You may need to scale up (vertically) your App Service plan before advanced features such as custom domains, SSL certificates, and autoscaling rules become available to you.

TECHNICAL
STUFF

APP SERVICE DOMAINS

As a convenience to its customers, Microsoft partnered with GoDaddy to sell public DNS domains directly from Azure through a service called App Service Domains. Adding domains to Azure products is almost turnkey if you buy the domain from this service. The Azure DNS service allows you to host DNS domains you purchased elsewhere in Azure.

Along the same lines, the App Service Certificates service enables you to purchase and manage publicly trusted SSL certs from the Azure portal. Azure stores the certs in Key Vault and makes it simple to create SSL bindings for your App Service apps.

Suppose you want to configure your web app to scale out from one to three instances, depending on the App Service plan's CPU load over a 10-minute window. Just as important, you want to scale down to your minimum number when the usage spike settles. To complete that configuration, follow these steps:

1. **In your web app settings, select Scale Out (App Service plan), and then click Custom Autoscale, as shown in Figure 7-12.**

   The Custom autoscale options appear. Also notice the Manual Scale option, which instructs Azure Resource Manager to spawn identical web app instances without messing with VMs, DNS, or app configuration — PaaS at its best.

2. **For Scale mode, select Scale Based on a Metric, and configure instance limits.**

   It's important to understand the difference among the three instance limit options:

   - *Minimum:* The smallest number of instances you want running. Note that you're charged for each instance.

   - *Maximum:* The largest number of simultaneous instances you envision needing.

   - *Default:* The value that Azure uses as a fallback if it can't calculate a metric.

3. **Select Add a Rule to define a scale rule.**

   A scale rule is also called a *scale condition.* Use the following settings as a baseline, but feel free to experiment:

   - *Time Aggregation:* Average

   - *Metric Name:* CPU percentage

   - *Dimension Name, Operator, Values:* Instance: = All Values

   - *Time Grain Statistic:* Average

   - *Operator and Threshold:* Greater than 70

   - *Duration:* 10 minutes

   - *Action:* Increase count by one instance, with 5-minute cool-down

   The cool-down value specifies the amount of time that Azure waits before scaling again.

4. **Click Add.**

   You should see your scale condition in the Custom autoscale settings now. You've created one scale condition to define web app scale out, but don't forget about scale in.

5. Select Add a Scale to create a new metric rule that scales down the cluster when CPU use reaches 40 percent or less.

TIP

I advise you to rename the scale condition entries so that they're meaningful to you and your team. Click the pencil icon next to an entry to edit it.

FIGURE 7-12:
Scaling out of App Service.

Monitoring a Web App

In this section, I review how to monitor your App Service apps by using Application Insights, an Azure-hosted application performance management platform that provides rich, deep insight into just about any application, whether the app exists in Azure, on-premises, or in another cloud. Application Insights is a feature embedded within Azure Monitor.

Instrumentation refers to adding the Application Insights software development kit (SDK) to your application's source code. You then link the client-side SDK to an Application Insights resource in your Azure subscription.

Some of the intelligence Application Insights can give your developers include the following:

>> **Request and response times and failure rates:** You can see which web app pages are most or least popular at different times of day, as well as where your users connect from.

>> **Dependency rates:** You can visually plot any dependencies of your app on external components, which can ensure uptime when you need to perform maintenance or migrations.

>> **Exceptions with source-code analysis:** You can follow stack trace output to actual lines in your source code because Application Insights telemetry embeds directly in your Visual Studio project.

>> **Performance counters:** You can observe performance statistics gathered from your web app's underlying VM infrastructure.

>> **Dashboards:** You can plot your telemetry data in easily digestible formats.

>> **Profiler:** You can follow web application requests and responses operation by operation.

Adding the Application Insights resource

Follow these steps to create a new Application Insights resource in your Azure subscription:

1. **In the Azure portal, browse to the Monitor Blade, locate the Application Insights blade, and then click Create.**

   The Application Insights Configuration blade appears.

2. **Configure the resource details.**

   These details are pretty self-explanatory:

   - Subscription
   - Resource group
   - Instance name
   - Region

   The main point that you need to be aware of is that to ensure the lowest latency, locate your Application Insights resource in the same Azure region as the web app with which it'll be associated.

3. **Submit the deployment by clicking Review + Create, and then Create.**

Enabling instrumentation in a web app

In Azure nomenclature, instrumentation refers to linking your Azure App Service app to an Application Insights instance. Application Insights goes into immediate action gathering details about your application's environment and performance.

Follow these steps to connect your Application Insights instance to an Azure web app:

1. **Switch to Visual Studio, and load the last ASP.NET web application you worked with in this chapter.**

2. **In Solution Explorer, right-click your project, and choose Add➪ Application Insights Telemetry from the shortcut menu.**

   The Application Insights Configuration window opens.

   TIP

   If you don't see the Application Insights option, you probably don't have the Application Insights SDK installed. Choose Tools➪Get Tools and Features to open the Visual Studio Installer, where you can install Application Insights.

3. **In the Application Insights Configuration window, click Get Started.**

   The Register Your app with Application Insights window opens.

4. **Complete the form.**

   You provide your Azure account, subscription, resource name, and pricing tier.

   Be sure to specify the Application Insights resource you created earlier.

5. **Click Register.**

Viewing Application Insights telemetry data

You can take advantage of Application Insights telemetry streams in any of the following locations:

» **Visual Studio:** Open the Application Insights toolbar to explore the features. If you don't see the toolbar, choose View➪Toolbars➪Application Insights.

» **The Azure portal:** Open your Application Insights resource, and click Application Dashboard on the Overview blade.

» **Azure Log Analytics:** Log Analytics is a universal query and reporting platform that uses its own SQL-like query language called Kusto (pronounced COO-stow) Query Language. You can query Application Insights in combination with just about any other resource in Azure from one central point. On the toolbar of your Application Insights resource's Overview blade, click Logs (Analytics).

Figure 7-13 shows the telemetry data viewed in the Azure portal.

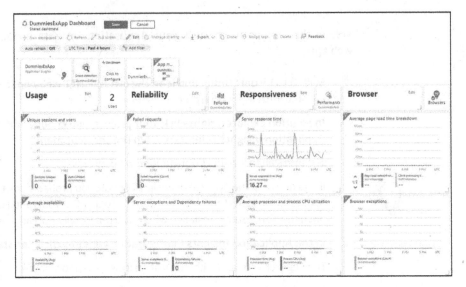

FIGURE 7-13:
Application
Insights telemetry
data in the Azure
portal.

Chapter **8**

Running Serverless Apps in Azure

This chapter moves into the wonderful world of serverless computing in Azure. I begin by demystifying the buzzword *serverless* and then discuss how to create Function Apps and Logic Apps in Azure.

Defining Serverless

The term *serverless* gets a lot of attention nowadays. What does it mean? I'll try to cut through marketing jargon and explain the concept succinctly.

App Service apps provide lots of flexibility, in that you don't have to manage the underlying infrastructure but you still have an entire application to deal with. The idea behind serverless apps is that Microsoft abstracts almost the entire environment from you. You can pretty much upload a single source-code function and instruct Azure to run it based on a predefined trigger event.

We all know that there's no such thing as *serverless* in a physical sense. All App Service apps rely on Linux or Windows Server virtual machines (VMs) under the hood. The term simply denotes an increased abstraction layer for Azure developers, administrators, and solution architects.

Getting to know Azure Functions apps

You can think of Azure Functions as being code as service, by which you upload your source code, and Azure runs it for you. Specifically, Azure runs your function based on a trigger, which is a type of event. The event could be a manually initiated trigger, a scheduled trigger, or some action that takes place elsewhere in Azure.

A *function app* is a container object; you can enclose one or more individual Azure Functions within the function app. The compute and application run time exist at the function-app level and are shared by all enclosed Functions.

TECHNICAL
STUFF

A *function* is a named section of a program that performs a specific task. Usually, applications consist of multiple functions. By contrast, Azure Functions are individual, named code blocks that are scoped to perform one action very well.

You have two ways to pay for an Azure Function:

>> **Consumption plan:** Azure allocates compute dynamically whenever your function runs. You're charged for the number of function executions per month; Microsoft has a generous free tier. The downside is that the consumption-cost model can be much slower than the App Service plan model.

>> **App Service plan:** This pricing model mirrors that of App Service web apps. The benefit is more-predictable performance because you have control of the underlying compute power.

ON THE
WEB

I don't provide much detail about Azure pricing in this book because Microsoft alters prices and pricing models often. To get the latest details, visit https:// azure.microsoft.com/pricing.

By default, Functions operate in a stateless way — that is, a Function is triggered, the source code runs, and the Function App platform pays no attention to maintaining persistence.

To suit longer-running tasks that do involve state, the ability to set and resume execution at checkpoints, and survive VM restarts, Microsoft offers Durable Functions, which are extensions to Azure Functions. They integrate with many common application architectural patterns, and at this writing, they support the programming languages C#, F#, and JavaScript.

Getting to know Azure Logic Apps

If you are a programmer looking to automate repetitive work without the overhead of an entire application programming interface (API) web application, consider using Azure Logic Apps. Azure Logic Apps solves a somewhat different problem, which is creating business workflows that integrate different third-party Software as a Service (SaaS) apps without requiring developers to know disparate APIs.

If you've ever heard of Microsoft BizTalk Server, Logic Apps is essentially a cloud variant of BizTalk. Both BizTalk and Logic Apps include an enormous connector library for all sorts of first- and third-party apps.

Suppose that your human resources department needs to move employee data from one database platform to another and then export selected results to another SaaS platform. Chances are good that Logic Apps has built-in connectors for each platform. Logic Apps Designer is a graphical control surface on which you can build your workflow.

Figure 8-1 illustrates Logic App behavior using a different business scenario.

Figure 8-1 shows that you can add conditional logic to your Logic App workflows. You can successfully mirror any desired business logic, no matter how simple or complex, without understanding different vendors' APIs.

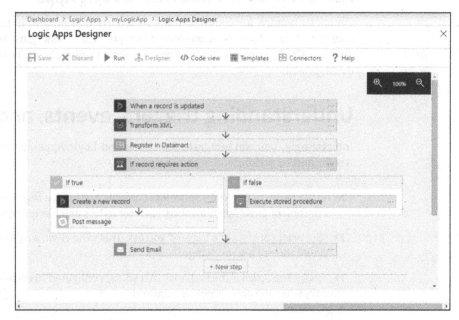

FIGURE 8-1: Logic Apps requires no API knowledge and uses a drag-and-drop workflow design surface.

Custom connectors

All Logic Apps, as well as their connectors, are described in JavaScript Object Notation (JSON). Therefore, it's not terribly difficult for your developers to define custom Logic Apps connectors if Microsoft's built-in library doesn't have a particular app. The restriction is that the app in question should expose a RESTful API that supports the OpenAPI standard.

Representational State Transfer (REST) is a programming methodology in which applications send and receive data by using the HTTP protocol. What's cool about REST is you need no special software to use it and the data transfer occurs over firewall-friendly ports and protocols.

Microsoft Power Automate versus Azure Logic Apps

Microsoft Power Automate (formerly known as Flow) is an SaaS platform built on Logic Apps and is a member of Microsoft 365. Stated another way, Power Automate is a simpler version of Logic Apps aimed at end users instead of developers.

Microsoft Power Automate is for business end users whose organizations aren't in Azure, whereas Logic Apps is for business end users or power users whose organizations are in Azure.

Azure Functions versus Azure Logic Apps

Functions require development skills with particular programming languages; by contrast, Logic Apps is a no-code solution. Also, Functions are for general-purpose CaaS, whereas Logic Apps is aimed squarely at business workflow development.

Understanding triggers, events, and actions

Interestingly, you can integrate Functions and Logic Apps, using either app as a trigger and/or action.

>> In the realm of the Azure serverless compute platform, a *trigger* defines how a Function or Logic App is invoked. Each serverless app has only one trigger.

>> "But what constitutes a trigger?" you ask. That's the *event*: a lightweight notification of a state change.

>> Finally, the *action* is the response that you've configured to occur automatically when the app's trigger is activated.

Working with Azure Functions

The first step in designing a Function is deciding what you want it to do. Suppose that you created a web application in App Service that allows users to upload image files. Your fictional app's source code places the user's uploaded image files in a container named (appropriately enough) Images, inside an Azure storage account blob (binary large objects) service container.

What if you want to take automatic action on those uploads? Here are some examples:

>> Automatically converting and/or resizing the image

>> Performing facial recognition on the image

>> Generating notifications based on image type

As it happens, it's possible to trigger a Function based on a file upload.

Azure Functions includes the following triggers, among others:

>> **HTTP:** Triggers based on a webhook (HTTP request)

>> **Timer:** Triggers based on a predefined schedule

>> **Azure Queue Storage:** Triggers based on a Queue Storage message

>> **Azure Service Bus Queue:** Triggers based on a Service Bus message

>> **Azure Service Bus Topic:** Triggers based on a message appearing in a designated topic

>> **Azure Blob Storage:** Triggers whenever a blob is added to a specified container (the trigger you need for the example)

>> **Durable Functions HTTP Starter:** Triggers when another Durable Function calls the current one

Creating an Azure Function

I mentioned that a Function App is a container object that stores one or more individual functions. Figure 8-2 shows the Function workflow.

First, you need to create the Function App. Next, you define the Function itself. Finally, you test and verify that your function is triggered properly.

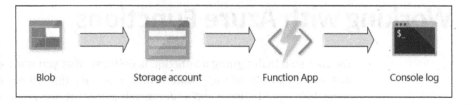

FIGURE 8-2:
Azure Function
for taking action
on uploaded
image files.

Blob   Storage account   Function App   Console log

Creating the Function App

Follow these steps to deploy a new Function App in the Azure portal:

1. On the Function App blade, click Add.

   The Basics tab of the Function App blade appears.

2. **Complete the Function App Deployment form (see Figure 8-3).**

   Here are some areas for which you will be required to supply appropriate values:

   - *App name:* This name needs to be unique because Function Apps are part of the App Services family and have DNS names within Microsoft's public azurewebsites.net zone.

   - *OS:* Choose the type of operating system you have.

   - *Hosting plan:* Consumption Plan is a good place to start. You can change this setting later if you want or need to do so.

   - *Runtime stack:* Your choices include .NET Core, Node.js, Python, Java, and PowerShell Core.

3. **Click Create to submit the deployment.**

Defining the Function

The next step in the Azure Function creation workflow is defining the Function itself. Here are a few things to consider:

- » A single Function App contains one or more Functions.

- » A Function Proxy allows you to present a single API endpoint for all Functions in a single Function app to other Azure or non-Azure API services.

- » Function Apps support deployment slots that serve the same purpose as deployment slots for App Service web apps, and they support slot swapping.

- » Function App Settings is where you specify settings for a Function App, Function, or Proxy, depending on the context.

Create Function App

Basics   Hosting   Networking   Monitoring   Tags   Review + create

Create a function app, which lets you group functions as a logical unit for easier management, deployment and sharing of resources. Functions lets you execute your code in a serverless environment without having to first create a VM or publish a web application.

Project Details

Select a subscription to manage deployed resources and costs. Use resource groups like folders to organize and manage all your resources.

Subscription * ⓘ   Jack Hyman - Microsoft Azure Account   ⌄

    Resource Group * ⓘ   DummiesBook   ⌄
                          Create new

Instance Details

Function App name *   DummiesFuncApp   ✓
                                            .azurewebsites.net

Publish *   ⦿ Code   ◯ Docker Container

Runtime stack *   .NET   ⌄

Version *   6   ⌄

Region *   Central US   ⌄

Operating system

The Operating System has been recommended for you based on your selection of runtime stack.

Operating System *   ◯ Linux   ⦿ Windows

Plan

The plan you choose dictates how your app scales, what features are enabled, and how it is priced. Learn more

Plan type * ⓘ   Consumption (Serverless)   ⌄

Review + create   < Previous   Next : Hosting >

FIGURE 8-3:
Creating an Azure
Function App.

The steps to create a Function are shown in Figure 8-4. First, look under the Function Blade (A) and select the Function option. Then follow the creation steps based on your configuration need. As for setting up configurations (B), you'll be able to assign settings from custom domains, certifications, Application Insights, and specific networking parameters.

Before you create the function, you should create the images blob container you'll need for this website-upload example. If you have Azure Storage Explorer installed, proceed! If not, see Chapter 3 for details on installing it.

REMEMBER

Azure Storage Explorer is a free, cross-platform desktop application that makes working with Azure storage accounts a snap. Obtain the tool at `https://azure.microsoft.com/features/storage-explorer`.

Follow these steps to create a blob container for the new Function:

1. **Open Azure Storage Explorer, and authenticate to your Azure subscription.**

FIGURE 8-4:
Creating a
function step
by step.

2. **Expand the storage account that you created for your Function App, right-click Blob Containers, and choose Create Blob Container from the shortcut menu.**

   Azure creates the container and places your cursor next to it, all ready for you to name the new object.

3. **Name the container images, and press Enter to confirm.**

Creating the Function

Excellent. You're almost finished. Now you need to create a function. Follow these steps:

1. **Open your Function App in the Azure portal.**

2. **Under the Functions Blade, press the Create (+) Button.**

   The details pane on the right leads you through a Function Wizard, the first step of which is choosing a development environment.

3. **Choose In-Portal as your development environment, and click Continue.**

   Both Visual Studio and Visual Studio Code have native support for writing Functions.

4. **Select the template type.**

   You'll want to select Azure Blob Storage Trigger.

5. Complete the Template Details.

Complete the following fields:

- *New Function:* I called mine BlobUploadFx. This is the name of the Function that will be contained inside the Function App. The name should be short and descriptive.

- *Azure Blob Storage Trigger Path:* This setting is important. You want to leave the {name} bit alone because it's a variable that represents any uploaded blob. The path should look like this:

```
images/{name}
```

- *Storage Account Connection:* Click New, and select your Function's storage account.

6. Click Create when you're finished.

When you select your function on the Function App's left menu, you can see your starter C# source code. For this example, the code should look like this:

```
public static void Run(Stream myBlob, string name, ILogger log)
{
    log.LogInformation($"C# Blob trigger function Processed blob\n Name:{name}
    \n Size: {myBlob.Length} Bytes");
}
```

This code says "When the function is triggered, write the name and size of the blob to the console log." This example is simple so that you can focus on how Functions work instead of getting bogged down in programming-language semantics.

The new Function contains the following three settings blades:

>> **Integrate:** This blade is where you can edit your trigger, inputs, and outputs.

>> **Manage:** This blade is where you can disable, enable, or delete the Function, as well as define host keys that authorize API access to the Function.

>> **Monitor:** Here, you can view successful and failed Function executions and optionally access Application Insights telemetry from the Function.

Testing

All you have to do to test your function is follow these steps:

1. **In Azure Storage Explorer, upload an image file to the images container.**

   To do this, select the container and then click Upload from the Storage Explorer toolbar. You can upload individual files or entire folders.

   Technically, you can upload any file, image or otherwise, because all files are considered to be blobs.

2. **In the Azure portal, select your Function App, switch to the Logs view, and watch the output.**

Configuring Function App settings

Before I discuss Logic Apps, I want to make sure that you understand how to tweak Function App settings. You may want to switch from Consumption to App Service plan pricing, for example, or vice versa. Or maybe you want to test a different run-time environment. In the last section, I pointed to the Settings Blade earlier in Figure 8-4. You'll notice that the Settings Blade is a specific area dedicated to Configuration activities. There are a lot of configurations packed under the Settings Blade. The sections you'll likely tinker with along the way to customize the Function App include

- » **Configuration:** Where you configure custom Application and Connection Settings.
- » **Custom Domains:** Where you map your own domain name (www.mydomain.com) to an Azure function.
- » **TLS/SSL Settings:** Where you connect a certificate to the Custom Domains.
- » **Scale-Out:** Where you set up scaling rules as an application grows (or possibly shrinks) dynamically.
- » **Properties:** Where you update the name of the Function App, change the region where it is housed, and modify the cost model if desired.

ON THE WEB

Function Apps are packed with many configuration options. To dig a bit deeper into the configuration type you are looking for, head to https://docs.microsoft.com/azure/azure-functions.

Building Workflows with Azure Logic Apps

Suppose that your company's marketing department wants to be notified any time a current or prospective customer mentions your corporate handle on Twitter. Without Logic Apps, your developers would have to register for a developer Twitter account and API key, after which they'd need to immerse themselves in the Twitter API to understand how to integrate Twitter with your corporate notification platform.

Instead, your developers can configure a Logic App to trigger on particular Twitter tweets and send an email message to an Outlook mailbox without knowing Twitter or Office 365 APIs. Figure 8-5 shows a workflow for this Logic App.

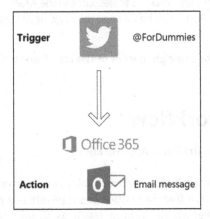

FIGURE 8-5:
The workflow for an Azure Logic App.

Creating an Azure Logic App

You're going to create a Logic App that triggers on mentions of the keyword *Azure* in public tweets. The resulting action sends email notifications to a designated email address. You'll develop your Logic App in three phases:

- » Deploying the Logic App resource
- » Defining the workflow
- » Testing the trigger and action

Deploying the resource in the Azure portal

Follow this procedure to create the Logic App resource:

1. **In the Azure portal, browse to the Logic Apps blade, and click Add.**

   The Create blade opens.

2. **Complete the Logic App Create blade.**

   There's not much to creating the resource. Provide the name, subscription, resource group, and location, and specify whether you want to monitor with Log Analytics.

3. **Click Create to submit the deployment.**

   When deployment is complete, click Go to Resource in the Azure notification menu to open the Logic App. You'll be taken to the Logic Apps Designer by default.

4. **Click the X button in the top-right corner of the interface to close the blade.**

Defining the workflow

Follow these steps to define the Logic App workflow:

TIP

If you want to follow along with this exercise, you need Twitter and Office 365 accounts. Twitter accounts are free, but Office 365 typically is a paid SaaS product. If you like, use another email account (such as Gmail). The Logic Apps connector library is so vast that chances are good that you'll find a service that works for you.

1. **Go to your new Logic App's Overview blade.**

2. **Choose Logic App Designer from the Settings menu.**

   This command takes you to the view you saw the first time you opened the Logic App.

3. **Scroll to the Templates section, and select Blank Logic App.**

   Starting with a blank Logic App enables you to become more familiar with the workflow design process, but Azure provides lots of templates and triggers that you can use for other purposes.

4. **In the Search Connectors and Triggers field, type** Twitter.

If the Logic App interface looks familiar, it should! It is eerily similar to the Power Automate user experience.

5. **In the search results, select the Twitter trigger category, and then click the When a New Tweet Is Posted trigger.**

6. **Click Sign In, and log in to your Twitter account.**

7. **Complete the When a New Tweet Is Posted form.**

For the example I outlined earlier, you want the Logic App to trigger whenever someone mentions the keyword *Hyertek* in a tweet, so you complete the options this way:

- *Search Text:* "Hyertek"

- *Interval:* 1

- *Frequency:* Minute

Configuring a Logic App to trigger on a keyword such as *Azure* will clog your inbox. Instead, I've selected a very discrete word, Hyertek, the name of my company, to trigger emails. If you chose a word such as Azure, be warned; you'll pay through the nose for these constant triggers because it will generate *lots* of events. More events, more money!

8. **Click New Step.**

9. **Scroll through the connector library list and look for Outlook.**

10. **When you find the Outlook connectors, click the Office 365 Outlook connector.**

11. **Search the actions list for Send, and select the Send an Email action.**

12. **In the Office 365 Outlook connector dialog box, click Sign In, and authenticate to Office 365.**

13. **Complete the Send an Email dialog box, preferably using dynamic fields.**

This step is where the procedure can get a bit messy.

(a) Put your destination Office 365 email address in the T: field.

(b) Place your cursor in the Subject field.

(c) Click Add Dynamic Content to expose the dynamic content pop-up window.

Dynamic fields allow you to plug live data into your workflow. Figure 8-6, for example, shows a customized email notification message.

14. **Click Save.**

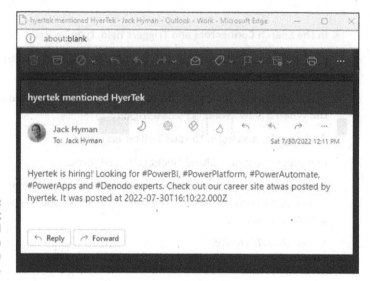

FIGURE 8-6:
Dynamic content
placed in several
fields to create an
email using an
Azure Logic App.

Testing the trigger and action

To trigger the action, follow these steps:

REMEMBER

1. **On the Logic App workflow toolbar, click Run.**

   You must— I repeat, *must* — switch the Logic App to a running state for it to catch the trigger.

2. **On Twitter, post a tweet that includes a reference to Azure.**

3. **Await notification.**

   The tweet should trigger an email to the address that you designated.

TIP

Another place to check workflow run status is the Overview page, which shows how many times the trigger was tripped, the workflow run, and/or any errors.

Chapter **9**

Managing Databases in Microsoft Azure

M ost line-of-business applications require a data tier to support data persistence, querying, and reporting, so the time has come for you to see how to implement databases in the Microsoft Azure public cloud. Databases in the cloud aren't new: SQL Data Services was the first cloud service that Microsoft made generally available. The year was 2008, even before Microsoft Azure came to market in 2010.

By the end of this chapter, you'll be up to speed on both relational and nonrelational database options in Azure, and you'll know the basics of their deployment and configuration.

Revisiting the IaaS versus PaaS Question

A common push–pull issue with customers in an Azure Cloud solution architect's life is making sure that a given workload belongs in Azure virtual machines (VMs) rather than in various hosted Platform as a Service (PaaS) services. The data tier is an excellent example of this dynamic.

The classical consultant's answer to questions such as "Should I host our app's SQL database in an Azure VM or Azure PaaS?" is "It depends." The answer typically isn't black-and-white. The following sections describe aspects Azure customers need to consider when making their decision.

Controlling the environment

When you host your database on Azure VMs in a virtual network, you have full-stack control of the entire environment. If you need to tweak your SQL Server's memory allocation, you're free to do that. If you want to make a Windows Registry–based performance enhancement, the VM enables you to accomplish that goal. The downside is that you also hold full responsibility for the updates to the VM software, including the database. That can be a full-time job.

By contrast, you lose that degree of administrative control when you use a hosted PaaS product such as Azure SQL Database. With PaaS, Microsoft strictly controls the degree to which you can access your database's underlying virtual server(s).

Running any version of any database

The main reason why some customers opt to run their data tiers on VMs is that a hosted version of their database isn't available. At this writing, Microsoft supports the following versions of Azure SQL Database for MySQL Servers:

>> MySQL Community Edition 5.6

>> MySQL Community Edition 5.7

>> MySQL Community Edition 8.0

What if your app requires an earlier or later version, or you've already paid for MySQL Enterprise Edition? In cases such as these, a VM is most appropriate.

By contrast, as long as your app supports an Azure-hosted PaaS database option, you can immediately take advantage of Azure's massive global scale and elastic compute power.

Using preinstalled VMs from Azure Marketplace

The Azure Marketplace is stocked with preinstalled VM images that run just about every relational or nonrelational database on the market.

The business advantage is that you don't have to spend additional time installing, licensing, and configuring the database server software because it's already installed on the image. Furthermore, SQL Server licensing is included in the per-minute VM run-time costs. But again, once you take the helm the VM, the database updates are all in your court. Not the case with a PaaS database option.

By contrast, with PaaS database options, the underlying server infrastructure is abstracted away from you. Thus, you don't have to worry about server performance tuning, backups, and the like. Instead, you can focus more squarely on your line-of-business applications and their back-end data.

Figure 9-1 shows a sample of the templates available in the Marketplace. Some partners offer "pay as you go" licensing that integrates with your Azure subscription costs.

FIGURE 9-1: You can save time by deploying a preinstalled VM from the Azure Marketplace.

Comparing Relational and Nonrelational Databases in Azure

This section goes deeper into Azure-hosted databases, starting with the difference between relational and nonrelational database systems. A full treatment of this subject is beyond the scope of this book, of course, but I can cover the essentials here.

TIP

For further information, please check out *SQL For Dummies*, 9th Edition, by Allen G. Taylor, and *NoSQL For Dummies*, by Adam Fowler (both Wiley). Fowler's book is a bit older than Taylor's, but between the two volumes, you'll gain wide skills in modern database systems.

Table 9-1 breaks down the biggest differences between relational and nonrelational database systems.

TABLE 9-1   ## Relational and Nonrelational Databases

	Relational	Nonrelational
Type of data	Large, unrelated, and volatile	Predefined schema
Uses	Mobile apps, real-time analytics, and Internet of Things (IoT) apps	Accounting, finance, banking, transaction processing
Scaling	Horizontal scaling across a cluster	Vertical scaling by adding more resources to VM
Data model	Key/value and wide-column	Related tables, with each table heavily constrained
Query languages	Various, including SQL-like	SQL

The following sections introduce Azure's relational-database PaaS products.

SQL Database

With SQL Database, Microsoft abstracts most of the server platform and allows you to focus nearly exclusively on the database itself. Table 9-2 describes the members of the SQL Database family.

TABLE 9-2   ## SQL Database Products

Product	Use
Azure SQL Database	Online transaction processing
Azure Synapse Analytics	Online analytical processing
Azure SQL Database Managed Instance	Online large-scale parallel processing

Generally, your selection of the appropriate product falls along the following lines:

>> If you need full control of the environment, choose SQL Database.

>> If you need a balance between Infrastructure as a Service (IaaS) and PaaS flexibility, choose SQL Database Managed Instance.

>> If you need massively parallel processing for intensive query workloads, choose SQL Synapse Analytics.

SQL Database for MySQL Servers

For businesses with apps that run MySQL, SQL Database for MySQL Servers — a fully managed, enterprise-ready MySQL Community Edition instance that's natively integrated into Azure — is a good fit.

This solution enables your developers to continue using the MySQL data platform with native tooling and to take advantage of the Azure platform's geoscale, security, and performance features.

Azure Database for MariaDB Servers

Since Oracle purchased MySQL in 2008, some businesses have moved their apps' data platform to another product or embraced the MariaDB project: an open-source fork of Oracle's proprietary MySQL relational database management system.

Azure Database for MariaDB Servers operates almost exactly like Database for MySQL Servers, except that you use MariaDB instead of MySQL. Otherwise, both database servers read and write the same files and even work in parallel versions.

Azure Database for PostgreSQL Servers

PostgreSQL (officially pronounced *post-gres-cue-el*) is a free open-source relational database system that ranks alongside MySQL in its popularity for use with open-source n-tier web application projects.

Azure's support for MySQL and PostgreSQL is a big deal; it wasn't too many years ago that it was unthinkable Microsoft would support any product besides its own SQL Server and Microsoft Access database products.

Implementing Azure SQL Database

This section gets some real work done with Azure SQL Database.

Understanding service tiers

Azure SQL Database has two service tiers and an elastic pool pricing model, all described in the following sections.

DTU-based service tier

In Chapter 7, I briefly mention the Azure Compute Unit (ACU), which is Microsoft's standardization metric for VM compute power. This value is a way to account for Microsoft's use of different hardware across its worldwide data-center network. Similarly, the Database Transaction Unit (DTU) is the SQL Database performance metric. The DTU is a composite value that takes into account server central processing unit (CPU), disk input/output (I/O), and memory allocation. The trick to the DTU model, of course, is forecasting the right service level for your database.

ON THE WEB

To help you determine how many DTUs you need for your SQL Database workload, Microsoft employee Justin Henriksen created the Azure SQL Database DTU Calculator, which you can find at https://dtucalculator.azurewebsites.net. Check it out!

vCore service tier

The vCore service tier enables you to specify discrete Azure VM instance sizes to power your Azure SQL Database databases. The advantage here is you have much more granular control over the compute layer than you do with the DTU tier.

With the Serverless option, your compute resources are autoscaled, and you're billed per second based on the number of vCores your database consumes.

Elastic pool model

The DTU and vCore service tiers pertain to single databases. Which pricing model should you choose if your business has several databases, each with its own usage patterns?

That's where SQL elastic pools come in. You populate your databases into an elastic pool, and the databases share an allocation of elastic DTUs. That way, quieter databases can help more active databases by surrendering DTUs that you would have paid for but not used.

Deploying an SQL Database and an SQL Database virtual server

This section takes you through the process of deploying an Azure SQL Database and its accompanying virtual server. In the past, you had to create the virtual server first before you could create the database. Since mid-2021, this process has been streamlined into a single unified interface, as shown in Figure 9-2.

FIGURE 9-2:
Deploying a new
Azure SQL
Database.

To deploy an Azure SQL Database, log in to the Azure portal with your administrative account and then follow these steps:

1. **In the Azure portal, browse to the SQL Databases blade, and click Add.**

   You are presented with a host of database options, including one labeled "SQL Database."

2. **Select the SQL Server option, which asks you to configure a database instance.**

   • *Subscription:* Select the subscription the database will bill against.

   • *Resource Group:* Select the associate resource group that the database can be tied to for a given project.

- *Database Name:* Enter a meaningful database name for your new database instance.

- *Server:* If you haven't already created a virtual database service instance, select Create New. Otherwise, select the instance from the drop-down menu with which the database is associated.

- *Want To Use Elastic Pools?:* Select Yes or No depending on your technical need.

- *Workload Environment:* Select whether your instance is associated with a Production-Grade database or Development.

- *Compute+Storage:* Select the service and compute tier to match your database architecture needs (see Figure 9-3).

3. **Click Review + Create, and then on the next page, click Create to submit the deployment to Azure Resource Manager (ARM).**

TIP

If you haven't created a virtual server instance, all you need to do is select Server ⇨ Create New. Then, you'll be prompted to provide the name of the server instance (not the database), along with the associated location. The final step is determining the security approach you want to utilize to authenticate with the database instances. Take a look at Figure 9-4 to understand the vanilla requirements to create the server instance.

FIGURE 9-3:
Configuring
Compute+
Storage
for an Azure
SQL Database.

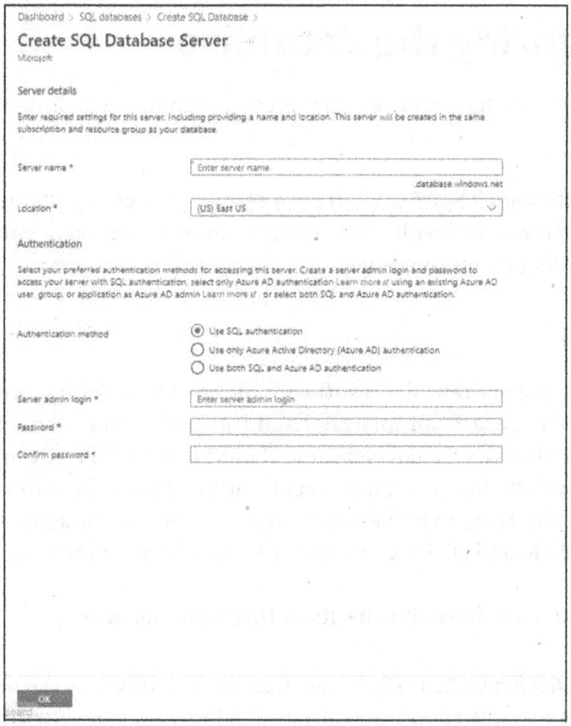

Dashboard > SQL databases > Create SQL Database >

Create SQL Database Server
Microsoft

Server details

Enter required settings for this server, including providing a name and location. This server will be created in the same subscription and resource group as your database.

Server name *   [Enter server name   ]
                                                           .database.windows.net

Location *   [(US) East US   ∨]

Authentication

Select your preferred authentication methods for accessing this server. Create a server admin login and password to access your server with SQL authentication, select only Azure AD authentication Learn more ⧉ using an existing Azure AD user, group, or application as Azure AD admin Learn more ⧉, or select both SQL and Azure AD authentication.

Authentication method   ⦿ Use SQL authentication
                             ○ Use only Azure Active Directory (Azure AD) authentication
                             ○ Use both SQL and Azure AD authentication

Server admin login *   [Enter server admin login   ]

Password *   [   ]

Confirm password *   [   ]

[OK]

FIGURE 9-4:
Configuring a
new Azure SQL
Database Server.

MAKING RESERVATIONS

TIP

Want to save a bit of money? Consider adding Azure Reservations into the equation if you know you'll be running a database for the long haul. Databases can be very costly to operate. A typical MySQL Server instance outside of a VM is about $150 to $200 per month. Azure SQL Server can run into the thousands of dollars per month. With Azure Reservations, you can cut the cost as much as 72 percent. The Reservations button on the Virtual Machines and SQL Databases blades enables you to prepay for a specified VM and/or SQL Database compute capacity over a yearly term. If you've already done due diligence and determined your compute needs, plus if you know you'll need the VM and/or database for that time period, you can save quite a bit of money over the agreement term as opposed to paying per-minute as usual. You can pay for the reservations either upfront or monthly; learn more by reading the "What are Azure Reservations?" Azure docs article at `https://docs.microsoft.com/azure/billing/billing-save-compute-costs-reservations`.

Configuring the database

This section covers some of the most common SQL Database configuration settings.

TIP

Check out the Quick Start blade from a resource's Settings list whenever you need to familiarize yourself with a new Azure resource. This blade provides tips, procedures, and documentation links.

Firewall

The SQL Database firewall is a software-defined networking component that protects your database from unauthorized inbound connections. You configure the firewall at either the virtual-server or database level. The advantage of setting the server firewall is that you can protect multiple databases with a single configuration. To configure it, open the server firewall from the database by browsing to the Overview blade and clicking Set Server Firewall on the toolbar.

The SQL Database firewall consists of three components:

- » **Allow Access to Azure Services:** This option enables connectivity traffic from all Azure-sourced public and private IP addresses. This setting doesn't constitute authorization, which you need to configure separately.

- » **Client IP Address and IP Rules:** These settings allow database connectivity from your local workstation's public IP address. You can also define a list of public IP address ranges that should be allowed to connect to the database.

- » **Virtual Networks:** If you defined an SQL Database service endpoint in your virtual network, you can complete the configuration here to constrain access to the virtual server from that network.

Connection strings

The database connection string represents the interface between your application and the database itself. SQL Database provides four driver choices:

- » **ADO.NET:** Generally used for .NET applications
- » **JDBC:** Generally used for Java applications
- » **ODBC:** General-purpose driver
- » **PHP:** Generally used for PHP applications

Choose the connection string that makes the most sense for your application and your development team's skill set.

Georeplication

In my opinion, the ability to configure asynchronous replication for SQL Database is one of the standout features of PaaS. Few businesses have the resources to do this configuration on their own.

You might replicate the database to another region for failover; this means that if the primary database goes offline, you can redirect connections to the secondary standby database copy. Another benefit of georeplication is the ability to run read-only queries against the replica database without creating blocking issues for your users.

Follow these steps to enable georeplication for SQL Database:

1. **Go to your database's Data Management blade and click Replicas.**

2. **Click Create Replicas.**

   The Create SQL Database – Geo Replica form appears, as shown in Figure 9-5.

3. **Fill out the form.**

   You'll likely need to create a secondary Database Virtual Server location if you intend to support georeplication.

4. **On the bottom of the page before creating the replication, select Geo-redundant backup storage.**

5. **Press Review+Create to activate Georeplication.**

6. **Click Create upon reviewing the replication configuration.**

TIP

Consider choosing the region designated as your primary region's pair. Microsoft puts additional high-speed network connectivity between paired regions to reduce latency. You don't have to use a paired region, but doing so is a good idea because of the reduced inter-region network latency.

TECHNICAL STUFF

You need to create a virtual server in the secondary region. That means if you are in a region such as East US, you can't be in East US for the replication. Creating a secondary database has pricing implications too, but to save money, you can run the secondary database on a lower pricing tier than the primary one.

7. **In the Replica instance, open the Failover Blade.**

8. **Complete the Failover Group configuration blade as follows:**

   - *Failover Group Name:* Enter a meaningful failover group name

   - *Server:* Select the non-replicated virtual server name (connects one region to the other).

   - *Read/Write Failover Policy:* Select Automatic.

- *Read/Write Grace Period (Hours):* This setting is the amount of time Azure waits before automatically failing over to your secondary database when data loss might occur. The decision here is setting a short enough grace period to uphold your service-level agreements, but not long enough to cause an undue denial of service.

9. **Click Create to submit the deployment to Azure Resource Manager.**

FIGURE 9-5:
Configuring
georeplication for
Azure SQL
Database.

TECHNICAL STUFF

Although these steps configure Azure to fail over a database automatically, you're responsible for changing the connection string in your application source code to point to the secondary instance. Azure may be smart, but it doesn't know everything until you feed it the right amount of information. To fetch your database's connection strings, open the database's settings in the Azure portal and browse to the Connection strings blade.

Figure 9-6 shows a completed georeplication configuration.

FIGURE 9-6:
Georeplicated
Azure SQL
database with
automatic failover
configured in less
than five minutes.

Configure

The Settings blade under Compute+Storage is where you can change your service tier. If you're using DTU, you can switch among Basic, Standard, and Premium levels. You can also switch between DTU and vCore purchasing models.

Inspecting the virtual server

This procedure helps you understand the relationship between a new SQL Database and its parent virtual server. Follow these steps:

1. **Navigate to SQL Database's Overview page.**

2. **On the Available Resources pane, click the Server Name hyperlink.**

    The virtual server name resides on the database.windows.net public DNS zone.

3. **Make these selections in the Settings list:**

    - *SQL Databases:* You should see your database, along with its status and current pricing tier.

    - *DTU Quota:* This setting shows you how many resources your database consumed during the current (monthly) Azure billing cycle.

4. **Make the following selection under the Data Management list:**

    - *Manage Backups:* Azure backs up your databases by default. You can select your database and click Configure Retention to adjust how often Azure backs up the database and how long it retains daily (point-in-time restore), weekly, monthly, and yearly backups.

Connecting to the database

To connect and manage your SQL database, you need to download and install Azure Data Studio from `https://docs.microsoft.com/sql/azure-data-studio/download-azure-data-studio?view=sql-server-ver16` (the free SQL

Server/Azure SQL Database management interface). When you have that product installed, follow these steps:

1. **On your database's Overview blade, copy your virtual server's Domain Name Service (DNS) name.**

2. **Start Azure Data Studio and authenticate with your administrative user account by selecting Create a Connection (see Figure 9-7).**

   You need to fill in the following information:

   - *Server Name:* Your virtual server name in the format *<server-name>*. database.windows.net

   - *Authentication:* SQL Server Authentication

   You can use Azure Active Directory authentication if you've configured it. You learn about Azure AD in a bit.

   - *Login/Password:* The administrative credentials you defined for your virtual server

3. **Expand the Databases container and select your database of choice.**

   For the purpose of this exercise, I use the Microsoft-provided AdventureWorks SQL Database.

   If you don't have an active database, you may want to acquire a sample database such as the Microsoft-created AdventureWorks. You can download and configure the instance by going to https://docs.microsoft.com/sql/samples/adventureworks-install-configure?view=sql-server-ver16&tabs=ssms.

4. **Choose File ⇨ New Query from Current Connection.**

   A new, blank SQL query window appears.

5. **In the query window, type the following Transact-Structured Query Language (T-SQL) query:**

   ```
   SELECT TOP (10) [CustomerID]
        ,[Title]
        ,[FirstName]
        ,[LastName]
        ,[CompanyName]
   FROM [SalesLT].[Customer]
   ```

6. **Select the query and then click Execute on the SQL Editor toolbar.**

   Alternatively, you can right-click your selected query and choose Execute from the shortcut menu.

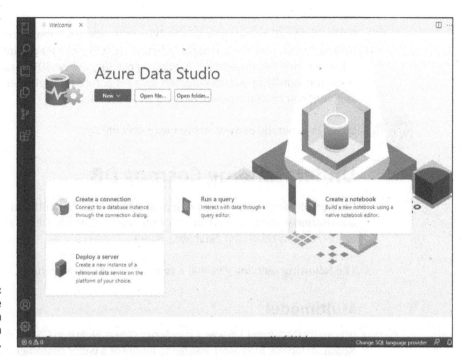

FIGURE 9-7:
Accessing the
Connection in
Azure Data
Studio.

REMEMBER

Azure SQL Databases are intended for public consumption and so they are fairly straightforward. Some organizations may require fully-managed deployment options because their applications are a smidge complicated. These are often the applications that are on-premises or hybrid in nature. In these instances, you'll want to consider Azure SQL Managed Instances because of their ability to support features such as linked servers or service brokers. Under these conditions, you'll need to account for pricing, connectivity, authentication, and provisioning, not just your database, as SQL Server options can become a bit hairy. To learn more about Azure SQL Managed Instances and when it's appropriate to use such a solution, go to https://docs.microsoft.com/azure/azure-sql/managed-instance.

Implementing Azure Cosmos DB

Relational databases are all about *schema*, or structure. I always say that to be a relational database administrator, you should be a micromanager, because every data row needs to be heavily constrained to fit the table, relationship, and database schema. Although relational databases offer excellent data consistency, they tend to fall down in the scalability department because of all the schema overhead. Enter the nonrelational database.

Rather than call a nonrelational database *schemaless*, it's more accurate to say that NoSQL databases have a flexible schema. At first, you may think that a flexible schema would make querying nearly impossible. But NoSQL databases can overcome this hurdle by partitioning the data set across multiple clustered nodes and applying raw compute power to the query execution.

NoSQL is generally understood to mean *not only SQL*.

Understanding Cosmos DB

Cosmos DB (originally called Document DB) is Azure's multimodel, georeplicated, nonrelational data store. You can implement Cosmos DB in conjunction with or instead of a relational database system.

The following sections give you a tour of Cosmos DB's features.

Multimodel

Originally Document DB was a JavaScript Object Notation (JSON) document-model NoSQL database. Microsoft wanted to embrace a wider customer pool, however, so it introduced Cosmos DB, which supports five data models/application programming interfaces (APIs):

» **Core (SQL):** This API is the successor to the original Document DB. The data store consists of JSON documents, and Core API provides an SQL-like query language that should be immediately comfortable for relational database administrators and developers.

» **Azure Cosmos DB for MongoDB API:** This API supports the MongoDB wire protocol. MongoDB, also a JSON document store, allows you to query Cosmos DB as though it were a MongoDB instance.

» **Cassandra:** This API is compatible with the Cassandra wide column store database and supports Cassandra Query Language.

» **Azure Table:** This API points to the Azure storage account's table service. It's a key/value data store that you can access with ARM's representational state transfer (REST) APIs.

» **Gremlin (graph):** This API supports a graph-based data view and the Apache Gremlin query language.

Do you see a theme? The idea is that just about any developer who needs a NoSQL data store should be able to use Cosmos DB without sacrificing original source code or client-side tooling.

Turnkey global distribution

With a couple of mouse clicks, you can instruct Azure to replicate your Cosmos DB database to however many Azure regions you need to put your data close to your users.

Cosmos DB uses a multimaster replication scheme with a 99.999 percent availability service–level agreement for both read and write operations.

Multiple consistency levels

Relational databases always offer strong consistency at the expense of speed and scale. Cosmos DB offers flexibility in this regard, allowing you to select (dynamically) any of five data consistency levels:

>> **Strong:** Reads are guaranteed to return the most recently committed version of an item. This level is the slowest-performing but most accurate.

>> **Bounded Staleness, Session, and Consistent Prefix:** These consistency levels offer balance between performance and consistent query results.

>> **Eventual:** Reads have no ordering guarantee. This choice is the fastest but least accurate.

Data consistency refers to the requirement that any database transaction change affected data only in allowed ways. With regard to read consistency specifically, the goal is to prevent two users from seeing different results from the same query due to incomplete database replication.

Creating a Cosmos DB account

This section gets down to business. The first task is getting Cosmos DB off the ground to create a Cosmos DB account. After you have the account, you can define one or more databases.

Follow these steps to create an account:

1. **In the Azure portal, browse to the Azure Cosmos DB blade, and click Add.**

   The Create Azure Cosmos DB Account blade appears.

2. **On the Create Azure Cosmos DB Account blade, complete the Basics page using the following settings:**

   ● *Account Name:* This name needs to be unique in its resource group.

   ● *API:* Select Core (SQL).

- *Geo-Redundancy:* Don't enable this option. If you do, Azure replicates your account to your region's designated pair.

- *Multi-Region Writes:* Don't enable this option. You can always enable it later if you need multiple read/write replicas of the account throughout the world.

3. **Click Review + Create and then click Create to submit the deployment.**

Running and debugging a sample Cosmos DB application

In my opinion, the best way to gain general familiarity with a new Azure service is to visit its Quick Start page. I'll now do this with Cosmos DB. Figure 9-8 shows the Cosmos DB Quick Start page.

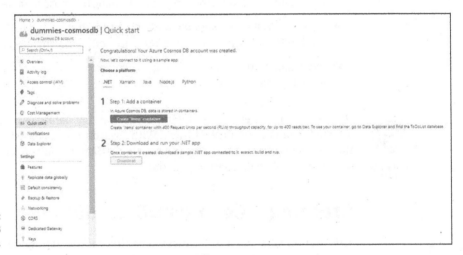

If you follow the Cosmos DB Quick Start tutorial, you can accomplish the following goals:

>> Create a new Cosmos DB database and container.

>> Download a .NET Core web application that connects to the Cosmos DB database.

>> Interact with the container and data store on your workstation by using Visual Studio.

To run a sample application, follow these steps:

1. **On your Cosmos DB account's Quick Start blade, choose the .NET Core platform, and click Create 'Items' Container.**

   Azure creates a container named 'Items' with 10GB capacity and 400 request units (RUs) per second. As you may rightly guess, the RU is the standardized Cosmos DB performance metric.

2. **Click Download to download the preconfigured .NET Core web application.**

3. **Unzip the downloaded archive on your system, and double-click the quickstartcore.sln solution file to open the project in Visual Studio 2022 Community Edition.**

4. **In Visual Studio, build and run the solution by choosing Build ⇨ Build Solution.**

5. **Choose Debug ⇨ Start Debugging to open the application in your default web browser.**

6. **In the To-Do App with Azure DocumentDB web application that is now running in your web browser, click Create New, and define several sample to-do items.**

   When you add to-do items, you're populating the Items container in your Azure Cosmos DB database.

7. **Close the browser to stop debugging the application.**

TIP

For extra practice, use the Visual Studio publishing wizard (which you find by right-clicking your project in Solution Explorer and choosing Publish from the shortcut menu) to publish this app to Azure App Service. This exercise is a great test of the skills you've developed thus far.

Interacting with Cosmos DB

To practice interacting with Cosmos DB and your database, return to the Azure portal and look at your Cosmos DB account settings. Here, I highlight some key settings to make sure you know where to find them:

» **Data Explorer:** Perform browser-based query and database configuration.

» **Replicate Data Globally:** Click the map to replicate your Cosmos DB account to multiple regions. (Additional costs apply.)

>> **Default Consistency:** Switch among the five data consistency levels.

>> **Firewall and Virtual Networks:** Bind your Cosmos DB account to specific virtual network(s).

>> **Keys:** View the Cosmos DB account endpoint Uniform Resource Identifier, access keys, and connection strings.

Now follow these steps to interact with your new Cosmos DB database directly from the Azure portal:

1. **In your Cosmos DB account, select Data Explorer.**

2. **Click the Open Full Screen button on the Data Explorer toolbar.**

   This button takes you to https://cosmos.azure.com in a separate browser tab, giving you more screen real estate to run queries.

   The ToDoList planet icon represents the icon, and the Items icon represents the container. The container is the Cosmos DB replication unit.

3. **Right-click the Items container and choose New SQL Query from the shortcut menu.**

TIP

   The Save Query button is handy for retaining particularly useful queries.

4. **View your existing items by running the default query.**

   The default query provided by Azure in the Data Explorer, SELECT * FROM c, retrieves all documents from your Items container.

TIP

   c is an alias for *container*. You'll find the alias to be super useful when you work with the Cosmos DB Core API.

5. **Experiment with different SELECT queries.**

   The double dash (--) denotes a one-line comment in Data Explorer. Try entering these queries in Data Explorer.

   ```
   -- select two fields from the container documents
   SELECT c.name, c.description from c
   -- show only incomplete todo items
   SELECT * from c WHERE c.isComplete = false
   ```

6. **Use Data Explorer to update a document.**

7. **Click the Update toolbar button to save your changes.**

CLEANING UP YOUR ENVIRONMENT

The Azure subscription model requires you to pay only for the resources you consume, so you need to understand how to remove your deployments when you don't need them anymore.

You've probably been using the Delete or Remove Azure portal commands to clean up your environments. A faster method is to invoke Azure PowerShell or Azure CLI from Azure Cloud Shell or from your own computer. To force-delete a resource group named 'DummiesBook' by using PowerShell, run the following command:

```
Remove-AzResourceGroup -Name 'DummiesBook' -Force -Verbose
```

To do the same thing with CLI, the command is

```
az group delete --resource-group DummiesBook --no-wait --yes
```

Bookmark the URL https://cosmos.azure.com so that you can easily access Cosmos DB Data Explorer in a full-window experience. Also, Microsoft offers excellent Cosmos DB SQL query cheat sheets at https://docs.microsoft.com/azure/cosmos-db/query-cheat-sheet.

Chapter **10**

Using Data Analytics and Machine Learning in Azure

Microsoft Azure isn't just a cloud solution provider to host workloads and transform data center applications in the cloud. As you'd expect, Microsoft added the horsepower of data analytics to ingest, analyze, and monitor data — and not just a few hundred records. I'm talking about millions of records that are stored in Azure each day, each hour, or even each minute. The data could come from a world-renowned business-to-business (B2B) or business-to-consumer (B2C) company or your smartphone using Internet of Things (IoT) sensors. To add the icing on the cake, Azure also offers a host of opportunities to intelligently learn from the data patterns and make intelligent recommendations with the help of Azure Machine Learning and Azure Cognitive Services. This chapter reviews the primary products you should become acclimated to and consider configuring when immersing yourself in Microsoft Azure.

Dipping into Data Analytics

No one ever said understanding data across many systems is easy, especially when systems likely don't communicate with one another. And that is the compelling reason for implementing big data solutions such as those Microsoft has added to the Azure arsenal of tools.

Instead of spending hours, days, or even weeks trying to create the perfect story, you can easily extract, transfer, and load (ETL) data from one system to another. It doesn't matter if the data is structured, semi-structured, or unstructured. Microsoft seems to have created a solution to handle the entire analytics lifecycle. You'll learn about these critical solutions in the following sections.

Azure Synapse Analytics

Data warehouses are notorious for housing large data sets that are mainly used for enterprise analytics. An organization can query and analyze the data based on the transaction source using business intelligence and data mining tools. An example of an enterprise business intelligence tool is Microsoft Power BI. But when the data is raw or highly curated, the data warehouse is necessary to scale the datasets up and down quickly. Sounds like the same concepts associated with a virtual machine (VM), right?

Long ago, organizations had to glue together their big data applications (which include the data warehouse) to build a usable data pipeline. Not anymore with Azure Synapse Analytics, a platform that brings the data warehouse together with one or more data analytics-driven applications in a single product.

TECHNICAL STUFF

Azure Synapse Analytics was formerly known as SQL Data Warehouse. Microsoft stitched together SQL Data Warehouse, Apache Spark tools for big data, and Azure Pipelines for data integration and ETL management to create a big data analytics warehousing solution. Other tools that can exchange data with Azure Synapse Analytics include Microsoft Power BI, Microsoft Cosmos DB, Azure Machine Learning, MariaDB, and PostgreSQL.

So what is the exact use case for Azure Synapse Analytics, as it seems so far and wide? The answer lies in the distributed querying capabilities of T-SQL, which enable data warehousing and virtualization to support streaming data and machine learning simultaneously. The other key benefit is that Azure Synapse Analytics offers two pricing models: a serverless model and a dedicated resources model. Of course, different consumption and pricing models are available depending on the chosen version.

TECHNICAL STUFF

The two consumption and pricing models are based on the following attributes:

>> **Predictable performance and cost** require you to create a dedicated SQL pool to reserve processing power for data stored in SQL tables.

>> **Unpredictable, burst-based workloads** enable you to configure the system to be available at all times using serverless SQL endpoints.

Four applications must be comingled to enable a single cluster in Azure Synapse: Synapse SQL, Apache Spark for Azure Synapse, Interop of SQL, and Apache Spark. All items work within the confines of a data lake, integrate with pipelines using Azure Data Studio, and are managed with Synapse Studio, a front-end interface for Azure Synapse.

ON THE WEB

An entire chapter or two could be written on the configuration process and components that make up Azure Synapse Analytics. To gain insight on how to use and architect a big data solution across this collection of solutions, check out https://docs.microsoft.com/azure/synapse-analytics.

Azure HDInsight

Keeping with the big data theme is Microsoft's introduction of Azure HDInsight, a cloud distribution of Hadoop components. HDInsight enables users to process massive amounts of data using a custom analytics-driven environment quickly and cost-effectively. Using popular open-source frameworks such as Hadoop, Spark, Hive, LLAP, and Kafka, users can collect, analyze, and evaluate data at scale while applying ETL with little effort. HDInsight is commonly used in conjunction with use cases involving data warehousing, machine learning, and IoT.

Following are reasons to use HDInsight over Azure Synapse Analytics and Azure Databricks (discussed next):

>> **HDInsight is cloud-native.** You can create optimized clusters for Hadoop, Spark, and Interactive Query. Kafka and HBase on Azure are both used as big data platforms. With HDInsight, you get a complete service licensing agreement (SLA) across all production workloads.

>> **HDInsight is scalable and affordable.** You can scale your workloads up or down while saving money, creating clusters on demand. Like other services in Azure, HDInsight is consumption-based, only requiring you to pay for actual usage.

>> **You can ensure secure compliance.** Using Azure's complete network and security products collection, enterprise data in HDInsight can be protected

with Azure Virtual Networks and Encryption. Azure Active Directory can also be integrated with HDInsight. Microsoft ensures that those using HDInsight will have tools that comply with all global industry and government compliance standards. To ensure these metrics are met, HDInsight works collaboratively with Azure Monitor, using a single interface to track all cluster activity.

>> **HDInsight is available globally.** As of this writing, HDInsight is the data analytics platform most available across Azure regions compared to Azure Synapse Analytics and Azure Databricks, Azure's other extensive data analytics offerings. HDInsight is available in all sovereign regions, unlike other big data analytics products.

>> **HDInsight is integrated, extensible, and productivity driven.** Users can integrate and be highly productive with Hadoop and Spark in their preferred integrated development environments, including Visual Studio, VSCode, IntelliJ, and Eclipse. HDInsight offers native Python, Java, and .NET support. HDInsight can also be integrated with big data platforms in as few as one click.

Azure Databricks

Extracting thousands of records to find the needle in the haystack is quite the feat. Can you imagine extracting and pulling together a clear message, especially if the data is 100 percent unstructured? When data comes from an array of sources, you'll find the problems escalate for even the most experienced data expert.

But suppose you have petabytes of data stored in a data warehouse or lake, and it's constantly flowing like a water spigot. You can be sure that building a complete data model and finding a logical answer is virtually impossible, especially when you are data mining or building a machine learning model. That's the use case for the Azure Databricks data analytics platform over other big data analytics solutions in Azure.

REMEMBER

To use Databricks, a user must select from two environments depending on their business need, either Databricks SQL Analytics or Databricks Workspace. What's the difference?

>> **Azure Databricks SQL Analytics** is intended for analysts looking to run SQL queries on targeted data lakes. The goal is to create visualizations, explore the query outputs across different perspectives, and architect dashboards.

TECHNICAL STUFF

Here's a secret. Microsoft makes you think that Databricks SQL Analytics is a separate product. It isn't! When you add users to the Azure Databricks instance, access to Databricks SQL is enabled. If you need to disable or re-enable Databricks SQL for users or group, you'll need to manage access for either the user or group. To learn more about configuring the environment, go to https://learn.microsoft.com/azure/databricks/scenarios/sql.

» **Azure Databricks Workspace** is purpose-built to support collaboration between data experts versus starting the analysis process using Azure Databricks SQL Analytics. A user can ingest data from Azure in batches using the Azure Data Factory built into Azure Databricks. Data streaming is also formidable using Kafka, Event Hub, or IoT Hub capabilities. Once the data is stored in an Azure storage container, a user can transfer data back and forth among data sources using a single data platform using Apache Spark, depending on the business use case.

To start with Databricks, you need to create a workspace. To get started, follow these steps:

1. **Go to the All Services blade and locate Azure Databricks under Analytics.**

2. **Select the Azure Databricks option.**

    An interface indicating that you need to create an Azure Databricks workspace appears, as shown in Figure 10-1.

3. **Next, fill out the Azure Databricks workspace creation form, making sure to select the appropriate pricing tier — Standard, Premium, or Trial — for your Databricks needs (see Figure 10-2).**

    There are significant differences between each pricing tier. Go to https://azure.microsoft.com/pricing/details/databricks for more information on what is included in each tier.

ON THE WEB

4. **Once you complete the form, click the Review+Create button and then Create to deploy the Azure Databricks workspace.**

5. **Upon full deployment, launch the workspace by pressing the Go to Resource button.**

6. **Once in the workspace, press Launch Workspace, as shown in Figure 10-3.**

    You might be asked to log in to Azure Databricks. If you already have an Active Directory account provisioned (most do), you should be let in without having to retype credentials.

WARNING

    Assuming your credentials are appropriately passed, you are taken into the Azure Databricks portal (shown in Figure 10-4) where you can import and export data, create a new data science notebook, or start querying, visualizing, and modeling your data leveraging the Azure Databricks SQL Analytics.

FIGURE 10-1:
An empty Azure
Databricks
workspace.

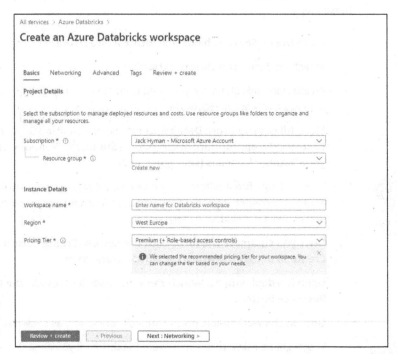

FIGURE 10-2:
Creating an Azure
Databricks
workspace.

TECHNICAL
STUFF

Many assume Azure Databricks is associated with the company Databricks and the Apache Spark platform. Surprisingly, it is not, as Microsoft built its Azure Databricks framework to run in Azure. The difference between Azure Databricks and Databricks by Apache is that Microsoft doesn't focus on storage exclusively. Azure Databricks is more concerned with analytics management.

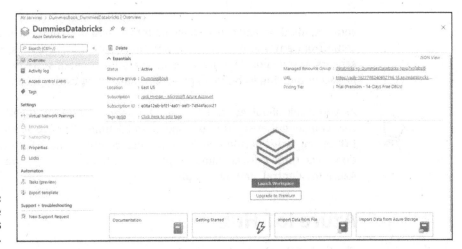

FIGURE 10-3:
Launching the
Azure Databricks
Workspace.

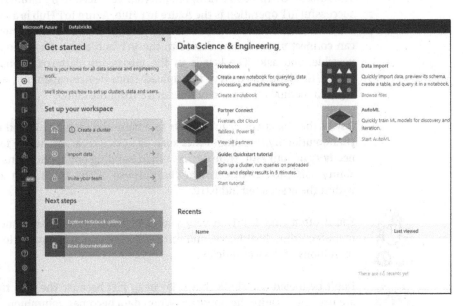

FIGURE 10-4:
The Azure
Databricks portal.

IoT in a Nutshell

When you hear the letters IoT, you probably think of big data. You are indeed correct. But big data in the context of Azure means a system of interrelated, internet-connected devices and sensor-oriented systems that collect — you guessed it — data over networks. The data is generated generally over wireless networks, without human intervention. The data sources from these networks are often noted as edge platforms. Some are also cloud in nature, where the devices will connect, monitor, and collect relevant bits of data from billions of assets. Data can come from anywhere — security solutions, operating systems, mobile devices, sensors, stand-alone applications, or analytic-oriented systems — to help businesses or individuals build, deploy, and manage typical applications.

TIP

As you think about Azure IoT, consider services working together across three core component areas: things, inputs, and actions. To have all components in an IoT setting work harmoniously, numerous solutions must help facilitate operations. The three critical solutions you'll need to be successful are Azure IoT Hub, Azure IoT Central, and Azure Sphere.

Azure IoT Hub

The first of the three IoT components that you need to be familiar with to build a successful IoT operation is the Azure IoT Hub. Azure IoT Hub is a managed service. With Azure IoT Hub, communication is bidirectional as a business or individual can connect virtually any device to the IoT hub and get a response. How is this possible, you ask? The key is in the messaging patterns supported, including device-to-cloud telemetry, file upload from device capability, and request-to-reply to methods that control the device from the cloud.

One of the objectives of IoT Hub is to ensure the monitoring and maintenance of your solution by tracking events such as device creation, device failure, and connectivity of your end-state device. When building out applications requiring scalability using IoT Hub, consider the purpose of the application and its patterns within the associated industry.

REMEMBER

You'll often find IoT Hub very useful in business segments such as industrial manufacturing, healthcare, and infrastructure management, as IoT Hub can scale to millions of devices quickly.

WARNING

Don't be fooled and think that it is cheap just because the data from IoT devices are itty-bitty. Quite the opposite. When data becomes voluminous, it gets expensive very quickly. You need to address the number of events per device and the scale of your solution at the start. The number of events determines the IoT Hub tier you'll need to utilize, which ultimately dictates pricing.

Azure IoT Hub is divided into two pricing tiers:

>> **Basic (B):** Intended for collecting data for devices and then analyzing it in a central hub

>> **Standard (S):** Intended when you have a variety of remote device configurations, distributed computing needs, or high-performance workloads

When it comes to pricing, there are a variety of variables to address. The biggest is data throughput. You'll need to get a handle on how your activity varies daily. Traffic varies, so your charges will change on a per unit basis. There is also the consideration of which messaging structure is best: device-to-cloud, cloud-to-device, or identity registration. As outlined in Table 10-1, throughput and send rates vary widely based on the IoT Hub tier. While there are other plans in public beta, these plans are generally available in this writing.

TABLE 10-1 **Select Data Throughput Edition for IoT Hub**

Tier Edition	Sustained Throughput	Sustained Send Rate
B1, S1	Up to 1,111K/minute per unit (1.5GB/day/unit)	Average of 278 messages/minute per unit (400,000 messages/day per unit)
B2, S2	Up to 16MB/minute per unit (22.8GB/day/unit)	Average of 4,167 messages/minute per unit (6 million messages/day per unit)
B3, S3	Up to 814MB/minute per unit (1,144.4GB/day/unit)	Average of 208,333 messages/minute per unit (300 million messages/day per unit)

REMEMBER

Scalability is paramount to ensuring the success of IoT Hub implementation. While the Basic tier supports unidirectional connectivity to the cloud, the Standard tier supports bidirectional communication functionality. This means a broader range of features, including security and communications, as outlined in Table 10-2.

TABLE 10-2 **IoT Hub Capabilities**

IoT Capability	Standard Tier	Basic Tier	Event Hub
Device-to-cloud messaging	Yes	Yes	Yes
HTTPS, AMQP and AMQP over Websockets	Yes	Yes	Yes
MQTT and MQTT over Websockets	Yes	Yes	
Per-device identity	Yes	Yes	
File upload from devices	Yes	Yes	
Device provisioning service	Yes	Yes	
Cloud to device messaging	Yes		
Device twin and device management	Yes		
Device streams	Yes		
IoT Edge	Yes		

IoT Hub does have limitations. It only supports one data throughput per edition. You can mix several data throughput editions with the same tier for many like-kind devices in each IoT Hub. For example, if you have many S3 IoT devices, you can't mix them with S2-tier IoT devices.

Configuring an IoT is a multi-step process. Follow these instructions to enable a new Azure IoT Hub:

1. **Go to the All Services blade and select All.**

2. **Locate the Internet of Things blade and among the list of items, select IoT Hub, as shown in Figure 10-5.**

3. **Fill out the form to create a new Azure IoT Hub (see Figure 10-6).**

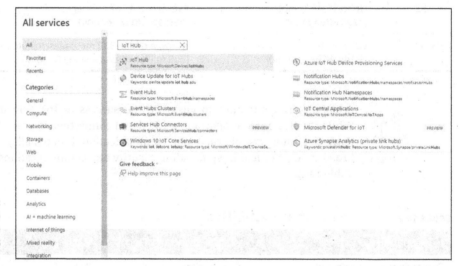

FIGURE 10-5:
Select IoT Hub
under the
Internet of Things
blade.

4. **Select the Management tab and the appropriate tier to manage your messaging units.**

   Remember, messaging units cost money based on volume, so pick the right option (see Figure 10-7).

5. **After selecting the appropriate messaging units, select the Review+Create tab and then press Create.**

   Your IoT Hub deployment is now on its way to being ready to add a new IoT device, which is found under Device Management ⇨ Devices.

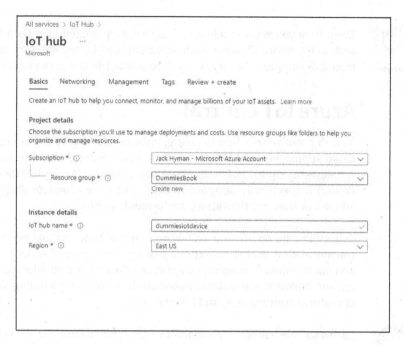

FIGURE 10-6:
Creating a new
Azure IoT Hub.

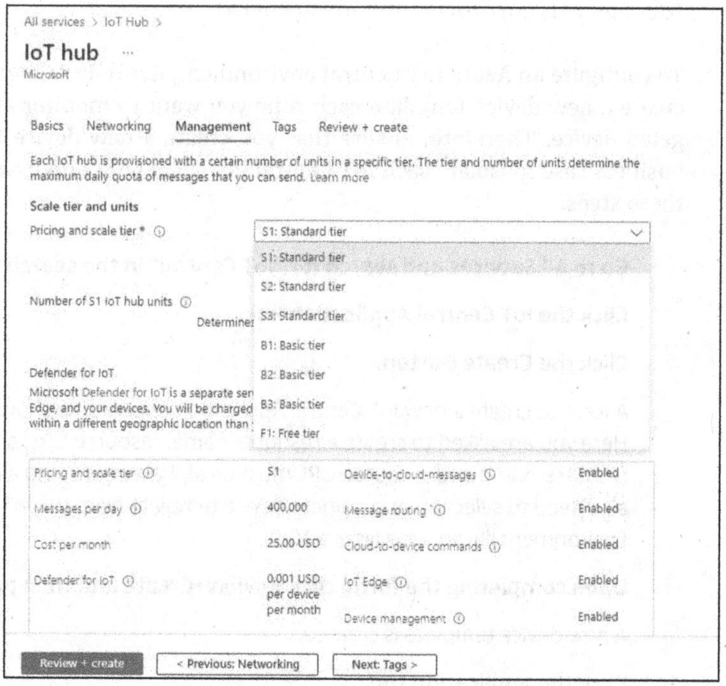

FIGURE 10-7:
Selecting
messaging units
in Azure IoT Hub.

REMEMBER

Every time you want to add a new device, be prepared to enter a few parameters such as the device ID name, authentication type, key parameters, and whether you intend to autogenerate keys to each connected device in the Azure IoT Hub.

Azure IoT Central

Now that you've seen how to create, manage, and deploy devices using messaged-based approaches with Azure IoT Hub, you'll want to monitor the devices post-deployment, right? That's the goal when you use Azure IoT Central. Azure IoT Central is specifically designed to help reduce the complete lifecycle activities of all devices from configuration, deployment, and usage.

Collecting data on all your IoT devices in real time enables you to focus on data transformation versus operations management-related tasks such as spending and maintenance management. Azure IoT Central also enables users to respond to line-of-business applications based on the user role, including Solution Builder, Operator, Administrator, and Developer.

ON THE WEB

Each user role has specific capabilities (and limitations, too, of course). To understand the range of capabilities, go to https://docs.microsoft.com/azure/iot-central/core/overview-iot-central.

To configure an Azure IoT Central environment, Azure IoT Central requires you to create a new device template each time you want to monitor and manage a targeted device. Therefore, ensure that you create a new device template for each business case to isolate each IoT Central instance. To set up new instances, follow these steps:

1. **Go to All Services and search for "IoT Central" in the search box.**

2. **Click the IoT Central Application link.**

3. **Click the Create Button.**

   A form to create a new IoT Central Application appears, as shown in Figure 10-8. Here you are asked to create a resource name, resource URL, and template. The resource name and resource URL must be alphanumeric and all lowercase. You also need to select an appropriate device template from the IoT Central Environment library (see Figure 10-9).

4. **Upon completing the form, click Review+Create and then press Create.**

   A new device template is created.

5. **Click the application URL.**

   The URL is located on the right side of the device page, as shown in Figure 10-10. From here, you are able to create the configuration for the IoT Central Application.

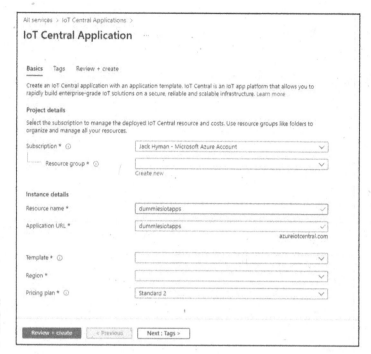

FIGURE 10-8:
Creating an Azure
IoT Central
Application.

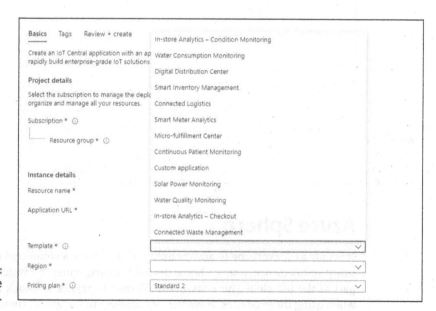

FIGURE 10-9:
Selecting the
device template.

WARNING

I can't stress this enough. The configuration is the easy part. The hard part is ensuring that you have the appropriate IoT device to match the template. Make sure you gather all the device specifications before creating the application template, which is quite detailed, as shown in Figure 10-11.

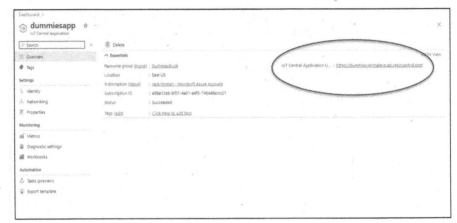

FIGURE 10-10:
Accessing the
IoT Central
Application URL.

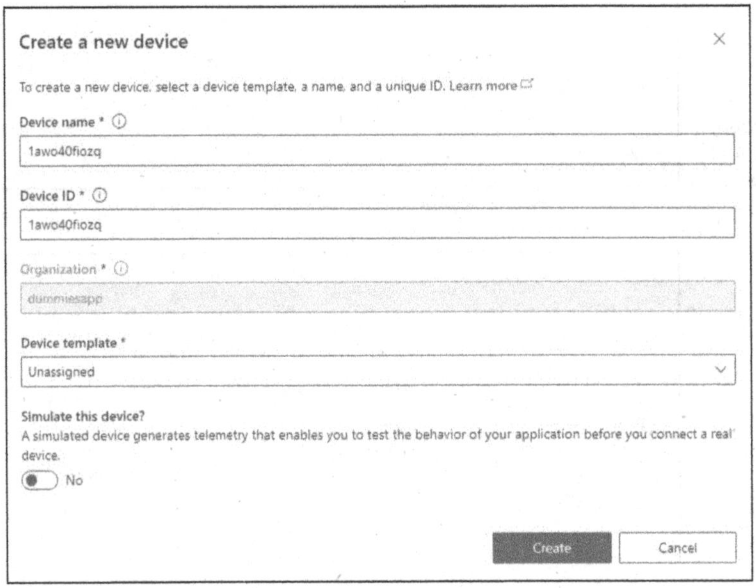

Create a new device

To create a new device, select a device template, a name, and a unique ID. Learn more

Device name *

1awo40fiozq

Device ID *

1awo40fiozq

Organization *

dummiesapp

Device template *

Unassigned

Simulate this device?
A simulated device generates telemetry that enables you to test the behavior of your application before you connect a real device.

No

Create   Cancel

FIGURE 10-11:
Azure IoT
Central device
configuration
example.

Azure Sphere

It seems as if everyone is always online if they have a connected device. Are you using an IoT device, a smart home device, a smartphone, or a watch? If so, you are part of the IoT club! There are many reasons to rejoice and look at the positives when using these devices. However, somewhere in the world, there are those with ill intent wanting to breach your privacy. Think of it as someone breaking into your home or car without permission.

Like every web application and computer with an operating system, IoT devices also have their security platform. The difference is that the programs are tightly integrated into the chipset. Each program on the chipset is designed to complete a set of tasks, not run the world. Although standardization is marginal with IoT devices, Microsoft needed a way to protect businesses from IoT vulnerabilities despite the program being stored on the chipset.

The answer is Azure Sphere, a highly secure application platform for internet-connected devices. Developers can intelligently create, connect, and maintain best-in-class secure applications for any IoT device from the edge to the cloud. The platform is made of connected, crossover microcontroller units, referred to as MCUs. Azure Sphere is built on a Linux-based operating system and a cloud-based security posture designed for continuous security, which is useful for mobile devices. Each time an operating system updates, every application running on the MCU is also updated.

WARNING

The device must be connected to a live network to receive an update using Azure Sphere. This includes complete application and operating system updates to the MCU.

To reiterate, for those looking to secure their IoT devices at the edge of the cloud, Azure Sphere is the appropriate route to take for the following reasons:

>> **A diverse catalog of devices:** Azure Sphere offers a diverse catalog of devices to connect existing or newly built intelligent-driven devices securely.

>> **Automated delivery:** Azure Sphere offers over-the-air update functionality, including a robust toolset to deliver and improve patches to every device.

>> **Best-in-class security:** When looking to build upon best practices, users get security improvements developed and deployed by Microsoft automatically to ward against threats across various devices.

>> **Interoperability:** Azure Sphere works with other IoT services, including Azure IoT Hub and Azure IoT Central, to simplify the deployment cycle.

Accessing Azure Machine Learning and Cognitive Solutions

Like many other vendors, Microsoft jumped on the machine learning, artificial intelligence, and cognitive services bandwagon with Azure. The difference with Microsoft is that it focuses on communicative solutions in the cloud, image analysis, speech comprehension, predictive analytics, and data ingestion approaches. Using either Azure Machine Learning or Azure Databricks, you can create a powerful machine learning and cognitive learning solution.

Your machine learning and cognitive solutions are only as smart as the amount of training and usage they get. A prerequisite for any machine learning solution is training and model development. Model refinement takes a bit of time. As the models are trained over time the solution becomes smarter.

Azure Machine Learning

Azure Machine Learning is a powerful platform to build, train, and deploy machine learning models so that computers can imitate human intelligence. Before exploring the machine learning tools within Azure, it's essential to get into the nitty-gritty with some definitions.

>> **Artificial intelligence:** Built using mathematical algorithms to support data model creation within Azure, most models are intended for predictive activity. An algorithm under this context applies passed data fields and then learns from the behaviors found scouring the algorithm's patterns. The result is a complication of data to make predictions using validated data sources. The model changes based on training and usage.

>> **Machine learning:** Combining data science techniques in Azure, machine learning takes mathematical calculations and applies them to existing data to forecast trends and analysis, entirely using compute power. Generally, machine learning solutions are powered by low or no-code solutions in Azure, which explains why Microsoft says that apps and devices become more intelligent based on more significant usage.

>> **Deep learning:** The most sophisticated form of machine learning, deep learning determines if predictive results are correct using the algorithms created with existing machine learning solutions. The scale at which machine learning must be applied in deep learning is extensive, as heavy data analysis is necessary.

The scale deep learning requires for analysis is far greater than that of machine learning. Deep learning evaluates data using artificial neural networks consisting of multiple layers of algorithms. Each algorithm layer looks at incoming data to perform specialized analysis. In addition, each of the layers in a neural network and multiple neural networks can learn through data processing.

The cost of running a deep learning model varies wildly depending on the needed optimization for a resource, such as compute, storage, or memory capacity. Similar to other Infrastructure-as-a-Service models like VM consumption, the more you use, including keeping the lights on 24/7, the more expensive it will be to run a model using Azure Machine Learning Data Studio.

Consider purchasing a Machine Learning Reservation if you intend to use data models and expect heavy traffic to the solution.

To use Azure Machine Learning, you must create a dedicated workspace as part of an Azure Machine Learning Studio project. The machine learning workspace is a centralized location for a machine learning project to manage all artifacts built using Data Studio. As the models evolve, a workspace ensures that updates are reflected in a single location.

To get started with Azure Machine Learning, follow these steps:

1. **Go to the All Services blade and select Azure Machine Learning under AI+Machine Learning.**

2. **Click the Create button.**

   A form appears that asks you to create the Azure Machine Learning workspace, as shown in Figure 10-12.

3. **When finished, click the Go to Resources button.**

   Your Workspace is now created, enabling you to launch Azure Machine Learning Studio once you press Launch Studio (see Figure 10-13).

4. **Press Launch Studio to launch the Azure Machine Learning Studio and select the project type appropriate for your business need.**

   Options include Notebooks, Automated ML, and Designer.

Knowing the difference between the three projects is essential.

>> **Notebooks** are code-based solutions meant for the data science folks wanting to code with the Python SDK with the intent of running experiments.

>> **Automated ML** provides a low-code approach to model creation, training, and tuning using data metrics.

>> **Designer** is a drag-and-drop interface to help developers prep their data so that a model can be easily deployed.

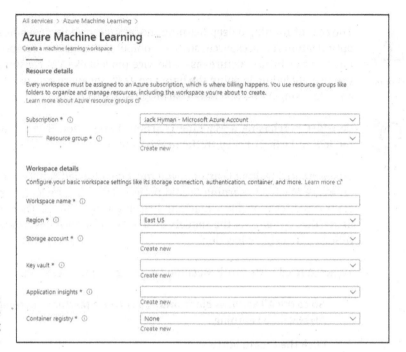

FIGURE 10-12:
Creating an Azure Machine Learning workspace.

FIGURE 10-13:
Launching Azure Machine Learning Studio.

TIP

If you've used the open-source platform Jupyter Notebook then you'll have no trouble getting used to these features in Machine Learning Studio.

For each project type, familiarize yourself with the concept of authoring, assets, and managing found in the Azure Machine Learning Studio navigation screen (see Figure 10-14).

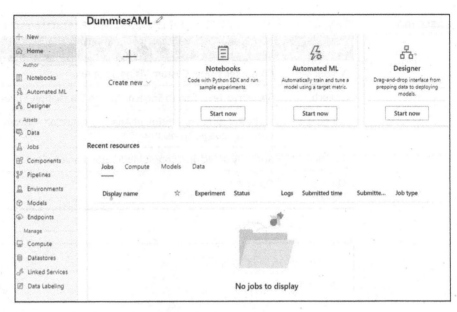

Azure Cognitive Services

Every vendor in the enterprise IT market claims to have cognitive services, and each vendor offers something unique. In Microsoft-speak, Azure Cognitive Services is a collection of APIs and Web-based services designed by Microsoft that contains machine learning algorithms to solve artificial intelligence–type problems. The packaged cognitive solutions are componentized into discrete activities such as speech, vision, and decision-making capabilities. The services are prebuilt for developers using a combination of REST APIs and client library SDKs. Such services are deployable using a few lines of code within a Web application, so the developer doesn't need to have programmatic knowledge beyond their core solution.

Table 10-3 explores the range of Cognitive Services available within the Azure portal. To access Azure Cognitive Services, go to All Services and search for "Cognitive" in the search box. You'll be presented with the full suite of cognitive offerings, as shown in Figure 10-15.

TABLE 10-3

Key Cognitive Services Offered in Microsoft Azure

Service	Solution
Vision	Computer Vision, Custom Vision, Face API
Speech	Speech to Text, Text to Speech, Speech Translation, Speaker Recognition
Language	Entity Recognition, Sentiment Analysis, Question Answering, Conversational Language, Translator
Decision	Anomaly detector, Content Moderator, Personalizer
OpenAI Service	OpenAI

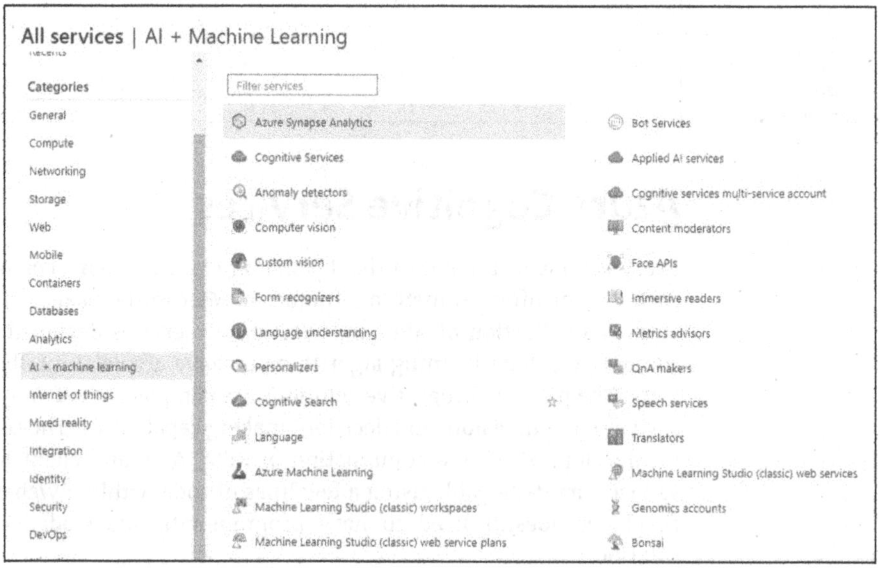

FIGURE 10-15:
Sampling of
Cognitive Services
accessible
through the All
Services blade.

Azure Bot Service

The Microsoft Azure Bot Service solution is grounded in the Azure machine learning and artificial intelligence areas. The goal is to build AI-capable conversational agents. You probably have seen at least one bot built using the Azure Bot Service on the Internet and not realized that it was built using Azure's framework solution (the Microsoft website, for example). Bots are commonly found on B2B or B2C websites.

Developers wanting to build a bot can complete all lifecycle activities from building, testing, deploying, and managing the intelligent solution right from Azure. A developer initiates the process by starting with the Bot Framework using the modular yet extensive SDK tools, templates, and AI services. Examples of supported features include qquestion-and-answer support, natural language translation, and speech translation.

Those looking for bots to handle conversations externally from Azure can use the core Bot Framework interface. Such conversational channels include social platforms such as Facebook, Slack, SharePoint, and Teams. The bot follows the same general process as outlined here and illustrated in Figure 10-16:

1. A bot model receives a request based on an input received.

2. The bot performs one or more tasks based on an action.

3. The bot asks one or more questions, hence targeted information, to access one or more services.

4. Once the requested activity occurs, the bot performs the tasks based on the appropriate recognition service.

5. The system interprets the request based on the programmed actions.

6. The bot concludes with the specific activity responding (or lack thereof if not enough information is available).

7. A likely outcome is a subsequent interaction via text, audio, or video.

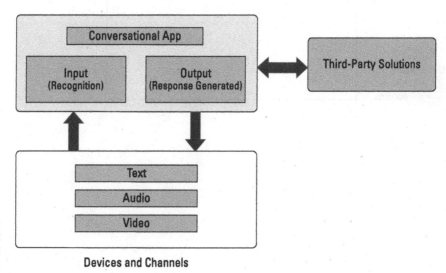

FIGURE 10-16:
The Azure Bot
Framework
process.

Figure 10-17 shows that configuring a bot in Azure is like that of a modern web application on the Internet, given that requests are API-driven. The critical difference is that a bot receives a message and must echo it back to a user. The code needed to communicate with that user is far less than a traditional web solution. The list of Azure Bot integration options includes those services Microsoft partnered with, so a developer has little coding to do besides interface integration.

FIGURE 10-17:
List of Azure Bot integration options.

4

Providing High Availability, Scalability, and Security for Your Azure Resources

Chapter **11**

Protecting the Azure Environment

isaster recovery is your business's ability to recover from an IT-related failure. Most folks need to learn that managing their cloud computing environment is a two-way relationship, known as a shared responsibility. For example, if you implement an Infrastructure as a Service (IaaS) environment, the hosting platform is managed by the cloud service provider. You are responsible for the virtual machines (VMs) and security running the application. The same is not true for Software as a Service (SaaS) applications. The shared responsibility varies slightly from vendor to vendor, including Microsoft. In this chapter, I review the protection strategies that are incumbent upon you to know under a variety of cloud computing situations.

All Azure services operate on the shared responsibility model. Microsoft is the cloud provider, and it gives you access to highly available resources that you use on a pay-per-use basis. In the scope of Azure, Microsoft's responsibility is to provide the infrastructure and specific degrees of high availability as outlined in the service-level agreements (SLAs), depending on the product offering. Product guarantees for uptime range from 95 to 99.99 percent, depending on product and geography. Take for example apps running on Microsoft Azure. Microsoft guarantees the following:

We guarantee that Apps running in a customer subscription will be available 99.95% of the time.

Is the same held true for storage? Absolutely not. Depending on the storage tier, guarantees vary from 99 percent (Cool Access Tier) to 99.9 percent (Hot Access Tier). But you might be wondering, what is behind a guarantee? In the case of storage, if your blob service falls victim to a cyberattack, Microsoft ensures that backups are made and available pretty quickly so that your system is operationally accessible virtually 24/7. Does this include disaster recovery, though? Not quite. Backup versus disaster recovery are two completely separate areas. And that is what I am going to address in this chapter.

The bottom line is that it's your responsibility as an Azure customer to take control of disaster recovery for your organization's Azure resources. Microsoft provides disaster recovery tools, but you need to put them into action. And, yes, there is always a fee associated with using the disaster recovery tools. After all, nothing in life is free, right?

By the end of this chapter, you'll understand the approaches Azure takes to secure your data, which includes protecting your storage accounts, VMs, app services, Azure SQL Database instances, and Cosmos DB databases.

Core Security Tactics in Azure

If you look at the news today, a week ago, a month ago, or several years back, one area tends to be a chronic pain point for enterprise technology. If you said security, you are absolutely on the money. Cloud computing is not immune to security issues, quite the opposite. Most organizations do their best to configure their cloud environments securely; however, there always seems to be one gotcha. If you are trying to secure your environments and data in Azure, it's important to know how to mitigate risk using key security and privacy tools.

Microsoft Defender for Cloud

Finding reliable security talent in the industry is a global challenge. There are simply not enough folks to address all the security vulnerabilities. Organizations such as Microsoft know this, as many of their problems are at the center of these security vulnerabilities. It's no secret that a unified infrastructure security management platform is desired. To the data center or the cloud computing operator, a way to address advanced threats across workloads is always needed. With Microsoft Defender for Cloud, global organizations can see all cloud computing operations in a single view.

Keeping up to date with the latest security requirements via patches, compliance notifications, regulatory requirements, or system updates across many applications can be daunting and also an outright security risk to the organizational posture. For organizations using Azure, Microsoft introduced Microsoft Defender for Cloud, a platform that supports network hardening, secure service management, and regulatory compliance monitoring controls.

Microsoft offers two tiers to the service: the free tier and one that utilizes the Azure Defender service, which is covered later in this chapter. A comparison of both services is provided in Table 11-1.

TABLE 11-1   ## Azure Security Center Feature Comparison

Service Level	Key Features
Free Tier	The free tier offers continuous assessment and security recommendations for basic services within an Azure environment subscription.
Azure Defender	Users of the paid tier are provided with all the free tier capabilities plus adaptive application control and network hardening, regulatory compliance dashboards for over 40 measures, threat protection management for any Azure VM environment, the ability to protect non-Azure servers when connected whether in the cloud or a data center, threat protection for PaaS applications and services, and Microsoft Defender for Endpoint support. On average, per server protection is $15.00 per feature. Some services are charged per gigabyte or based on bandwidth consumed.

To access Azure Security Center, go to the Azure navigation pane and select Microsoft Defender for Cloud. When you click on the menu options, a screen like the one shown in Figure 11-1 appears. Microsoft Defender for Cloud integrates a Secure Score, a Regulatory Compliance Pane, Azure Defender Pane, and Azure Firewall Pane. Other features are accessible from the Azure Security Center navigation on the left side: Security Alerts, Recommendations, and Inventory. If Firewall Service and Defender Service are enabled, those analytics will appear in the Azure Security Center as well.

TECHNICAL
STUFF

As part of the basic tier offering, a Secure Score is made available in Microsoft Defender for Cloud. The Secure Score evaluates the health of all resources across subscriptions. A sample Secure Score is shown in Figure 11-2. A score is derived from providing the user with a score based on predefined and custom rules set in the Azure subscription, combining over ten different health concerns. While the result is a maximum score of 100 percent, the actual score is not average weighting. Instead, a secure score weighs the posture of resources across subscriptions under several areas including Security, Regulatory, Workload, Inventory, Firewall Manager, and Information Protection. Based on a combination of factors, including resources in usage, importance, and criticality, a score is produced.

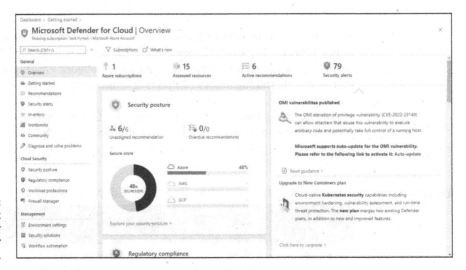

FIGURE 11-1:
Microsoft
Defender for
Cloud free tier
example.

It's pretty clear from the results shown in Figure 11-2 that the Azure environment is fairly unhealthy, which means a bit of time needs to be spent to reach a higher Secure Score. Can you imagine having to figure out which part of the environment is wreaking havoc on the health of the environment? It would be like finding a needle in a haystack. Microsoft takes care of that for you by explaining the features and functionality within the environment that require corrective actions. Microsoft even points out ways to easily correct the environment on a case-by-case basis. The solution, called Recommendations, is a line-time–based tool that helps mitigate all risks across the various Defender pillars (see Figure 11-3). As you make changes in Microsoft Defender for Cloud, the applicable areas requiring healthy resources to be achieved fluctuate.

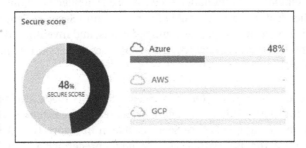

FIGURE 11-2:
The Secure Score
for Azure
Resources.

WARNING

You may assume that Microsoft updates the environment, including the secure score and recommendations, in real time. Not so! The Secure Score along with a series of recommendations are updated every 24 to 48 hours. Patience is of the essence.

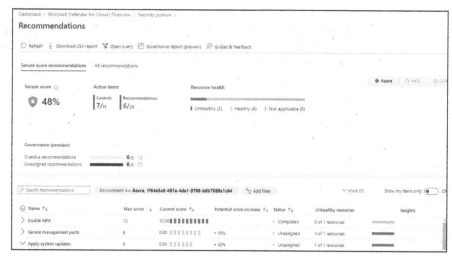

FIGURE 11-3:
Microsoft
Defender for
Cloud
recommendations.

Alerts, hygiene, and inventory

When resources become unhealthy, you might be notified by email or within your Azure portal that environmental hygiene is not up to par. If the situation is urgent, Microsoft provides a variety of alert types based on the triggered event.

WARNING

Don't think you are going to be told about every single alert by email, SMS, or in the Azure portal. While Azure does provide a baseline offering of key features requiring attention, the Azure Defender subscriptions are what drive frequent notifications. These notifications are not generic, either; they point to the specific resource while often making recommendations on how to fix the issue.

TECHNICAL STUFF

There are some major differences between a security *alert* and a security *incident*. Whereas an alert is a notification generated by Microsoft Defender for Cloud as soon as there is a threat detected on a resource, a security incident is a collection of related alerts brought together to signal that your attention is needed to resolve one-off issues that might lead to an eventual cyberattack.

In Microsoft Defender for Cloud, an incident addresses the attack path and the resources affected. An alert merely tells you that you need to quickly review the issue as there may be a mission-critical issue. Figure 11-4 represents an example from Microsoft Defender for Cloud based on a series of previous security alerts.

To take it a step further, every resource in your Azure instance should be scored based on resource hygiene health. The resource is deemed healthy, unhealthy, or not applicable. You can drill down into the unhealthy resource to find out what the alerts and recommendations might be so that the resource can be deemed healthy once again. By analyzing resource health and reliability, you are resolving resource hygiene issues in Azure. The quickest way to address the hygiene of each resource is to locate the Inventory, which is located under the General Settings in Microsoft Defender for Cloud (see Figure 11-5).

FIGURE 11-4:
Azure Defender for Cloud security alerts.

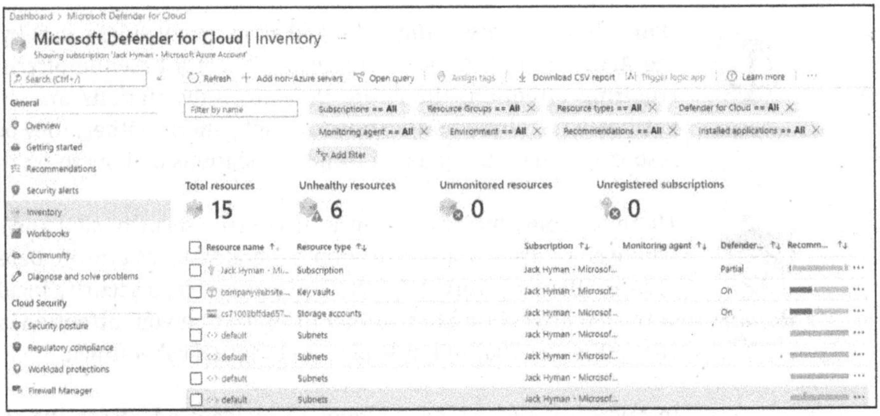

FIGURE 11-5:
Inventory in Azure Defender for Cloud.

Azure Key Vault

Password sprawl is not uncommon in the cloud. Applications in the cloud often connect to other services, such as a database or a web service. Each of those passwords is part of a connection string, which is often encrypted with yet another username and password. But when you have many usernames and passwords, each of those accounts having its own identity (hopefully) can yield a security risk.

TIP

To prevent credentials from getting out of control, you can utilize the Azure Key Vault. The Azure Key Vault offers users a safe method to hide credentials, including secrets, keys, and certificates. When using Azure Key Vault, you can apply a security policy that calls out the user or application requiring the specific credential. Because all keys are encrypted in Azure Key Vault, at least one layer of your security is protected.

To create a Key Vault, follow these steps:

1. **Search for "Key Vaults" in the Azure global search box at the top of the Azure portal, as shown in Figure 11-6.**

2. **Select Key Vaults in the list of results.**

3. **Click the Create button.**

   You will now be able to create a new Key Vault. On this page, you are asked to enter some information:

   - *Subscription:* Select the subscription appropriate to where resources are located.

   - *Resource Group:* Select the resource group where there is billable mapping.

   - *Key Vault Name:* Enter the name of the new vault.

   - *Region*: Select the geography where the vault is stored.

   - *Pricing Tier*: You'll have to pay, so pick the appropriate key type and tier for your vault.

   - *Days to Retain Deleted Vault:* This is the number of days a vault is kept after deletion.

   - *Purge Protection:* This option allows you to add an extra layer of protection before a vault is deleted.

4. **Upon completing the form, press the Review + Complete button, and then review the contents of the configuration.**

5. **At the bottom of the configuration review page, press Create.**

   At this point, the vault is deployed. Once complete, you'll press the Go to Resource button to open the vault and begin adding keys.

TIP

You might be curious about a few configurations for Azure Key Vault. The most obvious is the pricing tier. Is it worth the premium? With premium, keys are stored in a Hardware Security Module (HSM). The HSM is a separate component designed specifically to separate the content from its origination location, storage container, and how it processes cryptographic data.

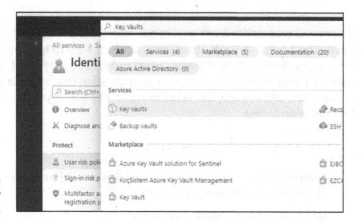

FIGURE 11-6:
Searching for
Azure Key Vault.

WARNING

If Federal Information Processing Standards (FIPS) 140-2 are mandated within your organization, you have no option but to use the Premium Key Vault, which allows for HSM.

Suppose you want to generate a self-signed certificate. To create the certificate, follow these steps:

1. **Click Certificate.**

2. **Click the Generate/Import button.**

   The screen shown in Figure 11-7 appears.

3. **Enter the following data:**

   - Method of Certificate Creation
   - Certificate Name
   - Type of Certificate Authority
   - Subject
   - DNS Name
   - Validity Period in Months
   - Content-Type Select either PKS #12 or PEM.
   - Lifetime Action Types
   - Percentage Lifetime
   - Advanced Policy Configuration
   - Tags

4. **When you are finished entering the data, click the Create button.**

Create a certificate

Method of Certificate Creation	Generate
Certificate Name * ⓘ	
Type of Certificate Authority (CA) ⓘ	Self-signed certificate
Subject * ⓘ	For example: "CN=mydomain.com".
DNS Names	0 DNS names
Validity Period (in months) *	12
Content Type	PKCS #12 PEM
Lifetime Action Type	Automatically renew at a given percentage lifetime
Percentage Lifetime *	80
Advanced Policy Configuration	Not configured
Tags	0 tags

Create

FIGURE 11-7:
Creating a
certificate in
Azure Key Vault.

TIP

Azure Key Vault is also used to store encryption keys for Azure VMs. For example, Microsoft Defender for Cloud will make recommendations to create a set of encrypted VM disks if you create a VM instance. A VM disk will need to create a virtual host disk file. Assuming the host operating system runs the VM, a security key to decrypt the virtual host disk and run it is required. Azure Key Vault acts as the orchestration agent for such encryption and decryption.

Microsoft Sentinel

Companies need a reliable way to monitor their systems and data. The two areas companies tend to invest in include SOAR (security, operations, automation, and response) and SIEM (security information and event management) systems. In 2020, Microsoft introduced a cloud-platform SOAR and SIEM platform called Microsoft Sentinel.

TECHNICAL
STUFF

Microsoft realizes that not all companies or individuals use Azure and Microsoft-only products. That's why Sentinel is plug-and-play with a variety of vendor solutions for analytics reporting and analysis of on-premises, third-party cloud hosting providers, and Azure-based solutions.

To get started with Microsoft Sentinel, you need to create an Azure Workspace. Once the Workspace is created, you must enable at least one Azure Log Analytics service to capture your data.

REMEMBER

SIEM and SOAR solutions require lots of log data, especially when looking at user behaviors. If you don't enable a log analytics capability, Sentinel will not operate.

To create a new Log Analytics Workspace, follow these steps:

1. **Search for Microsoft Sentinel.**

2. **On the introduction page, select Create Microsoft Sentinel, and then click the Create a New Workspace button.**

3. **Enter data for the following fields to create the Log Analytics Workspace (you'll want to call the workspace "SentinelAnalytics" for this example):**

   - Subscription
   - Resource Group
   - Instance Name
   - Instance Region

4. **Once you have entered all the data, press Review+Create at the bottom of the page.**

   You are now able to create a Microsoft Sentinel workspace, which requires you to connect your Log Analytics Workspace to Microsoft Sentinel.

5. **Select the SentinelAnalytics workspace you created in Step 4, and then click Add.**

   Microsoft Sentinel requires you to configure your environment against each cloud instance, data center instance, or data source. You are guided through each configuration step on the introduction page (see Figure 11-8) by first reviewing the connect steps and then creating the instance.

ON THE WEB

Microsoft Sentinel is a powerful technology. There are hundreds of configurations that you'll likely want to tinker with to ensure that your environment runs safely. To find the configuration that is most appropriate for your organization, go to https://docs.microsoft.com/azure/sentinel.

FIGURE 11-8:
Setting up
Microsoft
Sentinel.

Protecting Your Storage Account's Blob Data

Well, I have good news and bad news. The good news is that in addition to securing data using the core security infrastructure in Azure, Azure also has procedures to help you protect and back up your data. You can back up and restore individual blobs and even (with manual intervention) protect entire blob containers.

The bad news is that the tooling, despite years of tinkering by the Azure development team, isn't the most logical for the average user, in my humble opinion. In the following sections, I show you around so you can decide how you want to approach Azure blob storage disaster recovery in your environment.

Backing up and restoring individual storage blobs

A *blob* (binary large object) is an unstructured data file. Examples include document files, log files, and media files.

Soft delete in Azure storage accounts is effectively a recycle bin for deleted blobs. Enable the feature post-deployment by navigating to your storage account in the Azure portal, selecting the Soft Delete setting, enabling that feature, and determining your retention policy. The time span for soft-deleted blob retention ranges from 1 to 365 days.

TIP

If you're going to walk through the steps in the next couple of sections, I suggest that you create a container in a storage account and populate it with some unimportant files that you don't mind playing with. I cover creating Azure storage accounts in detail in Chapter 3.

In my environment, I created a storage account with the following properties:

>> **Storage account name:** wileyprimstorage

>> **Type:** General-purpose v2

>> **Blob soft delete:** Enabled

>> **Container name:** scripts

>> **Container contents:** Several Azure PowerShell script files that I had stored on my workstation

Creating and viewing snapshot backups

You can take manual snapshot backups of your Azure storage account blobs. The term *snapshot* denotes these backups as point-in-time file versions that you can download or restore as needed.

Within the Azure portal, follow these steps to take a snapshot backup:

1. **Browse to your target container, and select one or more blobs.**

The Azure portal allows multiple selections via the check box controls (see Figure 11-9).

2. **On the toolbar, click Create Snapshot.**

You won't see any confirmation within the storage account, but you should see a `Successfully created blob snapshot(s)` message in the Azure portal's Notifications menu, as shown in Figure 11-10.

FIGURE 11-9: Creating a storage snapshot.

3. **Select only one of the blobs you selected in Step 1, and then click View Snapshots on the toolbar.**

Figure 11-11 shows my snapshot list for a document file named DummiesExBlobDoc.docx. I've annotated the following:

- The Download button (A) helps when you need a copy of a blob's previous version. This command downloads the blob to your local computer.

- The Promote button (B) replaces your current blob copy with the selected snapshot backup. Be careful with this option because you will overwrite the current version of the blob.

- The Delete button (C) enables you to selectively remove snapshots that you don't want to use again.

- The Edit tab (D) enables you to modify snapshot contents.

- The Generate SAS tab (E) makes it easy to create a shared access signature Uniform Resource Identifier (URI) for the blob. A shared access signature allows you to provide time-limited public access to a blob; Azure developers use SAS tokens all the time to handle blob uploads and downloads with storage accounts.

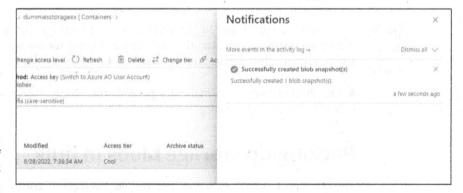

FIGURE 11-10: Notification of snapshot creation.

Deleting and restoring a snapshot

You can clean up your storage account blob list by deleting (and restoring, if you've enabled the soft delete setting) any blob. Follow these steps to delete a parent blob and then recover it:

1. **Chose the storage account for which you created the snapshot, open the context menu and locate Data Management.**

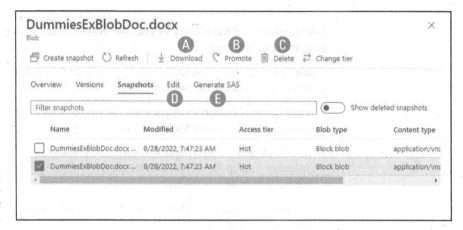

DummiesExBlobDoc.docx
Blob

A   B   C

🗐 Create snapshot   🔄 Refresh | ⬇ Download   ↻ Promote   🗑 Delete   ⇄ Change tier

Overview   Versions   **Snapshots**   Edit   Generate SAS

D   E

Filter snapshots   ⬤ Show deleted snapshots

Name	Modified	Access tier	Blob type	Content type
☐ DummiesExBlobDoc.docx ...	8/28/2022, 7:47:23 AM	Hot	Block blob	application/vn
☑ DummiesExBlobDoc.docx'...	8/28/2022, 7:47:23 AM	Hot	Block blob	application/vn

FIGURE 11-11: Managing blob snapshots in the Azure portal.

2. **Select the menu option Data Protection.**

   You are presented with a variety of options, including snapshot retention for containers and blobs in the Data Protection panel.

3. **Modify the time frame as desired for a blob or container.**

   In the use case, shown in Figure 11-12, the retention period for a snapshot is 7 days.

REMEMBER

You configure soft delete in the storage account settings. Navigate to the Data Protection settings blade, and then set the parameters for the soft delete for blobs and containers. Soft delete supports a retention range of from 1 to 365 days.

A soft-deleted blob is permanently purged from your storage account after it exceeds your retention policy.

Backing up storage blobs in bulk

The question I consider now is how to take backups of entire blob containers. There is no real fool-proof way of completing a bulk blob update. Most Azure administrators work around this problem by writing a shell script that calls AzCopy to copy blobs between two storage accounts, preferably in different regions.

First, install AzCopy (see the "AzCopy" sidebar later in this chapter), and then open an elevated command prompt and run the following PowerShell command to set a new environment variable that points to your AzCopy installation directory (in this example, AzCopy is in my C:\azcopy directory). You do this so that you can call the AzCopy command from any directory in a command-prompt session or script file:

```
[Environment]:SetEnvironmentVariable("Path",
        $env:Path + ";C:\bin", "Machine")
```

FIGURE 11-12:
Configuring soft
delete for Azure
storage account
blobs.

AZCOPY

TECHNICAL STUFF

AzCopy is a command-line tool for Azure storage that allows you to

- Work with Azure blob storage as well as Amazon Web Services S3 storage

- Integrate with Azure Storage Explorer

- Access verbose logging of all copy operations

- Throttle blob-copy speed

You can download AzCopy at https://docs.microsoft.com/azure/storage/common/storage-use-azcopy-v10. The tool is a stand-alone executable. You can place it in any directory on your system, but I suggest that you add the AzCopy directory path to your PATH system environment variable to ensure that you can start the tool from any command-prompt location.

Then restart your computer to enable the new system environment variable.

Here's the AzCopy command I used to copy my scripts container from my dummiesstorageex storage account to my scripts-backup container in my dummiesstoragesec storage account:

```
AzCopy /Source:https://dummiesstorageex.blob.core.windows.net/
       scripts /Dest:https://dummiesstoragesec.blob.core.windows.net/
    scripts-backup /SourceKey: F5IJHWI7==
       /DestKey: QAWSGFJF== /S
```

You authenticate to the storage accounts by passing in an access key.

Protecting Your Virtual Machines

That's enough about storage accounts. This section discusses protecting your precious Azure VM operating system and data disks that currently reside in Managed Disk storage.

Getting to know the Recovery Services vault

The Azure Recovery Services vault has two purposes:

>> Backup and recovery: Backing up and restoring individual VMs or VMs in bulk

>> Disaster recovery: Configuring warm standby instances of your Azure VMs and switching to them quickly if the primary instance(s) go offline

TECHNICAL
STUFF

Both the Managed Disk service and the Recovery Services vault are abstraction layers on top of the Azure storage account. Much of Azure Resource Manager deals with abstracting higher levels of administrative overhead for more-manageable levels.

Deploying a Recovery Services vault

Follow these steps to deploy a Recovery Services vault in the Azure portal:

1. Browse to the Recovery Services vaults blade, and click Add.

2. Complete the Create Recovery Services vault form.

The vault name needs to be unique at the Azure subscription level. Keep in mind that your VMs to be backed up need to be in the same region as your Recovery Services vault.

3. **Click Review + Create, and then click Create to submit the deployment.**

   The deployment is fast because the Recovery Services vault is essentially a container.

Azure Recovery Services vaults can automate the backups of SQL Server running in Azure VMs as well as storage account file shares, but you need to drill into VM backup.

WARNING

You can back up Azure VMs only to a Recovery Services vault in the same Azure region. If your VMs span regions, you need multiple Recovery Services vaults that do the same.

Creating a backup policy

A *backup policy* determines your backup schedule — that is, how often Azure makes backups and how long it retains them.

Follow these steps to create a simple backup policy to use for your VM backups:

1. **In your Recovery Services Vault settings, click Backup Policies.**

2. **On the Backup Policies page, click Add.**

   The Add blade appears.

3. **In the Add blade under Policy Type, select Azure Virtual Machine.**

   Notice that you can also create policies for SQL Server in an Azure VM and Azure File Share backups.

4. **Complete the Create Policy blade.**

   Here are the major policy options:

   - *Policy Name:* Use a descriptive name.

   - *Policy Sub-Type:* Select Standard or Premium depending on business need.

   - *Backup Policy:* Add a secondary schedule for setting up backups.

   - *Policy Details:* Enter specific configurations on the backup requirements including frequency, instant restore, retention points.

   - *Virtual Machine:* Select the appropriate VM that you'll add time-bound policies against.

5. **Click Enable Backup to commit your changes.**

Backing up VMs

You can configure VM backups using Recovery Services vault r on a case-by-case basis for each VM.

Note: To follow along with the exercises in this section, you need two VMs; it doesn't matter whether they run Windows Server or Linux. It's important that the VMs be in a running state so that the Azure VM Snapshot extension can back up files in use and provide for application-consistent backups.

Backing up a single VM

Follow these steps to back up a running VM in the Azure portal:

1. **In the VM you've selected, go to the Operations section and select Backup.**

2. **Complete the Welcome to Azure Backup blade.**

   All you need to do is choose your newly created Recovery Services vault and your new backup policy from the provided drop-down menus.

3. **Click Enable Backup.**

4. **When deployment is complete, return to the VM's Backup blade.**

5. **On the toolbar, click Backup Now (see Figure 11-13).**

   This step initiates a manual backup rather than waiting for the next backup window specified in your policy.

6. **Confirm the backup retention date.**

7. **Click OK to start the backup.**

Backing up multiple VMs

Follow these steps to back up one or more VMs from your Recovery Services vault:

1. **In your Recovery Services vault's settings list, select Backup.**

2. **Complete the following fields as shown here:**

   - *Where Is Your Workload Running?* Azure
   - *What Do You Want to Back Up?* Virtual machine

3. **Click Backup to continue.**

4. **On the Backup Policy blade, select your VM policy, and click OK to continue.**

   The Select Virtual Machines blade appears.

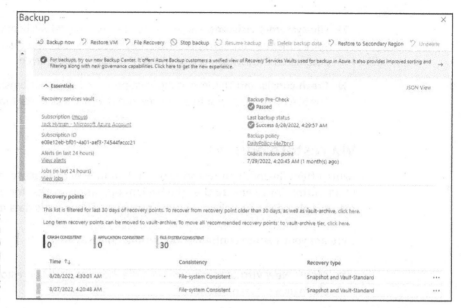

FIGURE 11-13:
An example of a
single backup
instance and
associated
history, including
manual activities.

5. **On the Select Virtual Machines blade, select the VMs you want to include in the batch backup job configuration.**

6. **Click OK.**

   The Backup blade appears.

7. **In the Backup blade, click Enable Backup to complete the configuration.**

TIP

You can check on the backup job status by clicking the Backup Jobs setting in your vault.

Restoring VMs

Before I explain the "clicky-clicky" procedure, I want to explain the VM restore options.

VM backup consistency levels

Azure offers three guarantees for VM restore, depending on the consistency level of the backup snapshots:

>> **Application-consistent:** This level is the most preferred snapshot consistency level. The guarantee is that the VM will boot up and that you won't suffer data corruption or loss.

>> **File-system-consistent:** The SLA stipulates that the VM will boot up and that you'll suffer no data corruption. You may need to implement manual or automated fixups, however, to ensure that your data is current.

>> **Crash-consistent:** This level is the least-preferred snapshot consistency level. The SLA offers no guarantees. The VM runs a disk check at startup.

VM restore options

Azure offers flexibility in restoring a VM. You may need to perform a trial restore of an entire VM to ensure that the backup operation works, for example, or you may simply need to pluck some files from one of your VM's data disks.

Here are your restore configuration options in a nutshell:

>> **Create New Virtual Machine:** Overwrite the existing VM or restore to an alternative virtual network.

>> **Restore Disks:** Copy the backed-up operating system and data disk(s) to a storage account blob service.

>> **Replace Disks:** Swap out your troubled VM's operating system and data disks for snapshot copies.

>> **File Recovery:** Mount snapshot operating system and data disks on your local workstation through some clever PowerShell scripting magic. Then you can recover individual files from backup quickly and easily.

ON THE
WEB

The File Recovery feature is exceedingly cool and useful. To learn more about it, take a look at the Azure documentation: https://docs.microsoft.com/azure/backup/backup-azure-restore-files-from-vm.

Backup and restoration

Restoring an item may take a bit of patience because you might have to go through several restore points to find what you are looking for. Let me show you how to work with the Azure VM restore experience. Follow these steps:

1. **In your VM's Settings list, select Backup.**

2. **On the Backup blade, click Restore VM.**

3. **On the Select Restore Point blade, choose a restore point.**

   The general guidance here is for you to choose the most recent application-consistent backup.

4. **On the Restore Configuration blade, choose a restore option (see Figure 11-14).**

   You can choose to restore the entire VM or only its disks to their original locations or to an alternative storage account and virtual network.

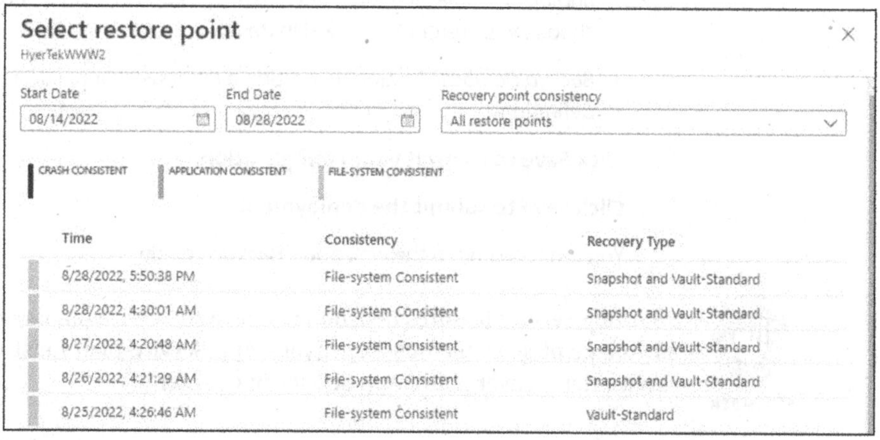
Select restore point

HyerTekWWW2

Start Date: 08/14/2022 | End Date: 08/28/2022 | Recovery point consistency: All restore points

CRASH CONSISTENT | APPLICATION CONSISTENT | FILE-SYSTEM CONSISTENT

Time	Consistency	Recovery Type
8/28/2022, 5:50:38 PM	File-system Consistent	Snapshot and Vault-Standard
8/28/2022, 4:30:01 AM	File-system Consistent	Snapshot and Vault-Standard
8/27/2022, 4:20:48 AM	File-system Consistent	Snapshot and Vault-Standard
8/26/2022, 4:21:29 AM	File-system Consistent	Snapshot and Vault-Standard
8/25/2022, 4:26:46 AM	File-system Consistent	Vault-Standard

FIGURE 11-14: Choosing a VM restore point.

Protecting Your App Services

One of the conveniences of the built-in backup in Azure App Service is that in addition to backing up the app's source code, Azure also backs up its associated configuration settings and support files:

- App file system artifacts
- App configuration data
- Database connected to the app

Backing up App Service apps

Note: To follow along with this section, you'll need a running App Service app and a general-purpose storage account. At this writing, App Service backup doesn't use the Recovery Services vault.

To back up App Service apps, follow these steps:

1. **On your app's Settings blade, click Backups.**
2. **On the toolbar, click Configure.**

3. **Complete the Backup Configuration blade.**

Complete the following information:

- *Backup Storage:* Select a storage account in the same region, and either create or designate an existing container to house your app backups.

- *Backup Schedule:* Schedule automatic backups every *n* days or hours, and choose your retention period in days.

- *Backup Database* (optional): Include a database connection in the backup definition.

4. **Click Save to commit your configuration.**

5. **Click Save to submit the deployment.**

You are returned to the web app's Backups blade.

Your App Service features depend on your App Service plan's pricing tier. To take advantage of scheduled backups, your App Service plan must run at least the S1 service tier. I cover Azure App Service in Chapter 7.

Restoring App Service apps

This section considers the other side of the proverbial coin: restoring apps. Perhaps you want to do a trial App Service restore to make sure that the backup is consistent.

To restore an App Service, follow these steps:

1. **Navigate to the Backups blade in your App Service app.**

2. **In the Backup section, select Restore.**

The Restore Backup blade appears.

3. **Complete the Restore Backup blade.**

- *Restore Source:* Choices are App Backup (choose this one), Storage, or Snapshot.

- *Select the Backup to Restore:* This lists previously taken backups.

- *Restore destination:* The choices are Overwrite or New or Existing App.

- *Ignore Conflicting Host Names on Restore:* Choices are No or Yes. Leave this set to No to prevent Azure from restoring an App Service app with a conflicting name to your environment.

- *Ignore Databases:* Choices are No or Yes. If your web app has a database connection string, you'll want to set this option to No.

4. **Click OK to finish the App Service restore process.**

Figure 11-15 shows the Restore Backup blade in the Azure portal.

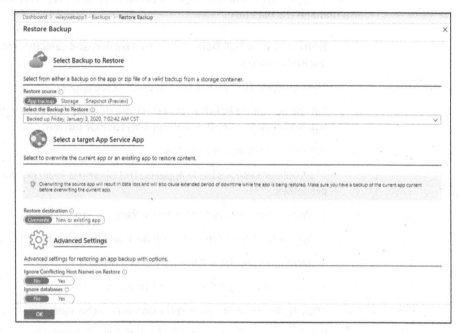

Dashboard > wileywebapp1 - Backups > Restore Backup

Restore Backup   ✕

Select Backup to Restore

Select from either a Backup on the app or zip file of a valid backup from a storage container.

Restore source ⓘ
[App backup] Storage Snapshot (Preview)

Select the Backup to Restore ⓘ
[Backed up Friday, January 3, 2020, 7:02:42 AM CST   ⌄]

Select a target App Service App

Select to overwrite the current app or an existing app to restore content.

ⓘ Overwriting the source app will result in data loss and will also cause extended period of downtime while the app is being restored. Make sure you have a backup of the current app content before overwriting the current app.

Restore destination ⓘ
[Overwrite] New or existing app

Advanced Settings

Advanced settings for restoring an app backup with options.

Ignore Conflicting Host Names on Restore ⓘ
[No] Yes

Ignore databases ⓘ
[No] Yes

[OK]

FIGURE 11-15:
Restoring an
Azure App
Service app.

Protecting Your Databases

The last things to back up and restore are the Azure SQL Database and Cosmos DB.

Backing up and restoring SQL Database

SQL Database creates full backups of your databases every week, differential backups every 12 hours, and transaction log backups every 5 to 10 minutes. The backups occur automatically with no intervention on your part.

Moreover, SQL Database places the backups in a read-access georedundant storage account to ensure that your backups remain available even if your primary Azure region becomes unavailable.

I teach you how to use an Azure SQL Database in Chapter 9.

Configuring SQL Database backup retention

You configure SQL Database backups at the virtual-server level. Follow these steps to manage the backups:

1. **Browse to your SQL Database virtual server, and select the Manage Backups setting.**

   The Configure Policies/Available Backups blade appears.

2. **On the Configure Policies tab, select the desired database in the database list, and click the Configure Retention toolbar button.**

   Figure 11-16 shows the interface.

   The Configure Policies blade appears. This blade has four configurable properties:

   - *Point in Time Restore Configuration:* Range is 7 to 35 days.

   - *Weekly Long-Term Retention (LTR) Backups:* Range is 1 to 520 weeks.

   - *Monthly LTR Backups:* Range is 4 to 520 months.

   - *Yearly LTR Backups:* Range is 1 to 10 years.

3. **Click Apply to submit your retention-policy changes.**

4. **On the Manage Backups blade, click the Available Backups tab.**

5. **Browse backups for all databases attached to the virtual server.**

Restoring SQL Database

To recover an accidentally deleted database, navigate to your Azure SQL Database virtual server and click the Deleted Databases setting. Next, select the deleted database, choose a restore point, and click Restore to bring back the database. You'll need to provide a new name for the restored database.

TIP

You can also perform SQL Database backups and restores by using native SQL Server client tools such as SQL Server Management Studio and Transact-SQL.

To recover a damaged database, browse to your SQL Database's Overview page, and click Restore. You'll be asked to confirm your desired restore point. You also can restore the database to another database server and/or elastic pool and can even change the pricing tier on the fly.

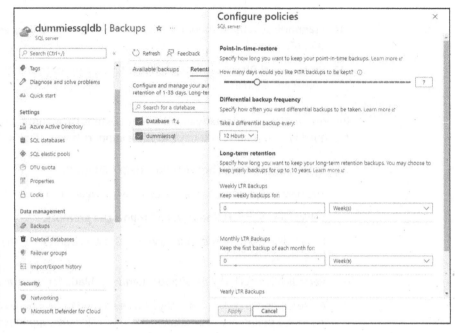

FIGURE 11-16:
Customizing
Azure SQL
Database
automatic
backup.

Backing up and restoring Cosmos DB

Like SQL Database, Cosmos DB takes backups of your data automatically, with no customer intervention required. Cosmos DB takes a database backup every 4 hours and keeps the latest two backups. Cosmos DB also retains snapshots for 30 days.

The Azure documentation recommends that you use Azure Data Factory to take manual backups of your Cosmos DB data by copying the data to another Cosmos DB account.

WARNING

If you need a backup of your Cosmos DB, better be prepared to reach out to Microsoft. This process is not automatic. The manual requirement is a good reason to check out developer support plans.

There are four Azure support plans. All pay-as-you-go subscribers start with the Basic support plan, which is free; the other three plans have a fixed monthly cost. Here's a quick rundown of the four plans and the SLAs associated with them:

>> **Basic:** No response-time SLA

>> **Developer:** Less than 8-hour response time SLA for minimal impact support issues

>> **Standard:** Less than 1-hour response time SLA for critical business impact support issues

>> **Professional Direct:** Shortest response times, plus Azure architecture and operations support

Suppose that you accidentally deleted your Cosmos DB account and need to restore it as quickly as possible. You have to file a support ticket. Here's the procedure:

1. **In the Azure portal, choose Help ⇨ Help + Support.**

   The Help + Support tool appears, as shown in Figure 11-17.

2. **Select New Support Request, and follow the prompts.**

   In this case, you'd choose your Cosmos DB instance and select the Backup and Restore problem type.

3. **Periodically check the All Support Requests blade for updates.**

   Azure support is likely to contact you via email and/or telephone call, depending on the preference you indicated when you filed the support request.

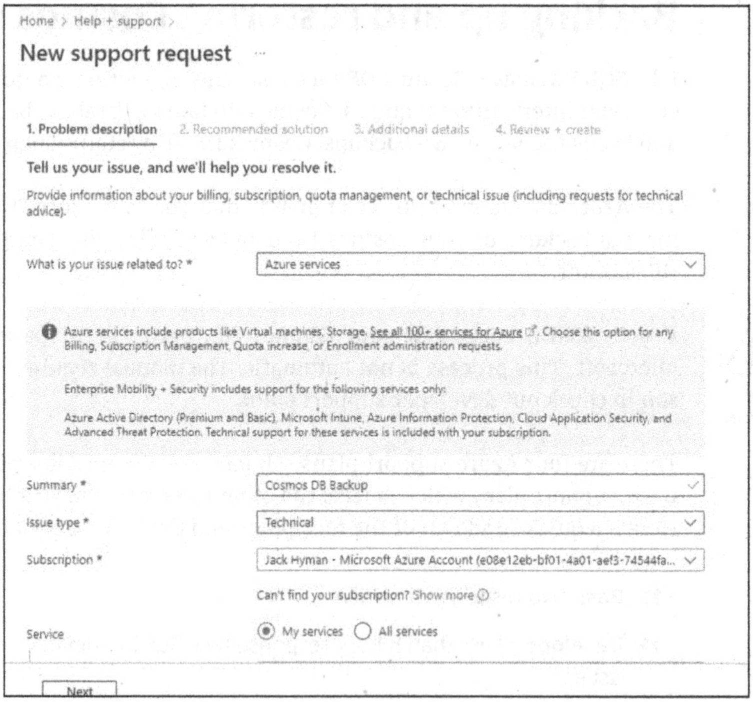

Home > Help + support >

New support request ...

| 1. Problem description | 2. Recommended solution | 3. Additional details | 4. Review + create |

Tell us your issue, and we'll help you resolve it.

Provide information about your billing, subscription, quota management, or technical issue (including requests for technical advice).

What is your issue related to? * [Azure services ⌄]

ⓘ Azure services include products like Virtual machines, Storage. See all 100+ services for Azure ⌐. Choose this option for any Billing, Subscription Management, Quota increase, or Enrollment administration requests.

Enterprise Mobility + Security includes support for the following services only:

Azure Active Directory (Premium and Basic), Microsoft Intune, Azure Information Protection, Cloud Application Security, and Advanced Threat Protection. Technical support for these services is included with your subscription.

Summary * [Cosmos DB Backup ⌄]

Issue type * [Technical ⌄]

Subscription * [Jack Hyman - Microsoft Azure Account (e08e12eb-bf01-4a01-aef3-74544fa... ⌄]

Can't find your subscription? Show more ⓘ

Service ⦿ My services ○ All services

[Next]

FIGURE 11-17:
Create and track
Azure support
requests on the
Help + Support
blade.

IN THIS CHAPTER

» Differentiating Active Directory products

» Describing the relationship between subscriptions and Active Directory

» Creating and managing users and groups

» Implementing role-based access control

» Configuring Multifactor Authentication and Conditional Policies

Chapter **12**

Managing Identity and Access with Azure Active Directory

E very time you work in Azure or use a Microsoft 365 application, you interact with Azure Active Directory (Azure AD) — a hosted identity service relevant to Azure architects, administrators, developers, business analysts, information workers, and even your customers. Azure AD is central in Azure because it forms the identity base for your subscriptions. Any person or process needing access to your Azure subscription must be defined in Azure AD.

By the end of this chapter, you'll have a strong grasp of the relationship between Azure AD and Azure subscriptions. You'll also have the skills necessary to protect resources with least-privilege security. The IT security principle of least privilege means you should give your users only enough permissions to do their jobs and no more.

Understanding Active Directory

Azure AD is a multitenant, hosted identity store used by Azure as well as other Microsoft cloud services, including

- >> Office 365

- >> Dynamics 365

- >> Power Platform

- >> Enterprise Mobility + Security

Any computer nowadays — whether it runs Windows, macOS, or Linux — has a local identity store that defines the users authorized to use that computer. Microsoft has offered Active Directory Domain Services (AD DS) in its Windows Server product since 1999; AD DS is a centralized identity store for on-premises networks.

The terms *tenant* and *multitenant* tend to confuse people, so let me clear up the confusion right away. With regard to Azure AD, a *tenant* is simply a single Azure AD instance. A single organization can have one or many Azure AD instances — one Azure AD instance for internal use and another for customers, for example.

Azure AD is called a multitenant identity store because

- >> You can have more than one Azure AD tenant.

- >> Each tenant can host user accounts from multiple sources, including other Azure AD tenants.

- >> One or more subscriptions can trust Azure AD (share a single identity store).

Another term that is often fuzzy is *cloud apps*. With regard to Azure AD, a cloud app is any application (web, desktop, or mobile) that relies on Azure AD as its user identity store.

Azure AD versus AD Domain Services

Azure AD may share part of a name with Active Directory Domain Services (AD DS) in your on-premises network, but these directory services are very different. Table 12-1 provides a high-level comparison.

Although AD DS and Azure AD are quite different, it's possible to combine them into a hybrid identity solution. You could deploy Azure AD Connect, Microsoft's free identity synchronization engine, to synchronize or federate local AD accounts to AD and thus provide single sign-on to cloud apps.

TABLE 12-1   **Azure AD and AD Domain Services Comparison**

	AD Domain Services	Azure AD
Access protocol	Lightweight Directory Access Protocol	Microsoft Graph REST API
Forest/tree domain structure	Yes	No
Group policy management	Yes	No
Organizational units	Yes	No
Dynamic groups	No	Yes
Multifactor authentication	No	Yes

ON THE WEB

For more information on using Azure AD Connect to extend your on-premises Active Directory to Azure AD, see https://docs.microsoft.com/azure/active-directory/hybrid/whatis-azure-ad-connect.

Relationship between subscriptions and AD tenants

You also need to understand clearly how the Azure AD tenant relates to Azure subscriptions. To create an Azure account, you need to use a Microsoft account identity. When you do, your trial subscription is linked to a default AD tenant typically labeled Default Directory.

The Azure AD tenant can exist separately from a subscription, but Azure won't let you deploy any resources unless and until the Azure AD tenant is linked to at least one subscription. Figure 12-1 shows what I mean.

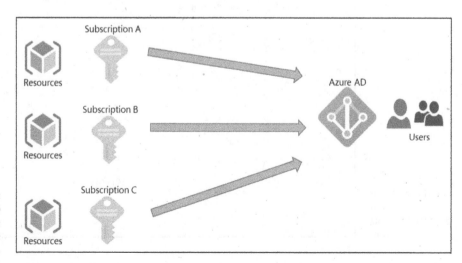

FIGURE 12-1: Relationship between Azure AD and Azure subscriptions.

Figure 12-1 depicts a trust relationship that exists between your Azure subscription and a single Azure AD tenant.

Multitenant Azure AD

Although Azure AD can be the identity store for more than one subscription, a single Azure subscription can trust only a single Azure AD tenant at a time. To understand these concepts, follow these steps:

1. **Log in to the Azure portal as the administrative user.**

2. **Select Create a Resource.**

3. **On the Azure Marketplace blade, search and select for Azure Active Directory, and consider the implications of having more than one Azure AD tenant.**

   You can deploy as many Azure AD tenants as you have use cases for, but you can't do anything substantial with them until you bind an Azure subscription to them. Azure AD tenants are resources much like any other resources in Azure Resource Manager (ARM).

4. **Use the global search box to browse to the Subscriptions blade, and select your subscription in the subscriptions list.**

   If you have only one subscription, this step is an easy one.

5. **On the Overview page toolbar, click Change Directory.**

   Now you're getting somewhere! This control allows you to unplug a subscription from its current Azure AD tenant and plug it into another. Figure 12-2 shows the directory change process in my environment.

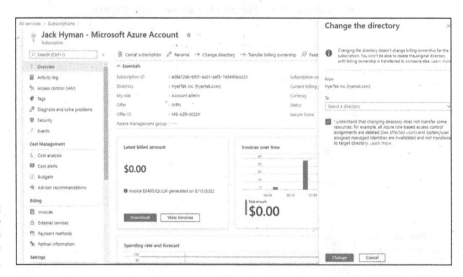

FIGURE 12-2: Moving an Azure subscription to another Azure AD tenant.

Perhaps your developers want to isolate their environment as they work on their cloud apps. Using a separate Azure AD tenant is great for providing isolation between Azure deployment environments.

WARNING

You have to redo all your role-based access control (RBAC) assignments when you move a subscription to another Azure AD tenant. The reason should be pretty obvious: You have a new group of Azure AD users and group accounts to work with.

The "other" Azure AD Directory family members

Before I dive into the topic of creating Azure AD identities, I'll differentiate among the other members of the Azure Active Directory product family:

>> **Azure AD Business-to-Business (B2B):** This collaboration technology simplifies inviting external users into your Azure AD tenant by allowing them to use their existing email IDs. Use this service when you want to give a contractor or temporary employee limited access to your Azure environment.

>> **Azure AD Business-to-Consumer (B2C):** This portable identity store is aimed at your line-of-business customers. This tenant includes turnkey integration with social media account sign-up and sign-in. Use this service when you want to simplify customer account management for public-facing Azure-based applications.

>> **Azure AD Domain Services:** Azure AD Domain Services is a managed, cloud-hosted Azure AD domain. You can take advantage of LDAP, Kerberos/NTLM authentication, organizational units, group policy, and other features normally reserved only for local AD. Use this service when you want to decommission your local AD DS environment and move entirely to the cloud while preserving your existing Active Directory management tools such as Group Policy.

>> **Azure AD Connect/Connect Health:** The former is a free application you install in your on-premises AD environment to synchronize or federate local accounts to Azure AD to support single sign-on. The latter is an Azure portal-based monitoring/reporting layer for Azure AD Connect. Use this product when you've configured hybrid identity between on-premises and Azure and you need to monitor the connection health.

Creating Users and Groups

This section gets to the good stuff. If you browse to your AD tenant's Properties page, you can change the tenant label from Default Directory to something more meaningful. (You may have noticed in the screenshots in this book that I named my directory "DummiesBook," as I wanted to isolate the examples presented in my Azure instance.)

A best practice is to have your users' sign-in names match their email addresses. The following sections describe how to accomplish this goal.

Adding a domain to your directory

Browse to the Custom domain names setting in your Azure AD tenant. You'll see your original directory name on Microsoft's onmicrosoft.com domain name. The *.onmicrosoft.com domain is the default sign-in suffix for your Azure AD users, but it doesn't make for a good user sign-in experience (unless of course you are trying things out in Azure).

WARNING

Once you create the domain name, you can't delete the *<tenant>*.onmicrosoft.com domain name. This is how Microsoft fundamentally identifies your tenant via the Domain Name System (DNS).

I highly recommend that you associate your business DNS domain with your Azure AD tenant. You will then have a choice of which sign-in suffix you want your Azure AD users to use.

All you have to do to add your own business DNS domain to your tenant's is verify ownership. Follow these steps:

1. **On the Custom Domain Names blade, click Add Custom Domain.**

2. **In the Custom Domain Name blade, add your custom domain name, and then click Add Domain.**

   You're taken to a verification blade.

3. **Add a TXT or MX resource record to your domain's zone file.**

   REMEMBER

   You need to have administrative access to your DNS zone to complete this step. It doesn't matter which record type you choose for verification.

   Azure provides you the resource record details.

4. **Click Verify, and wait for Azure to verify the existence of the resource record.**

   The idea is that only the DNS domain owner is able to create the record; thus, you've verified to Microsoft that you own the domain.

5. **When verification is complete, delete the verification record from your domain registrar zone file.**

   You no longer need the record, and now you're free to use your custom domain as a user sign-in suffix.

Figure 12-3 shows my tenant's custom domains list. You can see I have my onmicrosoft.com domain, one verified domain I can use, and a few unverified names I cannot yet use.

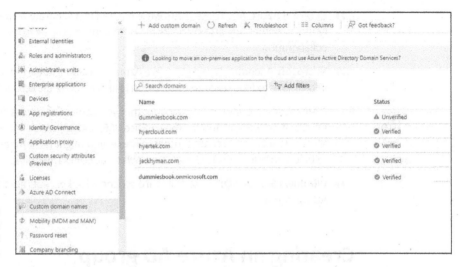

Understanding AD user and group types

An identity store is worthless without user and group accounts. User accounts represent individual identities, whereas groups aggregate multiple user accounts for easier management.

Next, let me explain how Azure AD users and groups work. In your Azure AD tenant, select the Users blade. Azure AD has two user account types and two group account types:

>> **Member user:** This account is a user created directly in the tenant or a synchronized/federated user from another directory (on-premises or AD).

>> **Guest user:** This account is a user invited into your tenant via AD B2B.

>> **Assigned membership group:** This group is one that you've statically populated with users.

>> **Dynamic group:** This group is one that Azure populates automatically based on predefined user account property values.

The Source column in your AD users list denotes where the user was created and where it is authenticated. This source of authority is important because you may want to treat cloud-native Azure AD accounts differently from federated or synchronized accounts. Options include

>> **AD DS:** These users were created directly in the local tenant.

>> **External Azure AD:** These users were created in a separate Azure AD tenant (yours or somebody else's) and invited into your tenant via AD B2B collaboration.

>> **Microsoft Account:** These users are Azure AD B2B invitees; the account that initially created the tenant/subscription is also a Microsoft account.

A Microsoft account is a free account that you can use to access several Microsoft services, including Xbox, Office 365, and, of course, Azure. The Microsoft account directory predates Azure; you might remember what used to be called "Windows Live accounts," which are the same thing.

REMEMBER

>> **Windows Server AD:** These users are synchronized or federated from a local AD DS domain.

Creating an Azure AD group

For the purposes of this book, I use the Azure portal to create and manage AD user and group accounts. Azure PowerShell and Azure CLI are alternatives you can use; these automation languages make for much shorter work when you need to create accounts in bulk.

You use Azure AD groups in Azure much the same way that you use groups in local Active Directory: to simplify administration. Follow these steps to create a sample Azure AD group:

1. **In your Azure AD settings, browse to the Groups blade, and click New Group.**

2. **On the New Group blade, complete the form.**

   Following are my recommendations for completing this form:

   ● *Group Type:* Choose Security. Office 365 is used for distribution groups in Microsoft Exchange Online. (Office 365 uses Azure AD as well.)

   ● *Group Name:* Give the group a meaningful name that's easy to type.

   ● *Group Description:* Describe the purpose of the group in the textbox.

   ● *Allow AD Roles To Be Assigned to this Group*: Select yes or no.

   ● *Membership Type:* Choose Assigned. The other options are Dynamic User and Dynamic Device. Dynamic groups instruct Azure to automatically populate these groups based on either user account properties (city, for instance) or their device type (desktop or mobile, for example).

- *Owners*: These are Azure AD users who will have the privilege to edit group membership.

- *Members*: If you chose Assigned as your group type, then you need to add Azure AD users to the group manually.

3. **Click Create to create the new group.**

Creating an Azure AD user

Now you can create a new Azure AD user account. Follow these steps:

1. **In the Azure AD settings list, select the All Users blade, and then click New User.**

2. **In the New User dialog box, click Create User, and fill in the Identity properties.**

   If possible, define the user name and domain parts to match your corporate email ID format. If you haven't added a custom domain, you have no choice but to use the *<tenant>*.onmicrosoft.com suffix.

   I explain how to associate a custom domain with Azure AD in the section "Adding a domain to your directory" earlier in this chapter.

WARNING

   Just because your Azure AD username matches an email name doesn't mean that Azure validates the address. Azure will send notification messages to this address but doesn't create a mailbox for the user. You have to handle email for your users separately.

3. **Decide how to handle the user's initial password.**

   Users need to supply this initial password the first time they attempt authentication against your AD tenant.

4. **Add the user to an existing group.**

   In the Groups and Roles section, click 0 Groups Selected, browse your directory, and select the AD group you created. The Groups property should read 1 group selected.

5. **Leave the other settings at their defaults, and click Create.**

REMEMBER

You might encounter a time when you need to set up a guest or an external account. These sound like they are the same thing but they aren't. An *external account* is an outside user who is assigned permission to specific resources in your Azure environment, which may include access to Microsoft 365. The external user is meant to collaborate using applications such as OneDrive and Teams. The external user must be invited to a group because they are outside the organization. The guest account allows an Azure AD administrator to invite people from outside the organization to collaborate and use the organization's applications.

TIP

Not all user accounts are going to connect with Azure-native environments. Synchronizing on-premises versus cloud-native environments is a bit different when leveraging Azure AD. With Azure Active Directory Synchronization, you are creating an identity that allows for one of three scenarios: creating an object based on a specific condition, trying to keep that object updated, or removing the object once the condition is no longer valid. In the case of synchronization, your on-premises AD will handshake with Azure AD each time one of those scenarios comes to fruition. To learn more about configuring AD Synchronization, go to `https://docs.microsoft.com/azure/active-directory/fundamentals/sync-directory`.

Working with Azure AD user accounts

In this section, I investigate some of the most important actions you can take with your Azure AD user accounts, such as assigning Azure AD licenses to users, logging in as a user, and changing a password.

Assigning licenses to users

All subscription owners start with their Azure AD tenant at the Free pricing tier. Table 12-2 shows a few distinctions among the various editions.

TABLE 12-2   Azure AD Edition Comparison

	Azure AD Free	Azure AD Premium P1	Azure AD Premium P2
Maximum directory objects	500,000	Unlimited	Unlimited
AD Connect synchronization	Yes	Yes	Yes
Company branding	No	Yes	Yes
Service-level agreement	No	Yes	Yes
Dynamic groups	No	Yes	Yes
Nonadministrative MFA	No	Yes	Yes

Keep the following things in mind:

>> Azure AD Premium has a fixed price per user, per month.

>> You get Azure AD Premium P1 for each Microsoft 365 license you purchase. Online standard users must pay the per month nominal fee.

>> Each user using a premium feature needs to be assigned the appropriate license.

WARNING

You need a native AD account rather than a Microsoft account. The account must also be assigned to the Global Administrator directory role. A directory role is a named collection of permissions that give the user greater control over Azure AD.

To purchase Azure AD licenses, follow these steps:

1. **Log in to the Microsoft 365 admin center (https://portal.office.com) using your Azure AD administrator account.**

2. **Choose Billing ⇨ Products & Services.**

   The Purchase Services gallery opens.

3. **Locate Azure Active Directory in the services list, and select P1 or P2.**

   Figure 12-4 shows the interface.

4. **Specify your desired license count, and complete the transaction.**

   You use your Azure subscription's listed payment method to pay for the licenses.

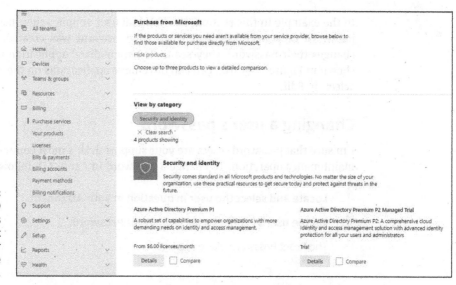

FIGURE 12-4:
You purchase AD Premium licenses in the Microsoft 365 portal rather than the Azure portal.

Distributing licenses

Now that you have some licenses to distribute, this section shows you how to do so in the Azure portal. Follow these steps:

1. **In your AD tenant, choose the Licenses setting.**

   The Get Started with License Management blade appears.

2. **In the Licenses Settings list, select All Products.**

3. **Select the type of license you purchased from the licenses list.**

   If you purchased Azure AD Premium licenses, for example, they show up in this list. You can see how many licenses you've assigned and how many licenses you have available.

4. **On the Licensed Users blade, click Assign from the toolbar.**

5. **On the Assign License blade, select the target user, and click Assign.**

Logging in as an Azure AD user

If you're not familiar with the Azure application access panel (https://myapps.microsoft.com), it's an authenticated site where your AD users can do the following:

>> Log in to Azure Cloud apps to which they've been assigned with single-sign on

>> Manage their user accounts, including changing their passwords or MFA options

In the example in this section, the fictional user supplies their username and the password they were assigned when their account was created. After the user changes their password, they see their personalized application access panel, as shown in Figure 12-5. You can add or remove applications on the myapps page by selecting Edit.

Changing a user's password

I'm sure that password resets are your support desk's most common user account maintenance operation. To change a password in Azure AD, follow these steps:

1. **Locate and select the user in question in your AD tenant.**

2. **On the user's Profile blade, click Reset Password.**

   The Reset Password blade appears.

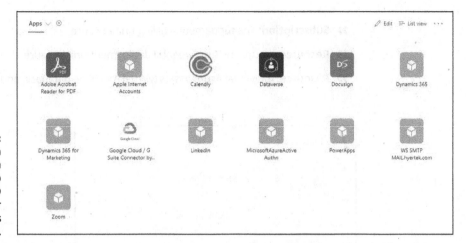

FIGURE 12-5:
The application access panel is a one-stop shop that lets Azure AD users access their profile properties and cloud apps.

3. **In the Reset password blade, click Reset Password.**

You can copy the temporary password and give it to the user or let Azure notify the user via email to the user's sign-in address. The user is forced to change their password at the next sign-in.

WARNING

You can't reset a Microsoft account's password from AD.

Configuring Role-Based Access Control (RBAC)

Microsoft uses a role-based access control (RBAC, typically pronounced *are-back*) authorization model. Authentication refers to credential validation, ensuring that the user is who they claim to be. A *role* is a predefined collection of authorizations typically aligned with a job role, so authorization defines the limits of that authenticated user's actions in your system.

Azure RBAC takes advantage of inheritance. In other words, an RBAC role assignment at a higher scope cascades via inheritance to lower scopes. Figure 12-6 shows the five Azure management scopes:

>> **Tenant root:** The highest scope level in ARM.

>> **Management group:** A container that can hold one or more subscriptions. This option is great for businesses that need to apply the same RBAC role assignments to multiple subscriptions simultaneously.

- » **Subscription:** The fundamental billing unit in Azure.

- » **Resource group:** The fundamental deployment unit in Azure.

- » **Resource:** Individual Azure assets (virtual machine, database, and so on).

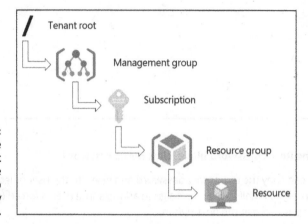

FIGURE 12-6:
Azure
management
scopes use
inheritance to
simplify
administration.

Implementing built-in RBAC roles

To avoid making a common rookie mistake, understand that Azure has two separate and distinct RBAC roles:

- » **AD roles:** Governing actions within AD
- » **Resource roles:** Governing actions with Azure resources at the tenant root, management group, subscription, resource group, and resource scopes

These roles are discussed in the following sections.

Azure AD roles

When you create an ordinary Azure AD user, that user has no directory roles assigned. The reason is simple: Only selected team members should have privileges in Azure AD itself.

Member-class user accounts can do basic things such as edit their profile properties and perhaps view the properties of other member user accounts. However, you may have people on your team who need the ability to register cloud apps with Azure AD or to create user and group accounts.

In your Azure AD tenant, select the Roles and Administrators setting to see the full list of built-in Azure AD roles. Some of the most common are

>> **Global administrator:** Role holders can perform all actions within the tenant. This role is the highest-privilege role in your directory, and you need to be extraordinarily careful to whom you assign it.

>> **Application administrator:** Role holders can manage cloud app registrations.

>> **Billing administrator:** Role holders can manage subscription invoicing and payment methods.

>> **Guest inviter:** Role holders can invite external users into your directory via AD B2B collaboration.

>> **Password administrator:** Role holders can reset passwords for nonadministrators.

>> **Reports reader:** Role holders can read Azure auditing reports.

>> **User administrator:** Role holders can manage AD users and groups.

Suppose that a new user is granted the user administrator role so that the user can create and manage Azure AD user accounts. To do so, follow these steps:

1. **Log in to portal.azure.com as the user.**

   Recall that the user is ordinary with no Azure AD role assignments.

2. **Browse to the Subscriptions blade.**

   You shouldn't see any subscriptions listed because the new user doesn't have sufficient permissions.

3. **In your Azure AD tenant, open the new user's settings, and click the Directory Role blade.**

   Choose the All Users setting, select the user, and then choose the Directory Role blade from within the user's settings.

4. **On the Directory Role blade, click Add Assignment.**

5. **Select the role in the Directory Roles list for User Administrator.**

6. **Click Add.**

   The user should be granted membership to the user administrator role.

7. **To test access, sign the user out of the portal and sign them in again to refresh the account's access token.**

The user interface technique of hiding or disabling controls to which the user has no privilege is known as *security trimming*.

Resource roles

Azure AD roles are named permissions collections usable within your Azure AD tenant. By contrast, resource roles are permissions collections associated with your Azure subscriptions and resources. Note that this is an entirely different set of roles from what you've seen thus far in Azure AD.

You can apply RBAC roles to any of the five management scopes discussed in "Azure AD roles" earlier in this chapter, and those assignments cascade via inheritance to lower scope levels.

You add role assignments for a user on the Subscriptions blade. The most common built-in resource roles include the following:

>> **Owner:** Lets you take any action at that scope, including editing the RBAC role memberships

>> **Contributor:** Has the same privileges as Owner except that you can't edit RBAC assignments

>> **Reader:** Lets you view resources but not change them

>> **Virtual Machine Contributor:** Lets you manage virtual machines (VMs) but not their associated network and storage resources

>> **Virtual Machine Administrator Login:** Lets you view VMs in a subscription and log in to them as an administrator

Adding an account to an Azure AD role

Follow these steps to add an account to the Reader role at the subscription level:

1. **To test the "before" state, log in to the Azure portal as a new user, and navigate to the Resource Groups blade.**

   Type **resource groups** into the Azure global search box to find this blade quickly.

   You shouldn't see any resource groups listed because the user hasn't been given any privileges yet.

2. **Browse to the Subscriptions blade, select your subscription, and click the Access Control (IAM) setting.**

3. **On the Check Access tab, type the user's sign-in name to view the user's current access level.**

   The Azure portal should show zero role assignments for this user.

4. **On the Role Assignments tab, choose Add ⇨ Add Role Assignment.**

5. **On the Add Role Assignment blade, assign the user the Reader role.**

   Use the following settings:

   - *Role:* Select the Reader role.

   - *Assign Access To:* Use Azure AD user, group, or service.

   - *Select:* Type the user's sign-in name to resolve the account, and click to select it.

6. **Click Save to commit your changes.**

7. **As your user, sign out of the Azure portal and sign in again to test access.**

   The Resource Groups blade should show limited access to all resources in the user's subscription scope. Azure prevents you from taking most actions, which you can test by attempting to shut down a VM or upload a blob to a storage account.

At any scope, you can visit the Access Control (IAM) blade and its Role Assignments tab to view which accounts have which degrees of access (see Figure 12-7).

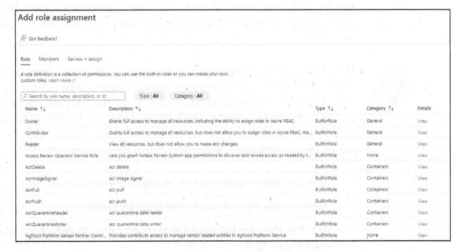

FIGURE 12-7: Viewing RBAC role assignments options to select from when adding a role assignment.

CUSTOM RBAC ROLES

TIP

The time will almost certainly arrive when the built-in RBAC roles don't precisely meet your needs. The good news is that you can define custom RBAC roles for Azure AD and Azure resources. Presently, Microsoft still requires an administrator to use Azure PowerShell or Azure CLI to create a custom RBAC resource role. By contrast, you can create Azure AD custom roles directly in the Azure portal. Learn more about custom roles in Azure by reading the docs article "Custom roles for Azure resources" at https://docs.microsoft.com/azure/role-based-access-control/custom-roles.

TECHNICAL STUFF

There is one more thing to consider when you have many Azure AD users and you must automate the management of the user accounts before they spiral out of control. That includes synchronizing the users with Custom RBAC roles among the AD forest. The capability is called Azure AD Connect Cloud Sync. To learn how to configure Cloud Sync Connect, go to https://docs.microsoft.com/azure/active-directory/cloud-sync.

Protecting Your Identity and Data with MFA

As I wrap up this chapter, I want to bring your attention to the use of Multi-Factor Authentication (MFA). It's also called two-factor authentication (2FA). Right now, you may be using MFA and not know it. Do you have a Microsoft account that asks you to check your phone or email for a six-digit code after you provide your username and password? If that's a big ol' yes, then you know what MFA is as an end-user.

TIP

It is important to configure MFA for any user who has access to Azure as any form of an administrator. Furthermore, many organizations require MFA for Microsoft 365 (and other Microsoft applications), too. Why, you ask? Because you may have access to the Microsoft 365 administrator account or control sensitive data.

To set up your MFA configuration, follow these steps:

1. **Use the global search box to locate Azure Active Directory.**

2. **Select Azure AD and locate the Security blade.**

3. **Scroll to the next blade under Manage called Multifactor authentication (see Figure 12-8).**

4. **Click Multifactor authentication.**

You are able to configure several settings here including Account Lockout rules, Block/Unblock Users, Fraud Alerts, Notifications, OATH Token setup, and Phone Call Verification settings.

FIGURE 12-8:
Access multifactor authentication.

For users who want to configure specific policies as to when MFA is applicable, go back to the Security blade and select Conditional Access. The Conditional Access blade, shown in Figure 12-9, is where you create specific conditions, hence Conditional Access, as to when MFA should be utilized.

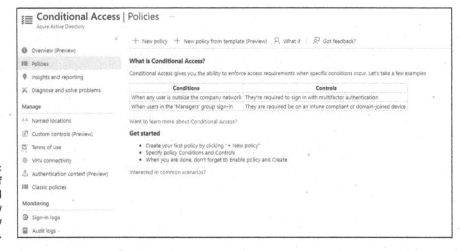

FIGURE 12-9:
Examples of Conditional Access and how to create a new conditional policy.

By default, Azure and Microsoft 365 set a basic condition that when any user is outside the company network, the user will be prompted for MFA credentials. For example, suppose I am logging into accounts tied with dummiesbook.onmicrosoft. com. If I decide to log off and switch accounts or go to another company, such as jackhyman.onmicrosoft.com, I'll be prompted to enter a second form of security verification. As part of your MFA setup, you establish the order and verification forms, which may include receiving an SMS text message, an email, or a phone call (or a combination of formats).

Chapter **13**

Implementing Azure Governance

Azure governance is how your organization approaches the management of your various Azure resources. For instance, how can you ensure that resources are deployed only to authorized regions? How can you limit resource sizes so you don't exceed your budget? In this chapter, you see how to use Azure's core governance tools: taxonomic tags and Azure Policy.

Implementing Taxonomic Tags

The resource group is Azure's fundamental deployment unit. The idea is that you place all resources that share a lifecycle in the same resource group to simplify management and auditing.

Life is rarely that simple, however. It's just as likely that you'll have deployments that span resource groups, regions, and even subscriptions. Satisfying your accounting and compliance departments to track these loosely coupled resources can be difficult. Using taxonomic tags is the answer. In Azure, a *tag* is a simple key/value pair. As long as a user has write access to a resource, the user can add existing tags to that resource or create a new tag.

For example, you may have tags to denote various cost centers in your organization, or perhaps your tags separate different Azure-based projects. Azure presents tags in the format key:value, such as CostCenter:Development.

Taxonomic tags in Azure are a bit fussy. Here are some facts about taxonomic tags to keep in mind as you go along:

>> Each resource group or resource can have a maximum of 50 tags.

>> Tag names are limited to 512 characters; tag values are limited to 256 characters.

>> Tags applied to a resource group don't flow by inheritance to lower management scopes.

>> Not all Azure resources support tags. You can't apply tags to management groups or subscriptions, for example — only to resource groups and most resource types.

>> Tag names can't include the following reserved characters: < > % & \ ? /.

WARNING

Unlike RBAC and Azure Policy assignments, tags applied to a resource group are not inherited to the resources inside that resource group. Although you can use Azure PowerShell or Azure CLI to work around this limitation, it's significant and worth noting.

Another pain point to consider is how easy it is to use Azure tags inconsistently. You'll find by bitter experience that some of your colleagues (never you, mind you, but your colleagues) do the following things:

>> Forget to add tags to resources during or after deployment

>> Accidentally use an incorrect tag name or value

>> Misspell a tag name or value

These problems can have big implications if you're using taxonomic tags for cost tracking because inconsistent tagging leads to inconsistent (inaccurate) reporting results. The good news is that you can use Azure Policy to standardize your tag application.

Applying tags to resource groups and resources

One of the most important governance conversations your team needs to have is about which Azure resource naming and tagging standard makes the most sense.

Refer to the following Microsoft online resources for guidance on resource and tag-naming best practices:

» Recommended naming and tagging conventions: https://docs.microsoft. com/azure/cloud-adoption-framework/ready/azure-best-practices/ naming-and-tagging

» Resource naming and tagging decision guide: https://docs.microsoft. com/azure/cloud-adoption-framework/decision-guides/resource- tagging

Table 13-1 summarizes a few ways to classify taxonomic tags and which tag names to use.

TABLE 13-1 **Common Azure Taxonomic Tagging Patterns**

Tag Type	Example Tags (name:value)
Accounting	department:legal
	region:europe
	project:salespromo
Classification	confidentiality:private
	sla:8h
Functional	app:prodsite1
	env:staging
	tier:web
Partnership	contact:jsmith
	owner:twarner
	owner:jhyman
Purpose	businessproc:development
	revenueimpact:high

Adding tags in the Azure portal

With no further ado, let me walk you through adding tags to resource groups and individual resources. I show you how to create resource groups in Chapter 2.

Make sure that you have a resource group with at least two resources inside and that you're logged in to the Azure portal with your administrator account, and then follow these steps:

1. **In your resource group's settings list, select Tags.**

2. **Type a new tag name and value, and then click Save.**

   You might use the name "project" and the value "learning," for example.

   Don't be surprised if you see other tag names and values, even if you're the only user in your subscription. Sometimes, Azure itself adds tags to resources.

   TIP

3. **Navigate to the resource group's Overview page, and verify its tag.**

   You should see a Tags field in the Essentials pane.

4. **Click the tag you named in Step 2.**

   Azure transports you to the project:learning blade, which lists any resources to which you've assigned this tag.

5. **Browse to a resource within your resource group, and click Tags from the resource's settings list.**

6. **Reuse the existing project tag, but change the name to testing.**

   The tag now reads project:testing.

   Azure tags are modifiable, which is both convenient and dangerous because a misspelling can result in incorrect reporting.

7. **Click Save to commit your changes.**

8. **Associate either tag or both new tags with a few other resources in different resource groups.**

You can (and should) add appropriate tags to new resources during deployment.

REMEMBER   Figure 13-1 shows the Create storage account's Tags deployment blade.

Adding tags programmatically

It's super-easy to add tags to resources programmatically with PowerShell. Chapter 2 talks about both Azure CLI and Azure PowerShell. First, use the following code to list existing tags on your resource group (mine is called 'wiley'):

```
(Get-AzResourceGroup -Name 'wiley').Tags
Name                 Value

----                 -----

project              learning
```

FIGURE 13-1:
It's best practice
to tag resources
during their
deployment.

REMEMBER

Log in to Azure with Login-AzAccount and set your default subscription with Set-AzContext before you try any of these steps.

Suppose you want to add a new tag (env:dev) to your resource group. If you use the Set-AzResourceGroup command to add the new tag, PowerShell overwrites any existing tags and replaces them with the new one, so you don't want to do that. Instead, you can first store the 'wiley' resource group's tags in a variable named $tags:

```
$tags = (Get-AzResourceGroup -Name 'wiley').Tags
```

Next, use the $tags object's Add method to include a new env:dev tag:

```
$tags.Add("env", "dev")
```

Finally, run Set-AzResourceGroup to commit the change:

```
Set-AzResourceGroup -Tag $tags -Name 'wiley'
```

Removing tags

If one of your colleagues misspelled a tag name and/or value, or if your team disposed of a project and you no longer need the tag, then you have an Azure governance problem to solve.

Just as it's easy to create tags and build new tags from existing entries, it's simple to remove a tag you no longer want. Again, you use PowerShell.

First, retrieve the existing tags (mine are on my `'wiley'` resource group):

```
(Get-AzResourceGroup -Name 'wiley').Tags
Name            Value
----            -----
env             dev
project         learning
```

Next, use the following code to try to delete the env tag and all its values with this command:

```
Remove-AzTag -Name env
```

The result is

```
Remove-AzTag : Cannot remove tag/tag value because it's being referenced by
    other resources.
```

Ouch! It looks as though you have to remove this tag from all related resources before you can delete it, which makes sense. You can run the following two commands to locate all resource groups and resources that have a specific tag:

```
(Get-AzResourceGroup -Tag @{ 'env' = 'dev' }).ResourceGroupName
(Get-AzResource -Tag @{ 'env' = 'dev' }).Name
```

TIP

You can leave a tag's name but delete a particular value by using the `-Value` parameter of `Remove-AzTag`. In this example, you could remove the `'projektY'` value from your `'project'` tag by running `Remove-AzTag -Name 'project' -Value 'projektY'`. That way, any other project values would persist in your subscription.

At this point, it's probably easier to look up the resources in the portal and delete the tag references. After you've cleared the tag from any associated resources, you can retry using the `Remove-AzTag` command to remove the tag.

Reporting via tags

The simplest way to report on which resources have been associated with a given tag is to open the Tags blade and click the appropriate tag, as shown in Figure 13-2.

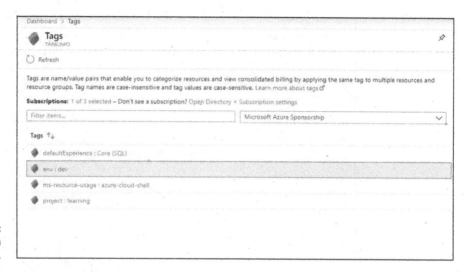

Each name:value pair shows up as a separate row in the Tags list. You might see project:learning or project:testing, for example.

One of the most important use cases for Azure taxonomic tags is cost reporting. As it happens, Azure makes it simple to generate this data in a visually appealing format.

Cost Management + Billing blade

You can see basic resource use/cost information on the Subscriptions blade in the Azure portal. To really dig into your spending and forecast future spend, however, use the Cost Management + Billing blade. Follow these steps to filter the view based on tag name/value:

1. **In the Azure portal, use global search to browse to the Cost Management + Billing blade, and then select the Cost Management setting.**

2. **In the Cost Management blade settings list, click Cost Analysis.**

3. **On the Cost Analysis toolbar, click the Add Filter button.**

   Azure creates a row to hold your filter expression.

4. **From the first drop-down list, choose Tag as your attribute, and from the second drop-down list select the appropriate tag names and/or values.**

   Azure applies the new filter immediately. Figure 13-3 shows my environment.

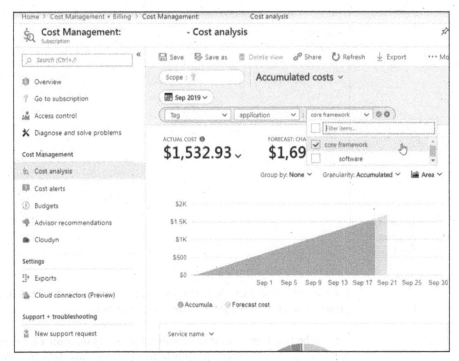

FIGURE 13-3:
Use tags to
perform Azure
cost analysis.

API access to tags and billing

Developers often prefer to use API access to find their answers as quickly as possible. To do this, they can use several billing-related APIs that include tags:

>> **Resource Usage API:** This API reveals your Azure service consumption data.

>> **RateCard API:** This API displays current prices for Azure services based on region.

>> **Cloud Cost Management API:** This API lies behind the Cost Management + Billing Azure portal blade.

ON THE WEB

Learn more about the Azure consumption APIs by reading the Azure documentation article "Azure consumption API overview" at https://docs.microsoft.com/azure/billing/billing-consumption-api-overview.

Implementing Azure Policy

Azure Policy is a simple JavaScript Object Notation (JSON) document that can protect your entire management group or subscription against deployment actions that violate your company policy. Policy limits what authorized users can do within their deployment scopes. You may deploy a Policy that prevents users from deploying virtual machines (VMs) outside your allowed Azure regions, for example.

Fundamental differences exist between role-based access control (RBAC) roles and Policy. RBAC roles enable your Azure users to perform particular actions on your Azure resources, such as deploying a VM.

You can define your own policies, but Microsoft offers existing policies that you can use. Here are some examples of built-in Policy definitions:

» **Allowed locations:** Restrict the locations that your organization can specify when deploying resources.

» **Disk encryption should be applied on VMs:** Apply whole-disk encryption to your Azure VM operating system and data disks.

» **Add a tag to resources:** Add the specified tag and value when any resource missing this tag is created or updated.

» **Allowed virtual machine SKUs:** Restrict which VM sizes users can deploy.

Policy definition structure

Like just about everything else in Azure Resource Manager (ARM), Policy definitions are JSON documents. It's a great idea to add parameters to your policies to make them more flexible. Consider the following example, which defines a parameter named listOfAllowedLocations:

```
"parameters": {
  "listOfAllowedLocations": {
    "type": "Array",
    "metadata": {
      "description": "The list of locations that can be specified when deploying
    resources.",
      "strongType": "location",
      "displayName": "Allowed locations"
    }
  }
}
```

You can learn more about Azure Policy JSON syntax by reading the Azure documentation article "Azure Policy definition structure" at https://docs.microsoft.com/azure/governance/policy/concepts/definition-structure.

At policy deployment, you specify a value for the `listOfAllowedLocations` parameter. The `strongType` element is a bit of ARM magic that creates a drop-down list containing all Azure regions. It's a handy trick to use in your ARM templates and Policy definitions.

Recall that Azure Resource Manager (ARM) is the API that underlies anything and everything you do in Azure. As an alternative, you can create an enumeration of allowed values by substituting the `allowedValues` array:

```
"allowedValues": [
    "EastUS",
    "EastUS2",
    "CentralUS"
]
```

The guts of a policy is the condition statement. The next code block uses an `if` block with one or more constraints. In this example, all the conditions must evaluate to be `true` for the policy to take effect. The policy evaluates the location specified in the deployment. If the target location isn't in the list of allowed locations, then the policy denies the deployment.

```
{
    "if": {
      "allOf": [
        {
            "field": "location",
            "notIn": "[parameters('listOfAllowedLocations')]"
        }
      ]
    },
    "then": {
      "effect": "Deny"
    }
}
```

Policy includes quite a different policy effects. In Azure Policy, an effect determines what Azure does if a given policy evaluates to true.

With the Audit effect, you can allow deployments but track them closely for auditing purposes. The DeployIfNotExists effect is super-powerful because the policy can execute an ARM template deployment to enforce the policy. For example, you can have a policy automatically reenable resource diagnostics if a colleague accidentally or intentionally turns them off on a resource.

If you'd like to dive deeper on Policy, see "Understand Azure Policy Effects" at https://docs.microsoft.com/azure/governance/policy/concepts/effects.

Policy lifecycle

Deploying a policy occurs in three phases:

>> **Authoring:** Typically, you make a copy of an existing policy definition, attach it to a management scope, and edit it to suit your requirements.

>> **Assignment:** You link a policy to a management scope.

>> **Compliance:** You review and report on Azure resource compliance and take authoring, assignment, and remediated corrective actions as necessary.

In Policy, an *initiative* is a container object associated with one or more individual policy definitions. The initiative's use case is businesses that want to manage multiple related policy assignments as a single entity. This chapter, however, focuses on individual policies.

Creating a policy

You can define a policy linked to the subscription scope that limits the regions to which administrators can deploy resources. Follow these steps in the Azure portal:

1. **Browse to the Policy blade, and choose Settings ⇨ Definitions.**

2. **On the Policy - Definitions blade, type location in the search box.**

   You see a list of results for the search term as you type. Spend a moment browsing the results list. I show you this interface in Figure 13-4.

3. **Select the Allowed Locations built-in policy definition, and click Duplicate Definition from the toolbar.**

   The policy definition appears. The built-in templates are read-only, so you need to duplicate it to make it your own.

4. **Complete the new policy definition.**

   Here is some guidance on the properties:

   - *Definition Location:* Options are management group and subscription. I recommend that you choose your subscription.

   - *Name:* Make the policy name meaningful in accordance with your corporate Azure naming convention.

   - *Category:* Store the policy in a built-in category or create your own.

5. **Edit the policy rule to remove the following lines:**

```
{
    "field": "location",
    "notEquals": "global"
},
{
    "field": "type",
    "notEquals": "Microsoft.AzureActiveDirectory/b2cDirectories"
}
```

The only policy condition you need, strictly speaking, is the one that references the listOfAllowedLocations parameter value(s).

6. **Click Save to commit your changes.**

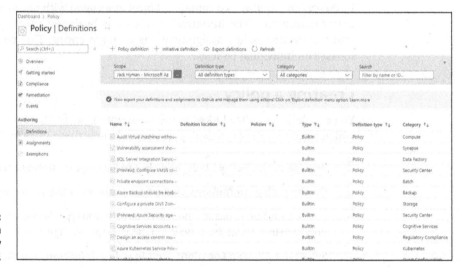

FIGURE 13-4:
Browsing built-in
Azure Policy
definitions.

TIP

Microsoft's Policy engineering team hosts an Azure Policy Samples GitHub repository that contains hundreds of policies across most Azure services. These policy definitions should give you a head start on governing your own environments. You can find them at https://github.com/Azure/azure-policy.

Assigning the policy

After you've created a custom policy definition, assign it to your subscription and test it. Follow these steps:

1. **On the Policy - Definitions blade, choose Custom from the Type drop-down list.**

   It's helpful to filter your view so that you see only your custom policies.

2. **Select your policy, and click Assign on the toolbar.**

   You can also edit or delete your policy definition from this configuration blade.

3. **Complete the form.**

   Here are my recommendations for filling out the form:

   - *Scope:* Because you linked the definition to the subscription level, select that subscription as your assignment scope. You can further limit policy scope to a particular resource group within the subscription.

   - *Exclusions:* You can exempt resource groups and individual resources from the policy. In this case, you may have resources already present in the subscription that have authorized to exist in disallowed regions.

   - *Assignment Name:* The assignment name can have a different display name from its underlying policy definition.

   - *Parameters:* In this case, you should see an Allowed Locations drop-down list populated with Azure regions. Choose whichever regions you want to allow.

   - *Create a Managed Identity:* This option is necessary only when your policy will perform deployment. A Managed Identity in Azure Active Directory (AD) is analogous to a service account in local AD (see Chapter 12).

4. **Click Assign to submit your policy.**

WARNING

Open the notification menu; you may see an information message informing you that Policy assignments take around 30 minutes to go into effect.

If you browse to the Assignments blade, you should see your newly assigned policy, as shown in Figure 13-5. To get a clearer view, open the Definition type drop-down list and filter for Policy.

Testing the policy

To test the policy, attempt to deploy an Azure resource to a disallowed location. For example, try to deploy a new storage account. Chapter 3 describes how to do this.

The deployment should fail. Notice that the Azure failure text explains that the desired storage account resource is disallowed by policy, and it even helpfully reminds you which policy was the protector.

AZURE BLUEPRINTS

TECHNICAL STUFF

Building a skyscraper takes a lot of work, and also requires a lot of planning. Much of the planning is spent on ensuring that the design is compliant with laws and regulations. Now, if you think about the role of the building architect and the cloud architect for Azure, there are an extraordinary number of similarities. The cloud architect aims to create repeatable assets that adhere to organizational patterns and requirements. Users like yourself can make repeatable cloud architectures using Azure Blueprints.

Azure Blueprints help the development team craft a new environment against specific compliance requirements, which also utilize components, including storage, databases, networking, and security. Collectively, the assets speed up the process, enforcing repeatability. Unlike Azure Policy and ARM Templates, Blueprints can orchestrate resource templates and artifacts using assignments.

So what's the downside, you ask? Unlike Azure Policy and ARM Templates, Blueprints must be stored in a globally distributed Azure Cosmos DB. The Blueprint objects are replicable across one or more Azure regions. That is not the case with Azure Policy or ARM Templates unless they are configured explicitly to handle such behavior.

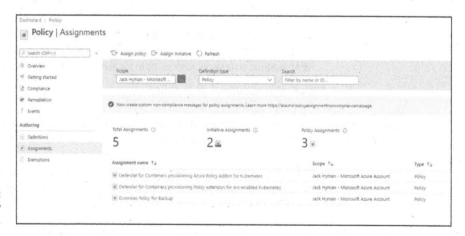

FIGURE 13-5: List of Policy assignments.

Dipping into Azure Security, Privacy, and Trust

What is often the biggest concern with organizations and their users when moving to the cloud? It's not the expense or time it will take. People understand that it costs time and money to migrate to the cloud. The heart of most concerns lies in security, privacy, and compliance, all of which are tenants of strong Azure governance.

REMEMBER

Moving to the cloud means that you are handing off responsibility for regulatory compliance to your cloud provider, including data protection standards. The cloud provider ensures that you are keeping up with the state, federal, and international requirements. That said, compliance is still a shared responsibility because the business still owns the data. If your data is improperly handled, you can't blame Microsoft, because it only handles the regulatory compliance for the infrastructure.

The scope of security, privacy, and trust compliance spans to several hundred control types. Ever hear of the European Union General Data Protection Regulation (GDPR) and California Consumer Privacy Act (CCPA)? Microsoft has solutions available to handle data transmissions between users for these two regulations. Not following the policy regulation comes with very stiff penalties. To mitigate the risks for these two regulations, for example, there are other controls that piggyback in enforcing the age-old problem of security, privacy, and trust in the cloud.

Other controls Microsoft may leverage to protect business data, especially in the context of U.S. Federal Government, include

» National Institute of Standards and Technology (NIST) SP-800 53

» National Institute of Standards and Technology (NIST) 800-171

» Cybersecurity Maturity Model Certification (CMMC)

In summary, all of these security, privacy, compliance and trust standards are further explored and cited in governance tools such as the Microsoft Privacy Statement, Online Service Terms and Data Protection Amendment, and Trust Center.

Reading through the documentation

Microsoft wants to impress upon its customers that it takes privacy, security, and trust seriously. To show how Azure commits to handling privacy across all its product lines, extensive details are provided in the Privacy Statement and Online Service Terms and Data Protection Addendum. Details on each of these governance sources are found in Table 13-2. These two documents are combined as part of the Microsoft licensing terms and conditions.

TABLE 13-2　Documentation to Support the Governance Process

Document	Purpose	URL
Azure Privacy Statement	Covers how Microsoft protects you in Azure under the scope of the following service areas: Azure services, websites, apps, software, servers, devices, and cloud solutions.	`https://privacy.microsoft.com/privacystatement`
Online Service Terms and Data Protection Addendum	Covers the terms you agree to by using a Microsoft product, specifically, online products. The goal is to describe how you can and cannot use Azure Services.	`https://www.microsoft.com/licensing/product-licensing/products`

Exploring the Trust Center

Looking for every single rule Microsoft has out there for security, privacy, and compliance information? Your one-stop shop is the Azure Trust Center (`www.microsoft.com/trust-center`). The Microsoft Trust Center, shown in Figure 13-6, isn't just for Azure; it's for the entire universe of Microsoft products. Of course, Azure touches most if not all Microsoft-based products. That's why you should familiarize yourself with key security principles as well as data management practices in Azure and even beyond.

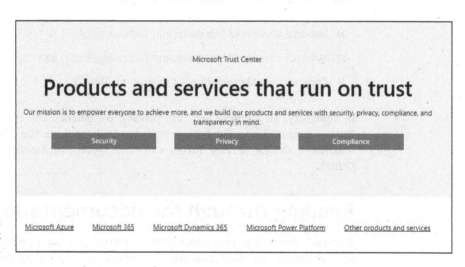

Microsoft Trust Center

Products and services that run on trust

Our mission is to empower everyone to achieve more, and we build our products and services with security, privacy, compliance, and transparency in mind.

Security	Privacy	Compliance

Microsoft Azure　　Microsoft 365　　Microsoft Dynamics 365　　Microsoft Power Platform　　Other products and services

FIGURE 13-6: Microsoft Trust Center.

TECHNICAL STUFF

Don't be surprised if every feature in the Azure stack is not listed as part of the Trust Center. Only publicly available features are documented, not those in private or public beta.

Touring Azure Advisor

Could you say for certain that your Azure infrastructure's cost, performance, security, and high availability is 100 percent accurate and compliant? I know I can't, as things are always changing within Azure. Fixing the issues as new products are rolled out or patches are enforced is alleviated by Azure Advisor. What makes Azure Advisor so unique is that it uses machine learning algorithms to make recommendations on how you can better optimize your Azure environment across cost, performance, high availability, and yes, security.

TECHNICAL STUFF

Azure Advisor is a recommendation engine that scans your subscriptions and provides guidance on high availability, security, performance, and cost. The service is free, so it's an economical way to get feedback on places where you may benefit from making changes in your subscriptions. You can create alerts that fire when Advisor makes particular recommendations, and you can tweak the recommendation engine to better suit your environment.

To work with Advisor, follow these steps:

1. **In the Azure portal, navigate to the Advisor Overview blade.**

   From this blade's toolbar, you can download reports in CSV (comma-separated values) or PDF format.

2. **Choose Settings ⇨ Recommendations ⇨ Security.**

   The Security Recommendations blade appears. Figure 13-7 shows the security recommendations Advisor made for me, listing impact, problem description, affected resources, and the date when it created the recommendations.

3. **Select a recommendation to view its details.**

   Notice the Security Center button at the top of the Advisor security recommendations. Azure Security Center also uses machine learning to make recommendations on your environment; Advisor includes Security Center recommendations as part of its logic.

You can't create your own Advisor recommendations, but you can customize the behavior of the built-in recommendations. To do so, follow these steps:

1. **In Advisor, select the Configuration setting.**

2. **Browse to the Rules tab.**

3. **Select a rule and then choose Edit from the pop-up menu that appears.**

4. **Make your change in the Edit Recommendation Rule blade.**

5. **Once complete, click Apply to finish the configuration.**

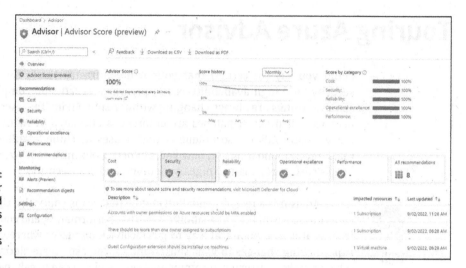

FIGURE 13-7:
Azure Advisor
provides detailed
recommendations
and sometimes
fixes problems
automatically.

5

Going Beyond the Basics in Microsoft Azure

Exploring DevOps solutions to plan, build, test, and deploy Azure Solutions and Resources

Extending your on-premises environment to Azure

Mastering how to migrate massive amounts of data from your on-premises network to Azure

Monitoring the health of your Azure resources

Chapter **14**

Discovering DevOps in Microsoft Azure

Moving to the cloud isn't something that can happen suddenly. Organizations must plan out the process. Whether creating a simple virtual machine (VM) or relocating an entire data center, you need to think about each stage of the process, including application planning, development, delivery, and operations.

Microsoft Azure includes a collection of Software as a Service (SaaS)–based development and operations (DevOps) tools to help organizations get to the finish line. Each phase of a cloud transition requires specific capabilities. Some transitions might require a place to store code, while others require project management. Built as a platform inside Azure, all Azure DevOps tools are cloud-based instead of on the desktop, so different project phases can be linked seamlessly. The old saying that there is an "app for that" is applicable in this case and is what this chapter covers.

Introducing the Azure DevOps Tools

Microsoft breaks the DevOps cycle into four stages: Planning, Developing, Deployment, and Operations, as noted in Table 14-1. Using Azure as an end user differs from trying to architect and build solutions in Azure. It takes a tremendous amount of planning and collaborating on code development to support the build-out of applications in Azure. Microsoft built Azure DevOps to help teams engage in the cloud's full lifecycle development and deployment process.

TABLE 14-1 **The DevOps Cycle**

Phase	Description	Azure DevOps Tool
Planning	During this phase, teams manage work across all of their Azure instances and projects. Planning incorporates all stages of the project management lifecycle that define and track work using the Kanban methodology. Features in Azure DevOps include boards, backlogs, dashboards, and reports.	Azure Boards
Developing	During this phase, teams use enterprise-class development tools or even low-code or no-code tooling to programmatically build solutions to use within Azure. Users can also collaborate with others using tools such as GitHub once the code is ready for distribution.	Azure Repos GitHub GitHub Actions Azure DevTest Labs
Deployment	During this phase, customers often use capabilities such as Kubernetes on Azure to automate deployments from the delivery stage. But when the cloud environment requires one stand-up multiple cloud instances, you want to focus on template-based design. That's when Azure Resource Manager becomes handy in conjunction with Azure Pipelines.	Azure Pipelines
Operations	This phase ensures that implementation runs as it should and requires constant monitoring. Your ability to gain complete visibility of your data can be accomplished using Azure Monitor. Where security and compliance are concerned, head over to Azure Defender for Cloud.	Azure Monitor Azure Defender for Cloud

WARNING

Microsoft prefers that customers use Azure DevOps Services, the online version, as it is easier to map cloud capabilities to the project management lifecycle. There is an alternate option for those organizations who want to use DevOps in the data center environment. The solution, called Azure DevOps Server, has an almost identical set of capabilities as Azure DevOps Services. However, linking cloud projects to the life-cycle is not as smooth, even with a robust integrated desktop environment (IDE).

The following is a high-level description of each of the Azure DevOps tools:

>> **Boards:** Using Scrum and Kanban methodologies, Azure Boards is an agile project management suite of tools for planning and tracking deliverables, including code and defects.

>> **Repos:** Repos is a method to support code delivery via Git Repositories or Team Foundation Version Control available in Visual Studio.

>> **Pipelines:** Pipelines helps organizations build and release services for Azure's continuous integration and continuous delivery (CI/CD) applications.

>> **Test Plans:** Test Plans is a collection of tools to support Azure's development and delivery testing lifecycle.

>> **Artifacts:** Artifacts enables a team to share code packages using various solutions including Maven, npm, and NuGet. Artifacts can be made available for public or private consumption. A team can also use Azure Pipelines to integrate code packages.

Azure Boards

If you have ever used IT service management or project management platforms for Agile development, such as Atlassian (Jira), Monday.com, Wrike, Smartsheet, Asana, Basecamp, and Trello, then you already have a head start on Azure Boards. Azure Boards takes some of the best features of Microsoft Project and adapts them for the cloud environment with a Scrum development–first approach. Using Azure Boards, you can create items including Kanban Boards, Story Items, Features, Backlogs, Sprints, and Queries within a project. Figure 14-1 illustrates a sample Azure board.

Think of Azure Boards as your cockpit to help manage a growing list of cloud computing responsibilities using the following Azure Boards features:

>> **Boards:** A board provides a complete view of all work items using a card-based approach. A user drags and drops the cards to make sense of all items on the board. Treat the cards as if they are sticky notes. The intention is to visualize the flow of activities for a team, similar to that of Scrum or Kanban.

>> **Work Items:** Work Items are discrete tasks that can be filtered or pivoted using a criteria-based system.

>> **Backlogs:** Backlogs enable you to review all items in a list format. The project backlog presents your project plan and the repository of all assets needed to guide your team's activities. Users can organize backlog data into hierarchies, such as an organizational chart.

>> **Sprints:** Sprints are short duration tasks. Consider using sprints if your team has a backlog of items and requires an even more granular view of the backlog, leading to an iterated work path. Users can assign work based on iterations. A user can manipulate any task using the drag-and-drop editor to fit the backlog schedule better.

>> **Queries:** The Queries feature behaves like a traditional search, but for items in your work list, it enables you to define a set of parameters to locate information in your Azure boards. Three options include grouping work items, listing work items based on sharing, and creating trend charts.

FIGURE 14-1:
An Azure DevOps
board.

Azure Repos

Have you ever met a team that didn't have some issue, even insignificant, with their code at some point? Code control issues are generally tied to version control. With the Azure DevOps suite, Azure Repos is the function that helps organizations with code control and version control.

REMEMBER

A version control system offers an organization an excellent opportunity to manage code. But the system doesn't do everything for you. A bit of setup is required to configure the system to manage the code. Azure Repos can handle such activities by taking a snapshot in time or creating a complete backup of files. To learn about how to configure Azure Repos, go to https://docs.microsoft.com/azure/devops/repos/?view=azure-devops.

One feature developers should have at their fingertips is the ability to roll back code easily. The reason is simple: Why rework something if you already developed the product in the past? To support code management and storage, users have two options to handle version control in conjunction with Azure Repos: Git for distributed version control and Teams Foundation Version Control (TFVC) for single-point version control. The configuration interface for Azure Repos is shown in Figure 14-2.

FIGURE 14-2:
Azure Repos
configuration
interface.

TECHNICAL STUFF

As you find out later in this chapter, Git is a cloud-based version control system that offers distributed computing capacity. TFVC requires a server and operates using an IDE. Ever since Microsoft acquired GitHub Labs in 2018, most organizations have shifted their preference to Git, as TFVC is quite expensive to set up and maintain relative to Git.

Azure Pipelines

Picture a time when you can build and test your projects automatically without human intervention. A few years ago, automated testing was considered science fiction. Now, if you want to make a code project available to others, especially if the code is platform-agnostic, you can use a tool such as Azure Pipelines.

The development team requiring the code may intend to change the code base to an entirely different language or platform. That's why organizations ensure that their code is available to support continuous integration and delivery (CI/CD) using Azure Pipelines. CI/CD allows for any time or person code deployment based on a specification.

Reasons to use Azure Pipelines are plentiful:

>> It offers consistent and quality code deployments.

>> It enables users to automate the delivery of projects and the associated code in a variety of settings.

>> It supports multi-target deployment.

>> You can build your platform on multiple operating systems, including Windows, Linux, and macOS, while integrating with GitHub.

Azure Test Plans

Suppose your enterprise application in Azure wasn't tested before it was deployed. The lack of quality control and testing will likely wreak havoc on your cloud environment and support team. Azure Test Plans is a documentation-centric testing solution that enables users to author test plans for a targeted audience in DevOps.

Azure Test Plans requires Visual Studio Enterprise Test Professional or an active MSDN Platform Account.

The Azure Test Plans feature set offers the following opportunities:

>> **Planned manual testing:** Enables a user to organize test plans and test suites. A project owner is responsible for assigning testers to the testing instance.

>> **User acceptance testing:** A process where test plans are manually written and established before using Azure Test Plans. The test plans are validated to ensure that customer requirements are met, including the appropriate creation of artifacts.

>> **Exploratory testing:** Usually carried out by a team of developers. Each member of the exploratory team is assigned the responsibility to test one or more facets of an application without requiring a test plan. Data collection is then brought together using Azure Test Plans as a series of artifacts created.

>> **Stakeholder feedback:** Users outside the organization carry out the testing. The results are then brought into Azure DevOps as a series of artifacts.

An example of an Azure Test Plans use case interface is shown in Figure 14-3.

Azure Artifacts

Done with your project? Wanting to share your code with other developers? If you said yes, peek at Azure Artifacts. Azure Artifacts enables developers to share code and manage all their packages from a single location. Developers can publish packages to their feeds and share them with a team, an organization, or even the world. Developers can also acquire the packages of others using feeds and public registries such as NuGet.org or npmjs.com. Most importantly, Azure Artifacts is not native to Microsoft-based packages; you can access Maven, Python, npm, NuGet, and Universal packages.

If you are looking for the Packages Page, which used to be under the Build and Release Group page, Microsoft repackaged this experience under Azure Artifacts. The Azure Artifacts experience replaces the navigation of Azure DevOps Services and Team Foundation Server (TFS).

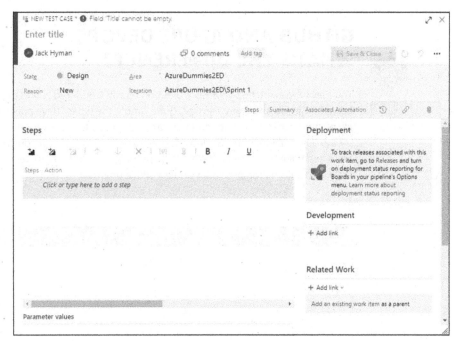

Collaborating with GitHub

Microsoft recognized that the open source world was alive and well a few years back with its acquisition of GitHub Labs in 2018. While Azure DevOps is intended for developers to collaborate natively inside Azure, many cloud users want to share resources beyond their little communities. To accomplish this, GitHub was started in 2008 with the mission to be the world's largest open-source developer community.

The GitHub web portal, known as Git, is a fast way for teams to collaborate on software projects when they are distributed. A shared code repository accessible to the masses (and we are talking millions of developers and organizations) gives new and experienced users the opportunity to learn from and engage with not only their code but also with other developer's code if it is made publicly available. Microsoft has embraced GitHub by embedding the repository solution within many Azure solutions.

As shown in Figure 14-4, a user can search for any asset with Microsoft in its title on GitHub.com. The search results indicate that there are almost 70,000 assets available on GitHub matching the query. Interestingly, the search offers users not only code but also access to VMs and Docker containers.

GITHUB AND AZURE DEVOPS: WHAT'S THE DIFFERENCE?

You may have scratched your head a few times and wondered what's the difference between GitHub and Azure DevOps. Quite simply, the typical developer needing a variety of approaches to handle source control and a broader code repository almost always uses GitHub. While GitHub offers an excellent platform for source code management and editing capabilities, Azure DevOps integrates and automates the testing, build, and automation processes under a single umbrella.

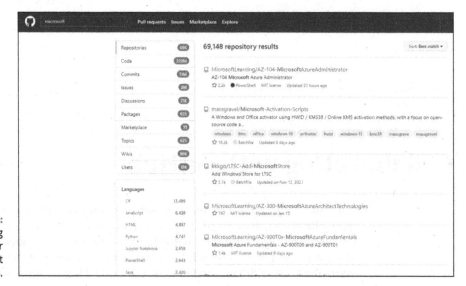

FIGURE 14-4:
Searching
GitHub for
Microsoft
assets.

You'd think Microsoft would have converted the name of GitHub to something new once it acquired GitHub Labs in 2018. It hasn't! You can still access www.github.com to create a new account. There are numerous places in Azure where GitHub is called out, but you still need to go to a website outside the Azure portal.

GitHub Actions is the open-source automated workflow solution for the Git environment. With GitHub Actions, users create event-driven workflows to automate processes, including CI/CD, build, test, and deployments inside of GitHub. If users are looking to support code reviews, branch management, and issue triaging exclusively in Git versus Azure DevOps, then GitHub Actions is a great secondary option. Because developers manage events, they define workflows using a text file scripted in YAML. Many preconfigured templates are also available in the GitHub Marketplace (see Figure 14-5).

To get started with GitHub Actions, follow these steps:

1. **Navigate to www.github.com.**

2. **Click on a repository you've created.**

   In this example, the repository is called "AzureDummies2ED."

3. **Select the Actions tab at the top of the page, as shown in Figure 14-6.**

   You'll be provided with some recommended actions assuming you have an open repository.

4. **Create a simple workflow by selecting Simple Workflow and following the prompts.**

   The process will vary from user and repository.

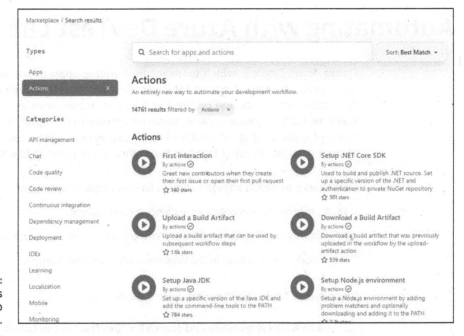

FIGURE 14-5:
GitHub Actions within the GitHub Marketplace.

TIP

If you've come to the end of this section and thought to yourself, it sounds like both applications offer just about the same features. You aren't incorrect. The key takeaway to determine which platform is most suited for your needs boils down to integrations and timing. If you are going to be integrating many solutions, I strongly suggest GitHub. However, if early on, you are looking for a single platform that grows over time, you should consider DevOps.

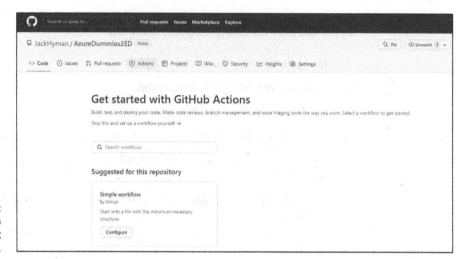

FIGURE 14-6:
Creating a GitHub
action with a Git
repository.

Automating with Azure DevTest Labs

Unlike Azure DevOps, which is meant for building applications and other code-based products, Azure DevTest Labs helps to automate the entire product lifecycle from the build, setup, and removal of Azure resources, such as the VM environment (which may contain one or more configurations for a project). Similarly, you can deploy and manage other Azure resources, such as ARM templates, from provisioning to testing using DevTest Labs. With Azure DevTest labs you can

>> Quickly provision any environment for repeatable consumption

>> Reduce quota and policy issues among environments

>> Automate the shutdown of resources, especially VMs, to reduce total spending

>> Build Azure resources in the Windows and Linux environment

To create an Azure DevTest Lab, follow these steps:

1. **Go to All Services blade and search for "DevTest" in the search box (see Figure 14-7).**

2. **Select DevTest Labs.**

3. **Press the Create button in the Navigation menu.**

   A form is displayed, allowing you to initiate a new DevTest instance, as shown in Figure 14-8. Once created, it will take a few moments to deploy the environment.

4. **Upon completion, select Go to Resource.**

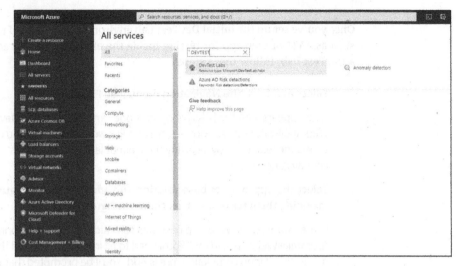

FIGURE 14-7:
Accessing Azure
DevTest Labs.

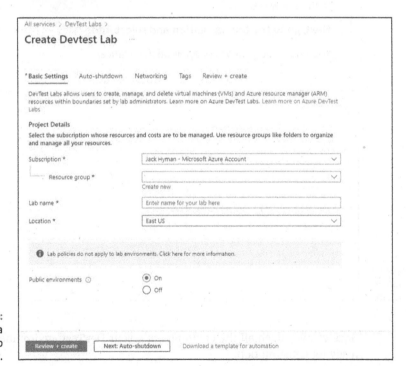

FIGURE 14-8:
Configuring a
new DevTest Lab
environment.

Once you've set up the initial DevTest Lab environment, you need to add a resource such as a VM or web app for testing inside the environment. To add a resource to a DevTest Lab, follow these steps:

1. **Select Add from the Navigation menu (see Figure 14-9).**

   A list appears with the possible options one can test against in DevTest labs for Web Applications (these options are also known as the *base*). You can also access these options by selecting the Claimable Virtual Machines blade in the left navigation pane.

2. **Select the appropriate base solution and add it to the configuration, including the environment, as shown in Figure 14-10.**

   In the example, the Web App base was selected using the environment name "DummiesWebAppDevTest." You'll need to fill in the form to Add the Web Application. Upon completion, press Add. You'll be prompted that the environment is now created.

3. **Next, go to the top navigation and select Add.**

   You'll now add your VM or application instance.

FIGURE 14-9:
Adding resources to a DevTest Lab.

Once you've added all the environments, your DevTest environment will now be ready for consumption.

The base environment must be in place before you create the DevTest environment or else you won't be able to add the VM or application to it.

REMEMBER

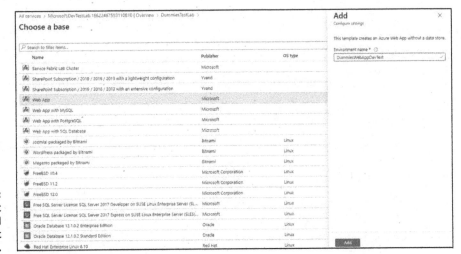

FIGURE 14-10:
Azure DevTest
Lab base and
environment
name.

Chapter **15**

Monitoring Your Azure Environment

This chapter explains how to check the pulse of all your Azure resources. Monitoring is an important skill for many reasons:

» Track the who, what, when, and where of deployments

» Generate performance baselines

» Manage resource usage costs

» Troubleshoot issues

» Identify and resolve security red flags

» Optimize your environment for cost, speed, security, and availability

By the end of this chapter, you'll be up to speed with Azure Monitor and Azure Log Analytics.

Azure Monitor

Azure Monitor is your baseline monitoring platform. I say *baseline* because Azure itself collects essential metric data and allows you to access it at no additional cost. By contrast, Application Insights and Log Analytics are premium monitoring services with their own pricing plans.

Azure Monitor collects two fundamental data types from your resources:

>> **Metrics:** Numerical time-series data that describes some aspect of your Azure resource

>> **Logs:** Text files or tables that describe various system events and metric data

The term *telemetry* gets a lot of press with regard to Azure; this term simply refers to a resource's ability to transmit its metric and log data to a collector resource.

**TECHNICAL
STUFF**

The word *telemetry* derives from two Greek words: *tele*, meaning *at a distance*, and *métron*, meaning *measure*. In contemporary English, you can say that telemetry signifies remote measurement.

Enabling diagnostic logging

For non-VM Azure resources, you can individually enable diagnostic logging metrics by visiting each resource's configuration blade in the Azure portal or by visiting Azure Monitor. You always enable diagnostics for your Windows Server and Linux virtual machines (VMs) at the VM resource level.

Azure Monitor Activity Log

The Azure Monitor Activity Log tracks what Microsoft calls "control plane events," which are administrative events issued by Azure itself or by you and your fellow Azure administrators. Some examples of control plane events include restarting a virtual machine, deploying an Azure Key Vault, or fetching storage account access keys.

I like to describe Activity Log as an operational/auditing log. With it, you can determine who executed which action in your subscriptions, at what time, and whether the action succeeded or failed.

WARNING

The Activity Log collects only subscription-level events. If you want to aggregate Activity Log data from multiple subscriptions, you need to look at Azure Activity Log Analytics, which is covered later in this chapter.

Follow these steps to tour your Activity Log environment:

1. **In the Azure portal, browse to the Monitor blade, and click Activity Log.**

2. **Click each filter button to gain insight into how to adjust the Activity Log view.**

I show you this interface in Figure 15-1.

You can type your Azure AD username in the search box to see only control plane events initiated by your user account, for example.

You can filter based on several criteria:

- *Resource Type:* Display VMs, web apps, databases, and so on.
- *Operation:* Display create, delete, write, or perform any other action that affects Azure resources.
- *Event Initiated By:* Search for an Azure AD username.
- *Event Category:* Show administrative, security, alert, etc.
- *Event Severity:* Show critical, error, warning, and informational.
- *Timespan:* List events that occurred within the last hour or month or a custom interval.

3. **Select an Activity Log event to view its details.**

In Figure 15-1 you can see exactly who successfully initiated the VM extension and when. The JavaScript Object Notation (JSON) source data shown in Figure 15-2 reveals the VM name and additional details regarding the triggered event.

The toolbar at the top of Figure 15-2 contains some useful buttons:

- **» Edit Columns:** Customize the display properties used in resource list views. You should get into the habit of using this control in all resource lists. Note that your customizations here affect only your Azure Active Directory (AD) account, not your colleagues'.

- **» Refresh:** Click to ensure that you see the latest data.

- **» Export Activity Logs:** Stream the current filtered Activity Log data into an Event Hub namespace. Then you can subscribe to this Activity Log stream by using other Azure resources and process the data according to your business requirements.

- **» Download As CSV:** Pull down a comma-separated value (CSV) representation of the current Activity Log view.

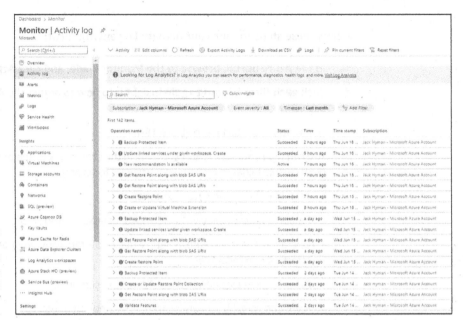

FIGURE 15-1:
Azure Activity
Log records
administrative
events initiated
by you or by
Azure itself.

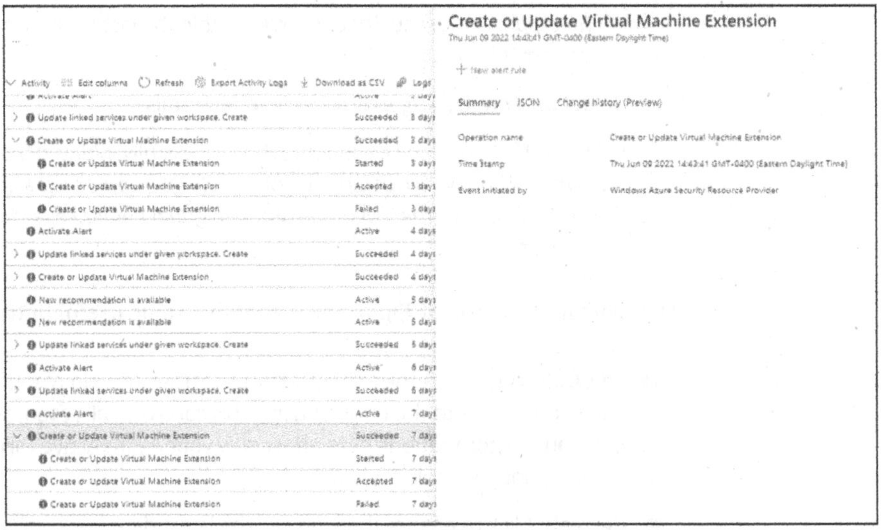

FIGURE 15-2:
Viewing the
JSON source for
an Azure Activity
Log event.

>> **Logs:** Takes you to Activity Log Analytics. You'll be prompted to create a Log Analytics workspace if you haven't already done so.

>> **Pin Current Filters:** Enables you to place the current filtered result set in a dashboard tile. This option can be convenient when you need to keep a steady eye on Activity Log data.

>> **Reset Filters:** Removes any user-defined filters and resets the view to the default.

Clicking an Activity Log event shows you a summary. The Summary tab, shown in Figure 15-2, shows general information. Click the JSON tab to reveal details in JSON format. This JSON provides deep details concerning the event and is useful when you perform forensic troubleshooting to figure out exactly who did what and when in your subscription.

TECHNICAL STUFF

Activity Log Analytics is a premium (paid) service that allows you to consolidate Activity Log data from multiple subscriptions; configure longer data archival policies; run interactive queries; and build dynamic reports on query data. You can find out more about Activity Log Analytics at `https://docs.microsoft.com/azure/azure-monitor/platform/activity-log-collect`.

Azure Monitor Diagnostics Settings

Azure Monitor Diagnostics Settings is a central control station for enabling non-VM resource diagnostics. Follow these steps to enable resource diagnostics in Azure Monitor:

1. **In Azure Monitor, select the Diagnostics Settings blade.**

2. **Use the filter controls to narrow your view, and select a resource from the list.**

   In Figure 15-3, you see three resources from one subscriptions. This example selects the `site-recovery-vault-rg` network security group.

3. **On the Diagnostics Settings blade, click Add Diagnostic Setting.**

   The two types of Azure Monitor diagnostics data are logs and metrics. Some Azure resources have both; others have one or the other.

REMEMBER

4. **Complete the Diagnostics Settings blade.**

   Compare what you see with Figure 15-4. Give the diagnostics stream a name; I always append -diag to the resource name.

   You can send diagnostics data to one or more of the following targets:

   - *Storage Account:* The benefit is long-term archival storage.

   - *Event Hub:* The benefit is subscribing to the diagnostics streams in real time.

   - *Log Analytics:* The benefit is the powerful querying/reporting functionality inherent in Log Analytics.

   You can revisit these settings later if you need to change them.

Besides the diagnostics settings targets, you need to specify which log(s) and metrics categories you want to collect. Different resources collect different types of metrics and logs. For example, network security group diagnostics logs any time an NSG rule is fired.

5. **Click Save to commit your changes.**

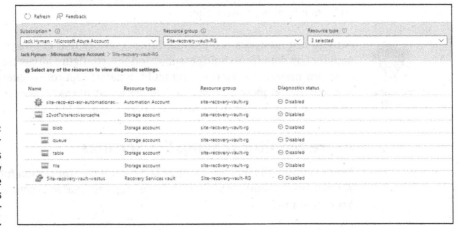

FIGURE 15-3:
Azure Monitor
Diagnostics
settings allow
you to enable
diagnostics
centrally for
several resources.

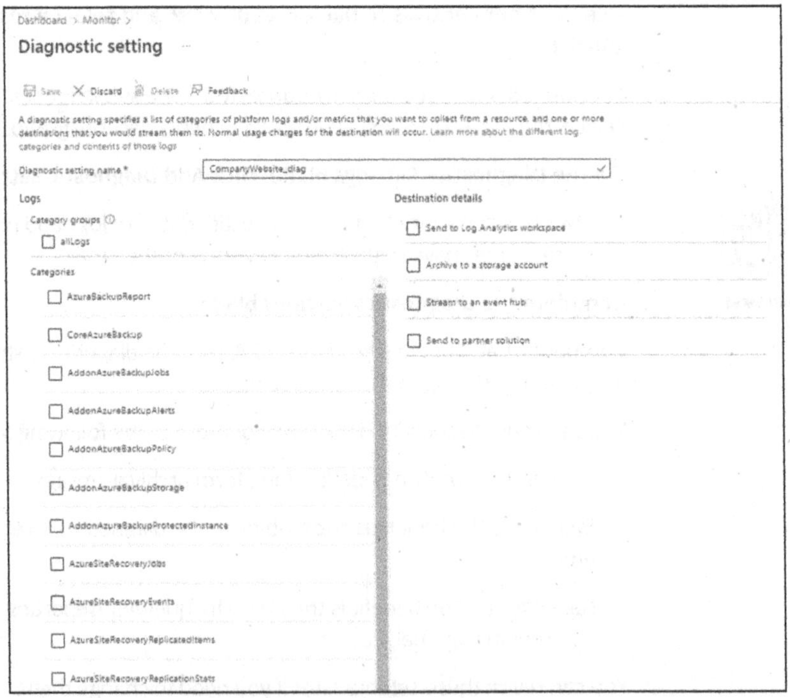

FIGURE 15-4:
Configuring
Azure resource
diagnostics.

VIEWING YOUR DIAGNOSTICS DATA

TIP

How you analyze your resource diagnostics data depends on which target(s) you chose for those data streams. If you choose Log Analytics, for example, you'd run KQL queries in Azure's Log Search interface. You can also use Monitor's metrics and alerting systems, which I cover later in this chapter.

WARNING

You'll be charged for using any other Azure resource, even as part of a separate configuration. In configuring diagnostics to store resource data in a storage account, for example, you're accepting those additional storage account-related charges.

VM diagnostic settings

VM resource diagnostics are handled separately from other Azure resources. Enabling VM diagnostics involves installing the Azure Diagnostics extension. As you might expect, the specific metrics and logs collected by this extension depend on the operating system (Windows or Linux).

To enable VM diagnostics, follow these steps:

1. **Navigate to the VM for which you want to enable diagnostics, and select the Diagnostics Settings menu item.**

2. **On the Diagnostic Settings Overview page, click Enable Guest-Level Monitoring (see Figure 15-5).**

   It's important to note that Azure collects very basic VM data with no agent required. By enabling guest diagnostics, you instruct Azure to collect more detailed, granular diagnostics data for the virtual machine.

3. **In the VM's settings list, click Extensions, and verify that the Azure Diagnostics extension has been installed.**

   In Figure 15-6, you can see there are various extensions tied to the virtual machine, which includes VM diagnostics and other extensions installed.

4. **Return to the VM's Diagnostics Settings blade, and review the configuration options.**

   You can collect the following data on Windows VMs:

   - Insights
   - Alerts

- Event logs

- Memory crash dumps

You can collect the following data on Linux VMs:

- System hardware metrics (processor, memory, network, file system, and disk)

- Syslog events from any enabled daemons running on the VM

TECHNICAL STUFF

You must have an existing storage account in a Linux VM's region to enable guest diagnostics on that VM.

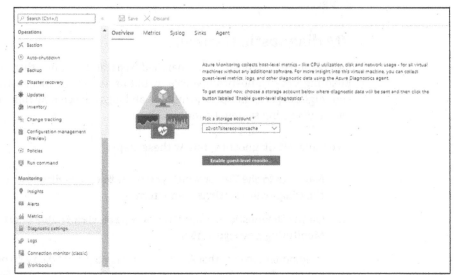

FIGURE 15-5:
Enabling
Guest-Level
Monitoring.

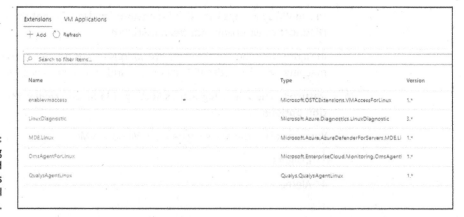

FIGURE 15-6:
Reviewing
the installed
extensions
on the virtual
machine.

VM boot diagnostics

I nearly always recommend that my customers enable boot diagnostics on Windows Server and Linux VMs. Boot diagnostics data is stored in a designated storage account's blob service. This feature provides two benefits to administrators:

>> Boot diagnostics periodically take a screenshot of your VM's screen — a convenient sanity check to ensure that your VM isn't in a stopped state.

>> Boot diagnostics enable the serial console — a diagnostic backdoor into your system whereby you obtain a command-line connection directly through the Azure portal. Serial console can be lifesaving when your VM's networking stack is offline and you can't reach the VM via the Internet or your VPN connection.

Plotting resource metrics and raising alerts

In this section, I return to Azure Monitor to examine Azure resource and VM diagnostic data. As mentioned earlier, the Azure platform gathers basic resource metrics that are viewable in Azure Monitor. You gain much deeper insight, however, when you formally enable diagnostics on your resources.

Charting metrics

Metrics are time-series values sampled from your resource periodically. Follow these steps to use Azure Monitor's Metrics Explorer to plot CPU consumption on multiple VMs:

1. **Browse to the Azure Monitor settings list, and select Metrics.**

Metrics explorer appears on the Details blade.

2. **Click the pencil icon next to Chart Title, and give your chart a meaningful name.**

I called mine "Virtual Machine CPU Utilizations."

3. **Complete the first resource row as follows:**

- *Resource:* You can select multiple subscriptions and/or resource groups to get a wide span of resources to choose among. Make sure that you select the Virtual Machines resource type. Sadly, you can choose only one VM here; you'll need to create additional resource rows to plot metrics from other VMs on the same chart.

- *Metric Namespace:* Select Virtual Machine Host. This value depends on the resource you've loaded into the Resource property.

- *Metric:* Select Percentage CPU. The metrics are specific to the resource and may be a longer or shorter list depending on whether you've enabled resource diagnostics.

- *Aggregation:* Select Average.

4. **If you have more than one VM, add at least one more resource row to plot metrics from additional VMs.**

   To do so, click Add Metric on the toolbar and then choose the same properties you selected when you defined the first resource row. Figure 15-7 shows a resulting chart.

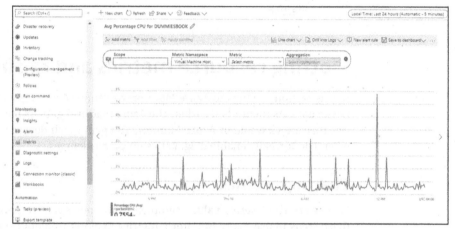

FIGURE 15-7: Metrics Explorer in Azure Monitor gives you at-a-glance diagnostics and performance data.

TIP

Your metrics charts disappear when you click away from Metrics Explorer in Azure Monitor. Click Share and then select Copy Link, and save that link in your web browser's Favorites list. That way, you can get your chart back when Azure vaporizes it.

Configuring alerts

Alerts in Azure are super-powerful because you can configure Azure to take automated corrective actions whenever an alert is triggered. An action group can contain one or more of the following action types:

>> **Automation Runbook:** Runs your Azure PowerShell or Python script

>> **Azure Function:** Runs your Function App function

>> **Logic App:** Runs a designated Logic App workflow

>> **Email/SMS/Push/Voice:** Notifies one or more accounts in various ways

>> **ITSM:** Creates a ticket in your IT service management platform

>> **Webhook:** Sends a particularly formatted HTTP(S) response to a receiving service (Azure Event Grid, Function App, Logic App, and so forth)

Suppose that you need to configure an alert such that you receive an email notification whenever your winserver VM is restarted. You define your action group, create the alert rule, and restart the VM to test the alert.

Creating an action group

Follow these steps to create an action group that sends you an email notification:

1. **In Azure Monitor, select the Alerts blade, and then click Manage Actions.**

2. **On the Manage Actions blade, click Add Action group.**

   You can consider an action group to be a container that holds one or more individual action rules.

3. **Complete the Add Action Group form.**

   After you supply an action group name, short name, subscription, and resource group, the real work begins: defining your action. Here's how I set my email-alert Action group action rule:

   - *Action Name:* Send-email.

   - *Action Type:* Email/SMS/Push/Voice. You're prompted to specify the destination email address.

   As you'd expect, each action type has its own subconfiguration.

4. **Click OK to confirm your configuration.**

Now it's time to create the rule, which you bind to the action group.

TIP

Microsoft intentionally separated the action groups and action rules from your alerts. This way you can easily reuse the same action groups and rules with different alerts. Pretty convenient, eh?

Defining an alert rule

Azure alerts supports two signal types:

>> **Metrics:** These are the same metrics you've been working with throughout the chapter.

>> **Activity Log:** These are events tracked in Activity Log. For a VM restart condition, you need this signal type.

Due to Azure platform limitations, you're limited to two metrics signals or one Activity Log signal per alert rule.

Follow these steps to create an alert rule that triggers whenever a given VM is restarted:

1. **On the Azure Monitor Alerts blade, click New Alert Rule.**

   The Create Rule blade appears.

2. **In the Resource section of the Create Rule blade, click Select.**

3. **Choose the VM you want to monitor.**

   Use the filter controls to drill through your subscriptions, locations, and resource types.

4. **In the Condition section, click Add, choose the Restart Virtual Machine Activity Log signal, and then click Done.**

   The specific configuration options depend on which metric or Activity Log signal you selected. I show you this interface in Figure 15-8.

5. **In the Actions section, click Select Action Group, and choose your action group.**

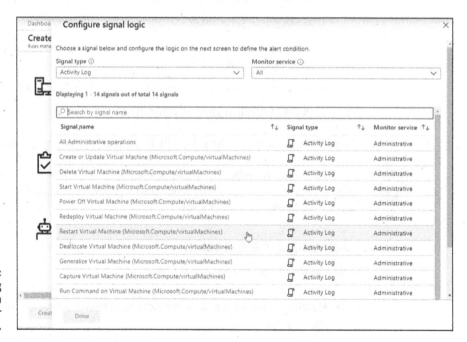

FIGURE 15-8: Configuring signal logic for an Azure Monitor alert rule.

6. **In the Alert Details section, complete the alert metadata.**

This metadata consists of the alert rule name, optional description, target resource group, and whether you want to enable the rule. Figure 15-9 shows my completed rule definition.

Be sure to select Yes for Enable Rule upon Creation so that you can test it out.

7. **Click Create Alert Rule to complete the configuration.**

FIGURE 15-9:
Completing the
alert rule
definition.

Testing the alert

You can view your alert rule definitions by revisiting the Azure Monitor Alerts blade and clicking Manage Alert Rules.

In my environment, I uploaded a very large image to the VM. The result was a trigger that available memory exceeded the normal threshold. Within a few minutes, I received my alert notifications. The composite screenshot in Figure 15-10 shows the Azure portal notification details.

APPLICATION INSIGHTS

An in-depth discussion of Application Insights falls outside the scope of this book. To give you the briefest possible introduction, however, let me tell you that Application Insights is an Azure application performance management product that works with all Azure App Service applications. Application Insights enables you to collect detailed telemetry from your applications and display the data meaningfully in numeric and/or chart views. It shows developers where users go in their App Service apps and what sorts of performance-related troubles happen so the developers can identify and resolve these bugs. For more information about Application Insights, visit https://docs.microsoft.com/azure/azure-monitor/app/app-insights-overview.

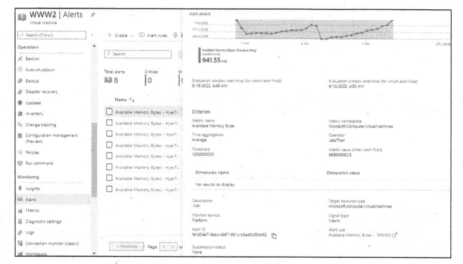

FIGURE 15-10: Example of triggered alert in Azure portal.

Azure Log Analytics

Having spent some time in Azure Monitor, you've seen some of the myriad log files that your Azure resources create. Think of all the ways that data is represented and imagine a way to put all your logs in a single data lake and run queries against it seamlessly.

Log Analytics is a platform in which you do just that: aggregate VM and Azure resource log files into a single data lake (called a *Log Analytics workspace*) and then run queries against the data, using a Microsoft-created data access language called Kusto (pronounced KOO-stoh) Query Language (KQL).

You'll find that Log Analytics somehow normalizes all these different log streams into a tabular structure. You'll also discover that KQL is similar to Structured Query Language (SQL), the data access language that is standard for relational databases.

Creating a Log Analytics workspace

The first order of business is to deploy a Log Analytics workspace. Then you can onboard as few or as many Azure resources to the workspace as you need. You can also deploy more than one Log Analytics workspace to keep your log data separate.

To create a new Azure Log Analytics workspace, follow these steps:

1. **In the Azure portal, browse to the Log Analytics Workspaces blade, and click Add.**

   The Log Analytics workspace blade appears.

2. **Complete the Log Analytics workspace blade.**

   You'll need to provide the following details:

   - Workspace name
   - Subscription name
   - Resource group name
   - Location
   - Pricing tier

3. **Click OK to create the workspace.**

4. **Click OK to submit your deployment.**

Pricing is beyond the scope of this book, but Log Analytics has a free tier as well as several paid tiers. The biggest free tier limitations are

>> Data ingestion limit of 5GB per month

>> 30-day data retention limit

Connecting data sources to the workspace

With your workspace online, you're ready to onboard Azure resources into the said workspace. To connect Azure resources to the workspace, go back to Monitor Diagnostic Settings, enable diagnostics, and point the log streams to your workspace. (Refer to Figure 15-4 to see what the interface looks like.)

You can connect VMs to the workspace directly from the workspace's Settings menu. Follow these steps:

1. **In your Log Analytics workspace settings menu, click Virtual Machines.**

   You see a list of all VMs in the workspace's region. You can see which VMs are connected to the workspace and which are not.

2. **If necessary, use the filter controls until you see the VM you want to connect.**

   You can link a VM to only one workspace at a time.

3. **Select the desired VM, and click Connect.**

   Behind the scenes, Azure deploys the Log Analytics agent (formerly called Microsoft Monitoring Agent) to the VM.

4. **Verify that the VM is connected to the workspace.**

   You can see this information in your workspace settings. Or you can revisit your VM's Extensions blade (see Chapter 5 for more information about how to do this) and verify that the MicrosoftMonitoringAgent extension is installed.

You can disconnect a VM from its current workspace and connect it to another one. This operation is trivial, taking only two minutes or so to complete. To do this, simply select the VM from within the workspace and click Disconnect from the toolbar.

USING BOTH DIAGNOSTICS AND LOG ANALYTICS

You may be thinking, "The Azure platform collects basic VM diagnostics with no agent required. Then you deployed the Azure Diagnostics agent to collect deeper metrics and logs. Now the VM is connected to a Log Analytics workspace. What now?"

Specifically, the question is whether you need both the Diagnostics and Log Analytics extensions installed simultaneously and what effect they have on performance. There's no noticeable performance penalty for having both agents installed on your VMs simultaneously. Diagnostics tracks metrics and log data, whereas Log Analytics stores only log/table data.

Writing KQL queries

You need to know a bit about how to access your Log Analytics workspace data with KQL. KQL is fast and easy to learn, and it should seem familiar to you if you've used Splunk Search Processing Language, SQL, PowerShell, or Bash shell.

Touring the Log Search interface

You can get to the Log Search interface by opening Monitor and selecting the Logs blade. Another way to get there (and the way I prefer) is to go to your Log Analytics workspace and click the Log setting.

A third method is to use the Log Analytics Query Playground where you can work with an enormous data set, getting to know Log Analytics before generating a meaningful data set.

Follow these steps to run some sample KQL queries:

1. **Open a new browser tab, and navigate to** `https://portal.loganalytics.io/demo`.

   This site is authenticated but don't worry: You're using Microsoft's subscription, not your own.

2. **Expand some of the tables in the Schema list (shown in Figure 15-11).**

   There's a lot in this list. Log Analytics normalizes all incoming data streams and projects them into a table-based structure.

   Expand the LogManagement category; then expand the Alert table, where you can use KQL to query Azure Monitor alerts. The *t* entries (shown under the expanded SecurityEvent item in Figure 15-11) are properties that behave like columns in a relational database table.

3. **On the Log Search toolbar, click Query Explorer, expand the Favorites list, and run the query Security Events, Count, by Computer During the Last 12 Hours.**

   This environment is a sandbox. Microsoft has not only onboarded untold resources into this workspace but also has written sample queries to let you kick the tires.

4. **In the results list, click Chart to switch from Table to Chart view.**

   You can visualize your query results automatically with a single button click. Not every results set lends itself to graphical representation but the capability is tremendous.

TECHNICAL STUFF

AZURE SOLUTIONS

You may have noticed tables that reference Azure products beyond VMs and individual resources in the Log Search query interface. I'm talking about categories such as DNS Analytics, Office 365, Security Center, SQL Assessment, and Network Monitoring.

These Log Analytics tables appear when you enable Azure Solutions. In the Azure Marketplace, for example, you can load the Azure SQL Analytics solution, which gives Log Analytics insight into your SQL Servers (virtual, physical, on-premises or cloud) along with their databases.

The idea is that, eventually, all monitoring roads in Azure will lead to Log Analytics. This platform is extremely wide-reaching and powerful; dive into it with gusto.

5. **Click Export, and save your query results (displayed columns only) to a CSV file.**

Note the link to Power BI, Microsoft's cloud-based business intelligence/dashboard generation tool.

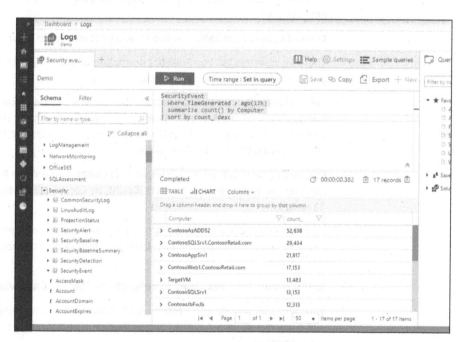

FIGURE 15-11:
Azure Log Analytics Log Search interface.

Writing basic KQL queries

For fun, I want to put you through an obstacle course of common KQL queries. Click the plus sign in the Log Search query interface (visible in Figure 15-11) to open a new tab — a multitab interface like those in Visual Studio and Visual Studio Code.

To get a feel for a table, you can instruct Azure to display any number of rows in no particular order. To display 10 records from the SecurityEvent table, for example, use the following command:

```
SecurityEvent
| take 10
```

Did you notice that the query editor attempted to autocomplete your query as you typed? Take advantage of that convenience by pressing Tab when you see the appropriate autocomplete choice appear.

Use the search keyword to perform a free-text query. The following query looks in the SecurityEvent table for any records that include the string "Cryptographic":

```
search in (SecurityEvent) "Cryptographic"
| take 20
```

When you press Enter, you'll notice the pipe character (|). This character functions the same way here as it does in PowerShell or the Bash shell. Output from one query segment is passed to the next segment via pipe — a powerful construct for sure.

You can ramp up the complexity by finishing with filtering and sorting. The following code both filters on a condition and sorts the results in a descending manner based on time:

```
SecurityEvent
| where Level == 8 and EventID == 4672
| sort by TimeGenerated desc
```

If you're thinking, "Wow, these KQL queries act an awful lot like SQL!" you're right on the money. Welcome to Log Analytics!

ON THE WEB

I adapted the KQL examples in this chapter from the Microsoft docs. For more information, see the "Getting Started with Log Queries in Azure Monitor" tutorial at https://docs.microsoft.com/azure/azure-monitor/log-query/get-started-queries.

Monitoring and Tweaking Your Azure Spending

So far you have learned about the tools to monitor system performance. As you may have noticed in your configuration of these monitoring tools, you are often charged a small fee for Azure to watch over the environment. For example, a notification that triggers CPU utilization may cost 20 cents per month per virtual environment. That's chump change when you think about it, but it can ensure that you and your organization's resources remain healthy.

But, these little costs can add up to quite a handsome bill at the end of the month. No one likes surprises, and Microsoft knows this.

You have another set of tools available to you to help you monitor your Azure spending. Unlike system monitoring, which costs a few pennies here and there, Azure Cost and Billing Management tools are one-hundred percent free. Go to the Cost Management & Billing pane to review your Azure costs. You'll want to select Cost Management to review your spending under various scenarios.

Cost analysis

Once you select Cost Management + Billing, a secondary pane appears in which you find all the Cost Management monitoring tools under this category. The most important is the Cost Analysis tool. Why, you ask? With this tool, you can view your past, present, and even forecasted spending. An important observation is to look where your money is being allocated. In the example shown in Figure 15-12, you find the current monthly bill, forecasted bill, and your past invoice date. An essential series of metrics to review are

>> Service

>> Location

>> Resource Group

PART 5Going Beyond the Basics in Microsoft Azure

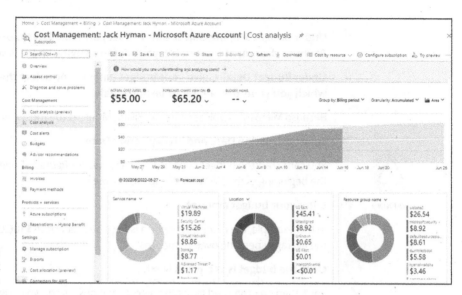

FIGURE 15-12:
Azure Cost
Analysis example.

In this case, a significant amount of spending is being allocated to Virtual Machines and Azure Security Center. The majority of resources are located in the US East. The resource group with the highest spending is the group website2.

Cost alerts and budgets

Sometimes you may use Azure for occasional development and application testing. Other times, your Azure deployments are intended for always-on production activity. What happens when you want to limit your spending for specific VM instances for a given month? Or perhaps you want to set an alert to indicate that your monthly budget has reached a certain percentage (and dollar amount). With Cost Alerts and Budgets, two options under the Cost Management + Billing pane, you can configure both options quickly.

To set a cost alert, follow these steps:

1. **Select Cost Management ⇨ Cost Alerts.**

   A screen appears that requires you to add an alert.

2. **Select Add ⇨ Add Budget from the navigation bar.**

   The Create Budget screen appears, as shown in Figure 15-13.

3. **Under Budget Scoping, select that the scope should have more than one Azure environment (otherwise, your default environment is set).**

4. **Under Budget Details, give your budget a name and select the period in which you want the budget to be applicable.**

   Because Microsoft invoices monthly, Billing Month is the most common option.

5. **Select a Creation Date and an Expiration Date.**

WARNING

   You can't start the budget cycle the very day you configure it. Budgets start at the beginning of the following complete invoice cycle.

6. **Enter your budget amount.**

   In this example, the recommendation is for a budget above $106.00, as this is the average spending over 12 months.

7. **Once the budget is set, press Next.**

   You'll then be prompted to set the alert conditions, as shown in Figure 15-14. You'll need to select the following:

   - Type (Actual or Forecasted Budget)

   - % of Budget, which requires a value to be entered

   - Action Group (assign to the appropriate group for storage)

TIP

   An essential part of an alert is the email notification. Every time the alert triggers, the selected users will be notified by email that the monetary threshold has been breached.

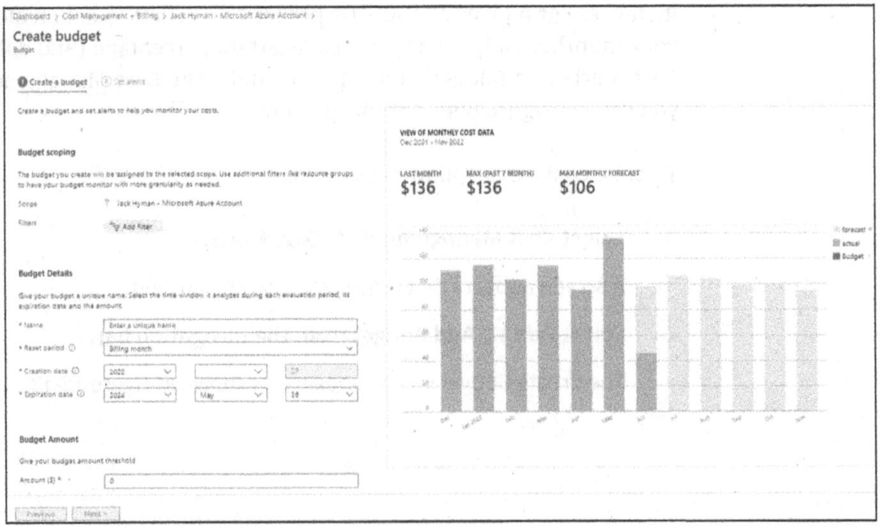

FIGURE 15-13:
Azure Budget
Creation.

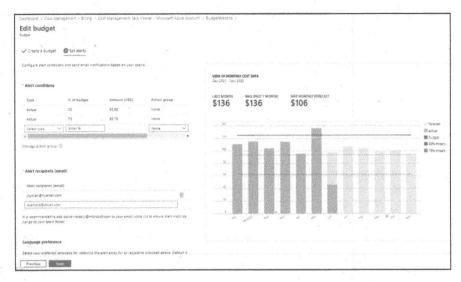

FIGURE 15-14:
Azure Budget
Alerts.

8. Once you have entered the email address, select the language preference for the notification.

9. To complete the alert creation, press Create.

Azure Advisor

One last monitoring tool that helps users improve their environment reliability, security, and performance while reducing spending is Azure Advisor. By using Azure Advisor, a user can evaluate a specific subscription and resource group. Advisor looks to optimize the subscription using its known telemetry against Azure resources and configurations.

Azure Advisor is accessible using the Azure portal or one of the command-line tools. In the example shown in Figure 15-15, the Advisor Score is 90 percent. The advisor recommends that I tweak two system components to ensure operational reliability. For all other areas, best practices are being enforced.

FIGURE 15-15:
Azure Advisor.

IN THIS CHAPTER

» Migrating on-premises data and
databases into Azure

» Migrating on-premises physical and
virtual servers into Azure

» Establishing a VPN to connect your
on-premises network to Azure

Chapter **16**

Extending Your On-Premises Environment to Azure

I n this chapter, I cover the task of migrating on-premises data and applications into Azure. The good news is that Microsoft provides many tools to make the process easier. I also discuss how to create a hybrid cloud in which you extend your on-premises network infrastructure into an Azure virtual network.

Data Migration Options

Managing data on-premises can be both expensive and stressful. There's data resiliency to consider, as well as disaster recovery. You have security issues such as data encryption, and you have to be concerned about running out of space and having to make additional capital expenditures to expand your local storage fabric.

For these reasons and more, you may want or need to move local data into Azure. You have three options for doing that:

>> Blob copy

>> Azure Data Box

>> Azure Migrate

Blob copy

The most straightforward way to get local blob data into a storage account is to do file copies. You could use Azure Storage Explorer, but a better option is the AzCopy command-line tool, available free at https://docs.microsoft.com/azure/storage/common/storage-use-azcopy-v10.

Suppose you have 2TB of data in a server directory called D:\backup-archive, and you want to copy these files to a container on Azure named backup-archive in your azuredummies storage account.

After you open an elevated command prompt on the file server, you authenticate to Azure with AzCopy this way:

```
azcopy login
```

Next, you perform the copy (note that the following code should be on one line; I had to break the line so it would fit on the printed page):

```
azcopy copy "D:\backup-archive" https://azuredummies.
        blob.core.windows.net/
        backup-archive
        --recursive --put-md5
```

The --recursive flag ensures that you copy all subfolders inside the parent folder. The --put-md5 flag instructs AzCopy to verify that the copied files match their local versions through MD5 checksum verification.

The upside to this data migration method is that it's very inexpensive, barring network bandwidth. The downside is that the process could take hours or days to complete. Also, although AzCopy includes retry logic in the event of a copy interruption, the program will abort after a 15-minute timeout, which can make your data migration process take longer yet.

Azure Data Box

Azure Data Box is a collection of physical storage appliances (and one virtual option) that you rent from Microsoft. The high-level Data Box workflow is

1. Order your Data Box from the Azure portal.

2. Connect Data Box to your local computer or network.

3. Use Data Box's local web portal to structure how you want the Azure-side data to look (storage accounts, containers, and so on).

4. Copy data from your local environment to Data Box.

5. Ship the Data Box to your primary Azure region.

   Microsoft unpacks your data into your Azure subscription.

Here's a rundown of the Data Box family members:

>> **Data Box Disk:** 8TB SSD drive, available in packs of five (40TB). Plug the disks into your local workstation by using a USB/SATA interface. Data Box Disk offers 128-bit encryption.

>> **Data Box:** Ruggedized appliance with 100TB capacity; connects to your LAN with high-speed Ethernet ports. Data Box features AES-256 encryption.

>> **Data Box Heavy:** Wheeled drive cart with 1PB capacity.

>> **Data Box Gateway:** A virtual appliance version of Data Box Edge.

TIP

Azure has a legacy offline data migration product called Import/Export Service whereby you prepare your own hard drives and ship them to Microsoft. I chose to ignore this option for this book because Data Box is much more flexible and cost-effective. Check the documentation for more information at https://docs.microsoft.com/azure/storage/common/storage-import-export-service.

Figure 16-1 shows the various physical Data Box form factors. The Data Box Gateway is a software appliance; therefore, it's not shown.

The advantage of Data Box is that it's a convenient way to get large data volumes into Azure. The disadvantage (with the exception of Data Box Gateway) is the latency between ordering, filling, shipping, and unpacking the appliance. You may not be able to afford that kind of data latency.

What is your alternative, then? In the "Hybrid Cloud Options" section, I describe the virtual private network (VPN) and ExpressRoute options for establishing secure, high-speed, always-on connectivity to Azure.

Data Box

This ruggedized device with 100-TB capacity uses standard NAS protocols and common copy tools. It features AES 256-bit encryption for safer transit.

Order Data Box >

Data Box Disk

Our 8-TB SSD with a USB/SATA interface has 128-bit encryption. Customize it to your needs—it comes in packs of up to five for a total of 40 TB.

Order Data Box Disk >

Data Box Heavy

This ruggedized, self-contained device is designed to lift 1 PB of data to the cloud.

Sign up for Data Box Heavy >

FIGURE 16-1:
The Data Box
product family.

Azure Migrate: Database Assessment

Instead of, or in addition to, blob (file) data, you likely have on-premises SQL Server databases that you want to migrate to Azure in an offline or online manner. The Microsoft-supported database migration workflow involves two phases:

>> **Assessment:** Evaluate your current workload parameters and determine which Azure product is the best fit and at which pricing tier/scale.

>> **Migration:** Determine your tolerance for network latency, and then decide on an offline or online migration method.

Performing the database assessment

Practically all data migration options nowadays happen under the Azure Migrate product umbrella. Follow these steps to create a new database migration project and kick off an assessment:

1. **In the Azure portal, browse to the Azure Migrate blade.**

   If the blade is not visible, search the word Migrate and select Azure Migrate.

2. **In the Migration Goals section, click Databases Only**

   The Getting Started blade appears.

3. **Click Create Project.**

   The Create project screen appears, as shown in Figure 16-2.

4. **Assuming you've never created an assessment project before, enter the following to initiate a project:**

   - Subscription
   - Resource group
   - Project name
   - Geography
   - Connectivity method

5. **On the Details pane in the Getting Started section, click Add Tool(s).**

6. **On the Select Migration tool blade page, choose the Assess button under Azure Migrate: DatabaseAssessment.**

7. **Click the link to download Data Migration Assistant (DMA).**

   DMA is a free desktop app that you download and run on your administrative workstation. Figure 16-3 shows the DMA interface.

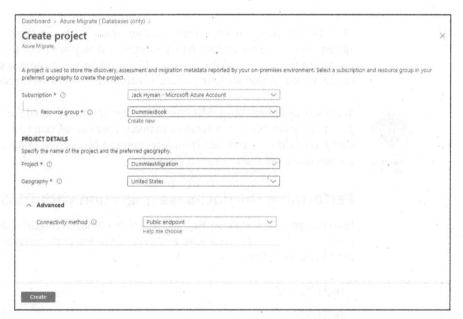

FIGURE 16-2:
Create Project for
Azure Migrate.

When you run DMA, you model your local SQL Server database against one of four targets:

>> Azure SQL Database

>> Azure SQL Database Managed Instance

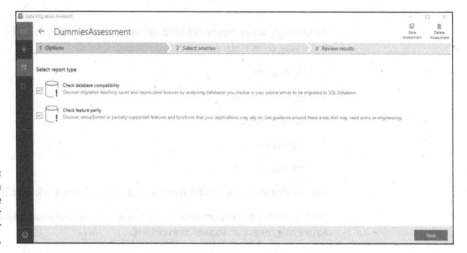

FIGURE 16-3:
Complete a
Database
Assessment for
Compatibility or
Feature Parity.

>> SQL Server on Azure Virtual Machines

>> SQL Server

DMA checks your database compatibility against your defined Azure database option, and it checks feature parity to ensure that you're not using features on-premises that aren't available in Azure. It also allows you to upload your assessment results to your Azure Migrate project, which feeds into the next phase: migration.

TECHNICAL STUFF

Microsoft designed Azure Migrate to work without the need for a secure virtual private network (VPN) connection. Instead, your connection to Azure is encrypted using the TLS/SSL protocol. Therefore, you can be assured of data privacy before, during, and after the migration process.

Performing the database migration with DMS

In Azure, you use Database Migration Service (DMS) to migrate your assessed on-premises SQL Server databases to Azure. DMS supports several other database platforms, including

>> MongoDB

>> MySQL

>> AWS RDS for MySQL

>> PostgreSQL

>> AWS RDS for PostgreSQL

>> Oracle

Follow these steps to get started with DMS in the Azure portal:

1. **Select Servers, Databases, and Web Apps on the Azure Migrate blade.**

2. **Select the Click here button to add tools under Migration tools.**

3. **Chose the Azure Migrate option that best suits your need.**

4. **Click the Add Tool button.**

REMEMBER

Whereas database assessment required no VPN, you need to have an existing, secure connection path between your on-premises database server and Azure to complete the database migration with Azure Database Migration Services. This could be a point-to-site VPN, site-to-site VPN, or an ExpressRoute circuit.

Performing database migration with DMA

If establishing a VPN isn't workable, you can perform the database migration with the DMA tool, which uses standard secure web protocols and requires no VPN. Figure 16-4 shows the interface.

TIP

If you need to migrate only a small number of SQL Server databases, you likely don't need DMS. But if you're operating on a large number of potentially gigantic databases across vendors, DMS is a great fit.

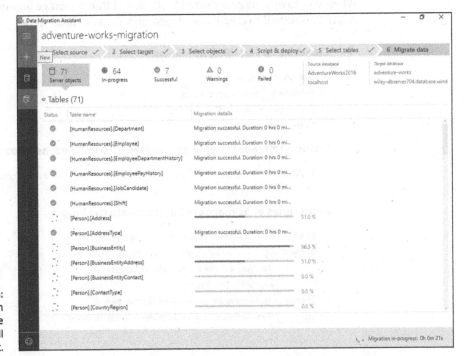

FIGURE 16-4:
The DMA tool can perform database migration as well as assessment.

Server Migration Options

The last category of migration is server migration. The most convenient way to migrate servers is with Azure Site Recovery (ASR), which supports physical and virtual servers, and also fully supports VMware and Hyper-V virtualization environments.

However, you also can migrate on-premises VHDs to an Azure storage account by using AzCopy; then you convert the uploaded VHDs to managed disks.

VHD upload

A common, still-valid use for a tool such as AzCopy is migrating generalized VHDs from on-premises into Azure to Azure virtual machine (VM) deployments. To do that, you first upload your generalized Generation 1 VHD.

WARNING

Azure has been steadily rolling out support for Hyper-V Generation 2 VHDX files since 2019. It's a safe bet to go with a Generation 2 VHDX file unless the environment requires light resources or is somewhat old in nature. You may need to do some format conversion on your VM disks before transferring them to Azure, especially if you use VMware or another non-Microsoft hypervisor.

When you have your generalized VHD tucked into a storage account, you can use Azure PowerShell to create a managed disk. Follow these steps:

1. **Create some variables, as follows:**

```
$vmName = "vm-template"
$rgName = "myResourceGroup"
$location = "EastUS2"
$imageName = "myImage"
```

2. **Create a reference to your generalized VHD in Azure, as follows:**

```
$osVhdUri = https://mystorageaccount.blob.core.windows.net/vhdcontainer/
    vhdfilename.vhd
```

3. **Run a series of AzImage cmdlets to create the image:**

```
$imageConfig = New-AzImageConfig -Location $location
$imageConfig = Set-AzImageOsDisk -Image $imageConfig
        -OsType Windows -OsState Generalized
        -BlobUri $osVhdUri
$image = New-AzImage -ImageName $imageName
        -ResourceGroupName $rgName -Image $imageConfig
```

When you have your managed image in place, you can deploy new VMs based on that image. On the Basics tab of the Create a Virtual Machine blade, click Browse All Public and Private Images, and switch to the My Items tab. Chapter 5 covers creating an Azure VM.

Azure Migrate: Server Assessment

The other alternative is to use Azure Migrate as your on-premises server migration base of operations. Follow these steps to get things rolling:

1. **In the Azure portal, browse to the Azure Migrate blade, select Servers, Databases, and Web Apps, and then click Add Tool(s).**

2. **Complete the Migrate Create Project tab.**

   You need to fill in metadata: subscription, resource group, migrate project name, and geography.

3. **When the project is created, go to the area on the page that indicates Assessment Tools.**

   You can either discover your current environments available to migrate or select an assessment tool. Microsoft allows certain independent software vendor partners to include their tools in this list. Figure 16-5 shows this interface.

4. **Select the best migration tool for your environment, and then press Add Tools.**

You can then kick off a discovery and assessment process that takes different forms, depending on whether you have a Hyper-V or a VMware environment on-premises.

The discovery and assessment workflow

You download a Migrate VM appliance, stand it up in your local network, and let it do its work. The appliance does a good job of enumerating all your local servers and reporting on how they might translate into Azure VMs.

The collector appliance also sends its discovery and assessment data to your Migrate project for centralized tracking. The deliverables are a series of Microsoft Excel spreadsheets and Migrate data sent to your project.

Figure 16-6 shows an example server assessment report. Besides giving you VM size recommendations, the server assessment engine gives you cost estimates. In my work as an Azure solutions architect, I've never yet met a customer for whom minimizing cost wasn't a principal concern.

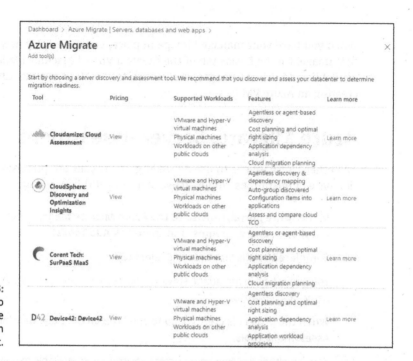

FIGURE 16-5:
Adding tools to
an Azure Migrate
server migration
project.

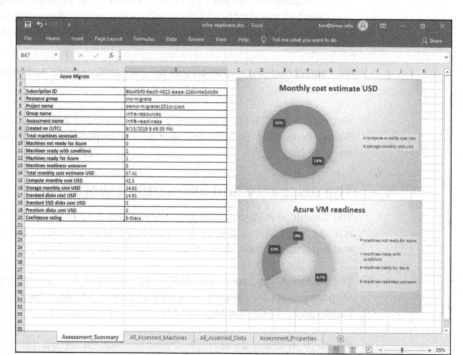

FIGURE 16-6:
Azure server
assessment
reports include
graphs and
table data.

In its documentation, Microsoft advises you to run your assessment for as long as possible to gather all peaks and valleys of your on-premises servers' performance. It isn't uncommon to run an assessment for two weeks to a month or more.

Azure Migrate: Server Migration

Before Migrate came along, the option for migrating on-premises servers via replication was using the Recovery Services vault and ASR. The ASR and Recovery Faculty functionality are now part of Azure Migrate as a configurable step.

Here is a high-level overview of what happens:

1. Create a virtual network environment in Azure for your on-premises VMs and physical servers.

2. Replicate your on-premises servers' disks to Azure until their data is synchronized.

3. Perform a failover from your local environment to your Azure virtual network.

4. Stop replication.

5. Decommission your on-premises servers because you no longer need them.

6. Continue to use your services in Azure.

You don't need a VPN or ExpressRoute connection to perform this Azure Migrate replication.

Replication is agentless for VMware environments as well as for Hyper-V.

The upside of Migrate server migration is that replication means nearly zero downtime. The downside is that the initial replication hit can be substantial and costly if you have a metered internet connection.

In Migrate terminology, *server migration* translates to "Replicate, failover, and don't fail back to the on-premises environment."

Hybrid Cloud Options

I'm closing this chapter with a survey of the two primary ways you can extend your on-premises environment into Azure:

>> Site-to-site (S2S) VPN

>> ExpressRoute circuit

Deploying a hybrid cloud is cost-, labor-, and time-intensive, so I can't get into the minute details of the process in this book, but I want to give you a global understanding of these technologies.

Site to Site (S2S) VPN

A VPN is a secure connection across an unsecure medium: the Internet. Azure S2S VPNs are always-on secure connections that tunnel your internet traffic by using the Internet Protocol Security (IPSec) and Internet Key Exchange (IKE) security protocols.

The value propositions of establishing a VPN tunnel between your local network and an Azure virtual network are manifold. The VPN allows you to do the following:

>> Join Azure VMs to your on-premises Active Directory domain.

>> Manage Azure VMs with System Center or other configuration management and monitoring platforms.

>> Administer on-premises VMs by using Azure management solutions.

>> Ensure data confidentiality between the local environment and Azure.

Extend is an appropriate word for an Azure hybrid cloud because the hybrid cloud enables you to make your on-premises network available to your Azure subscription, and vice versa.

Let me walk you through the parts and pieces of the S2S VPN. Figure 16-7 shows a high-level view of an Azure hybrid cloud:

>> The on-premises gateway

>> The virtual network gateway

>> The local network gateway

>> The connection

On-premises VPN gateway

Azure needs to know your local VPN gateway's public IP address as well as the network addresses of all your local virtual local area networks (VLANs). Azure stores this information in a resource called the local network gateway; you're responsible for configuring your on-premises VPN gateway with the Azure gateway's public IP address and preshared key.

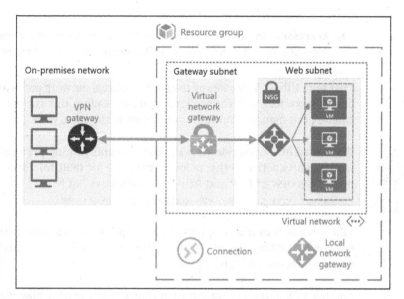

FIGURE 16-7:
Representative
Azure S2S VPN
topology.

ON THE
WEB

I recommend that you read "About VPN devices and IPsec/IKE parameters for Site-to-Site VPN Gateway connections" (quite the mouthful of an article title, isn't it?) at https://docs.microsoft.com/azure/vpn-gateway/vpn-gateway-about-vpn-devices. That article lists all the validated VPN devices that Microsoft guarantees will work with Azure. You'll likely find a link to a detailed configuration guide provided by your device manufacturer or Microsoft.

Azure VPNs use garden-variety VPN and routing protocols such as IPSec, IKE, and Border Gateway Protocol (BGP), so you shouldn't have difficulty configuring your local side of the VPN tunnel even if your hardware isn't on Microsoft's list of validated devices.

Virtual network gateway

This Azure resource is called a virtual network gateway rather than a VPN gateway because it's multifunctional. With this single resource, you can create any combination of the following connections:

>> **S2S VPN:** You configure this secure IPSec tunnel between an on-premises network or another cloud-hosted network and your Azure VNet.

>> **VNet-to-VNet VPN:** You configure this secure IPSec tunnel between two Azure virtual networks. Strictly speaking, this gateway is no longer necessary thanks to VNet peering.

>> **Point-to-Site VPN:** You can configure specific client computers to create their own private VPN tunnels into your virtual network. See the sidebar "Azure P2S VPN" later in this chapter for details.

>> **ExpressRoute:** You can configure a high-speed, always-on connection from your local environment to Azure that bypasses the Internet entirely.

That said, I'll use *VPN gateway* to signify a virtual network gateway configured for one or more S2S VPN connections. You are reading this correctly: A single VPN gateway can manage multiple connections at the same time.

ON THE WEB

When used in conjunction with the BGP dynamic routing protocol, the VPN gateway supports active-active failover scenarios for fault tolerance. For more info, read "Overview of BGP and Azure VPN Gateways" at `https://docs.microsoft.com/azure/vpn-gateway/vpn-gateway-bgp-overview`.

VPN gateway is available in more than 15 options. If you want to see the variety of options available, go to `https://docs.microsoft.com/azure/vpn-gateway/vpn-gateway-about-vpngateways`.

Another VPN gateway configuration choice is to consider how the device handles IPSec traffic routing. Route-based gateways use static routing tables, whereas policy-based gateways take advantage of dynamic routing protocols such as BGP. Your choice largely depends on how old your on-premises VPN hardware is. The general guidance is that older VPN hardware normally requires you to select the route-based gateway for the Azure side of the tunnel.

Finally, know that your VPN gateway needs to be placed on its own subnet in your hub virtual network. You may have noticed the Gateway Subnet button in your virtual network's Subnets blade. You don't have to use this button to create your gateway subnet, but the subnet does need the name GatewaySubnet (with no spaces).

TIP

Microsoft recommends using the smallest possible IP address space for the gateway subnet so that you conserve your private IP addresses. A /29 network address is a common choice.

Local network gateway

In Azure, the local network gateway is a resource that represents your local network. The local network gateway contains two or three important configuration values:

>> Public IP address of your on-premises VPN endpoint

>> The IP address ranges of your local network(s)

>> (Optionally) BGP settings such as autonomous system number and peer IP address

When you think about this, it makes sense because Azure needs to be able to identify not only the VPN concentrator at the other end of the tunnel but also the remote network segments that facilitate hybrid cloud traffic routing.

WARNING

Be careful of the private IP address ranges you use in Azure. The last thing you want to do is troubleshoot/unwind IP address conflicts between your on-premises networks and Azure VNets. Always use nonoverlapping IP address ranges.

Connection

Finally, you have the connection. The Azure connection resource is the glue that binds together your local network gateway and VPN gateway and defines your hybrid cloud handshake.

Within the Connection definition, you define the connection type (S2S, VNet-to-VNet, or ExpressRoute) and the preshared key that both the local gateway and VPN gateway will store for mutual authentication and data encryption.

REMEMBER

All the Azure hybrid cloud parts and pieces I've discussed are part of the Azure product family, so all the stuff covered in the book thus far — including RBAC, Policy, taxonomic tags, and so on — applies here just as much as to any other resource. Don't be afraid to apply your new knowledge.

ExpressRoute

As noted earlier in the book, ExpressRoute is similar to the Azure S2S VPN in that it is an always-on private connection between your on-premises network and an Azure VNet. ExpressRoute is unique because it's a truly private Azure connection that bypasses the public Internet. ExpressRoute links require no tunneling protocols.

TIP

AZURE P2S VPN

You may want to give some of your IT staff remote access to your Azure environment but you need all their data encrypted within a VPN tunnel. One option is the point-to-site (P2S) VPN configured in your Azure VPN Gateway settings. The P2S VPN uses firewall-friendly security protocols and digital certificates to give users a VPN link to Azure no matter where they are in the world. Specifically, Azure creates a client installation package based on your VPN settings. You deploy this package to your remote users, and they can start and end P2S sessions at their convenience.

The ExpressRoute circuit bandwidth options go from 50 Mbps to 10 Gbps. This means that you can have a connection to Azure that's as fast as your local network's speed. Data ingress into ExpressRoute is free but you're charged for data download unless you purchase ExpressRoute's unlimited data plan.

ExpressRoute has two peering options that you can use separately or in combination:

>> **Azure private peering:** ExpressRoute link from on-premises into an Azure VNet

>> **Microsoft peering:** ExpressRoute link from on-premises into Office 365 or Dynamics 365

Figure 16-8 depicts a typical ExpressRoute implementation.

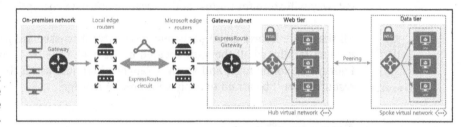

FIGURE 16-8: ExpressRoute representative topology.

You need two edge routers to build an ExpressRoute connection. You also need to work with a local third-party ExpressRoute connectivity provider to help you peer into the Microsoft cloud platform.

Most customers locate a local ExpressRoute service provider by asking their Internet Service Provider, consulting with a Microsoft Partner, or performing a good old-fashioned online search.

Introducing Azure Arc

Arc is a solution for deploying Azure services anywhere and extending Azure-based management to a hybrid, multi-cloud infrastructure.

The Arc use case

TECHNICAL
STUFF

In information technology, *governance* refers to the policies and procedures your business has in place to ensure compliance with organizational and legal requirements. In Azure, governance is also used to limit cost, maximize security, and understand which groups own which Azure-based resources.

The Azure VPN and ExpressRoute options extend your on-premises network into Azure so that you can integrate Azure-based VMs and other resources more directly into your local IT governance strategy.

By contrast, Arc brings core elements of Azure Resource Manager (ARM) into your local networks as well as those you maintain in other clouds. Figure 16-9 shows an overview of the Azure topology.

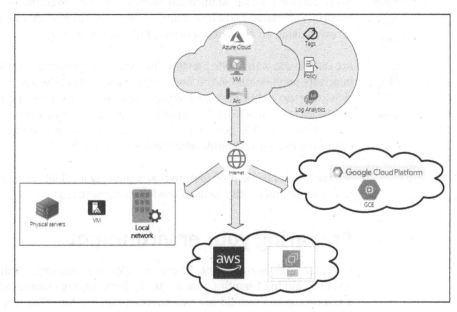

FIGURE 16-9: Arc topology overview.

In Figure 16-9, notice how the flow works. Without any VPN or ExpressRoute requirement, you can extend core Azure features such as tags, policy, and log analytics not only to your local network, but also to other clouds, such as Amazon Web Services and Google Cloud Platform.

The second value proposition that Arc brings to the table is the notion of deploying Azure resources directly in your local environment. You can use ARM templates, for example, to deploy VMs, databases, and Kubernetes clusters into your own data centers and then manage these resources right alongside your cloud-native resources using Azure tools.

Arc family members

As of this writing, the Arc product family includes three members that enable you to complete certain tasks:

>> **Azure Arc for Servers:** Manage virtual and physical machines that are outside Azure by using native Azure tools.

>> **Azure Arc for Data Services:** Run Azure data services such as Azure SQL Database and Azure Database for PostgreSQL on-premises or in another cloud environment.

>> **Azure Arc for Kubernetes:** Deploy and manage Kubernetes applications across environments.

Azure Arc for Enabled Application Services, which covers the ability to run App Service, Functions, and Logic Apps, is in preview as of this writing but can be accessed using an Azure Arc-enabled Kubernetes cluster.

Arc for Servers is in public preview, and Arc for Kubernetes and data platform are in private preview status. You normally have to apply to be a part of a private preview, whereas public preview features are available to some or all Azure customers. Be aware that Microsoft normally doesn't support or supply an SLA on Azure preview features. The general guidance is that you should run Azure preview features only in your testing/development environments.

Arc for Servers is the only feature that's publicly available at this writing; therefore, that product is the focus of the following sections.

Preparing your environment

In my local lab environment, I have two VMs: one running Windows Server 2019 and one running Ubuntu Linux 20.04. To keep my Arc environment tidy, I create a resource group to hold my two on-premises machines. In this section, I show you how to use Arc for Servers to onboard these machines into an Azure subscription.

Follow these steps to create a new resource group in the Azure portal:

1. **Search for resource groups, and browse to the Resource Groups blade.**

   The Resource groups blade appears.

2. **On the Resource Groups blade, click Add.**

   The Create a Resource Group blade appears.

3. **On the Create a Resource Group blade, fill out the Basics form, and then click Review + Create.**

All you provide here is the appropriate Azure subscription, resource group name, and region. As of this writing, Azure Arc is available only in selected regions. Don't be surprised by this; Microsoft rolls out preview features gradually with the goal of the product being available in all regions by its general availability date.

4. **Click Create to submit the deployment.**

This operation should take only a few seconds to complete.

Adding a Windows Server system to Arc

You can add a Windows-based server to your Arc environment. According to the Arc documentation, the service supports systems running Windows Server 2012 R2 and newer.

You don't need a VPN or ExpressRoute connection to Azure to add a server. All you need to do to make a local system manageable by Azure is install a single agent.

Follow these steps to onboard a Windows Server system to Arc. Of course, you can perform these steps only if you have local servers available:

1. **In the Azure portal, search for azure arc.**

The search results include entries for Azure Arc and Machines - Azure Arc.

2. **Click the first icon to see the full product.**

3. **On the Arc welcome page, click Manage Servers.**

The Machines - Azure Arc blade appears.

4. **On the Machines - Azure Arc blade, click Add.**

The Select a Method blade appears.

5. **On the Select a Method blade, click the Generate Script button for a Single Server in the Add Machines Using Interactive Script section (see Figure 16-10).**

The interface is continually evolving, and what you see may look different from Figure 16-10, such is the nature of Azure's evolving ecosystem.

When you click this button, the Generate Script blade appears.

Read the nearby sidebar "Adding servers at scale" for more information on the other Arc server onboarding method.

TIP

6. **On the Generate Script blade, complete the Basics tab.**

Choose your subscription, resource group, and region; then select your local computer's operating system (Windows or Linux).

7. **Click Review + Generate.**

The Review + Generate tab appears.

For Windows machines, you see the following script (or something like it if Microsoft updates the code after this book is published):

```
# Download the package
Invoke-WebRequest -Uri https://aka.ms/AzureConnectedMachineAgent
        -OutFile AzureConnectedMachineAgent.msi
# Install the package
msiexec /i AzureConnectedMachineAgent.msi /l*v
        installationlog.txt /qn | Out-String
# Run connect command
& "$env:ProgramFiles\AzureConnectedMachineAgent\azcmagent.exe"
        connect --resource-group "AzureArc" --tenant-id
        "133f6972-44a7-4037-8eea-1d9afd1ebfc8"
        --location "westus2" --subscription-id
        "2fbf906e-1101-4bc0-b64f-adc44e462fff"
```

The Azure portal dynamically populated this PowerShell code with the environment details you specified earlier in the deployment process.

PowerShell accomplishes the following three tasks: downloads the Azure Connected Machine Agent in Microsoft Installer (.msi) format, installs the agent on your system by using the msiexec command-line utility that's built into Windows, and links the local system to your Azure subscription in general and to Arc in particular.

8. **Click Download.**

9. **Copy the onboarding script to your target system.**

You run the script directly on the system.

10. **On the target system, start an elevated PowerShell console by opening Start, typing powershell, right-clicking the PowerShell icon, and choosing Run as Administrator from the shortcut menu.**

An administrative PowerShell console appears.

11. **Temporarily set the script execution policy to Bypass.**

For security reasons, Windows doesn't run all PowerShell scripts by default. To ensure that you can run the Arc onboarding script, type and run the following command:

```
Set-ExecutionPolicy -ExecutionPolicy Bypass -Scope Process -Force
```

This code relaxes the system's script execution policy for the duration of this PowerShell session.

12. Run the script.

All you have to do is type the full or qualified path to the script file. If you used the `cd` command to set your command prompt location to the same directory as the script file, for example, you could type the following to run the script:

```
.\OnboardingScript.ps1
```

On Windows and Linux systems, specifying the *dot slash* syntax instructs your computer to run the script from the present working directory.

Dashboard > Azure Arc >

Add servers with Azure Arc
Servers - Azure Arc

Azure Arc allows you to use Azure tools to manage on-premises servers and servers from other clouds. We'll start with some prerequisites and deploy the Azure Connected Machine agent. Learn more

Add a single server

This option will generate a script to run on your target server. The script will prompt you for your Azure login, so this option is best for adding servers one at a time.

[Generate script]   Learn more

Add multiple servers

To add multiple servers to Azure, we will generate a script that handles authentication through a service principal. You will see that and other prerequisites next.

[Generate script]   Learn more

Add servers from Update Management (preview)

Non-Azure servers managed by the Update Management service can be easily connected to Azure via Azure Arc. Once you have selected the servers, the deployment will happen automatically.

[Add servers]   Learn more

Add servers with Azure Migrate

Discover servers in your VMware vSphere environment and automatically add them to Azure Arc with the Azure Migrate: Discovery and assessment tool.

Learn how to add servers with Azure Migrate

FIGURE 16-10:
Choosing a server onboarding method for Arc.

Over the past few years, Azure has added more than ten prerequisite operating system connection types which have come a long way from being Linux-Only in 2019 when this book was last published. To review the prerequisites and configuration options, go to https://docs.microsoft.com/azure/azure-arc/servers/prerequisites#supported-environments.

ADDING SERVERS AT SCALE

Microsoft understands that some Azure administrators need to add dozens, hundreds, or thousands of their local machines to Arc. If you need to add many machines, you can use PowerShell to script the deployment and target as many local systems as you need to onboard. You can automate the script by using a *service principal* — a special Azure AD identity that uses a digital certificate for authentication.

For more information on onboarding systems to Arc at scale, see "Quickstart: Connect machines to Azure using Azure Arc for servers - PowerShell" at `https://docs.microsoft.com/azure/azure-arc/servers/quickstart-onboard-powershell`.

Managing local systems with Arc

Now it's time to answer the question "What can I do with onboarded machines with Arc for Servers?" Key capabilities that Arc for Servers supports for management actions on onboarded systems include

>> Role-Based Access Control (RBAC)

>> Azure Monitor

>> Taxonomic tags

>> Azure Policy

Implementing Azure Policy

Policy is a powerful platform for Azure resource governance. Suppose that your business is located in the western United States. You need to ensure that all systems are assigned the Pacific time zone by using Policy.

Follow these steps to configure a Windows Server–based Arc machine for policy assignment:

1. **On the Machines - Azure Arc blade, select your Windows server.**

   The server's Overview blade appears.

2. **Select the Policies setting, and then click Assign Policy on the toolbar.**

   The Assign Policy blade appears.

   Figure 16-11 shows the VM's settings interface. If you're thinking that managing an on-premises system works exactly as it does for managing an Azure native VM, you understand the Arc for Servers use case.

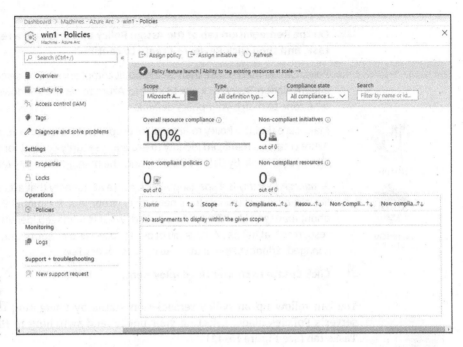

win1 - Policies
Machine - Azure Arc

Search (Ctrl+/)

- Overview
- Activity log
- Access control (IAM)
- Tags
- Diagnose and solve problems

Settings

- Properties
- Locks

Operations

- Policies

Monitoring

- Logs

Support + troubleshooting

- New support request

➕ Assign policy   ➕ Assign initiative   ↻ Refresh

Policy feature launch | Ability to tag existing resources at scale. →

Scope	Type	Compliance state	Search
Microsoft A...	All definition typ...	All compliance s...	Filter by name or id...

Overall resource compliance ⓘ

100%

Non-compliant initiatives ⓘ

0 out of 0

Non-compliant policies ⓘ

0 out of 0

Non-compliant resources ⓘ

0 out of 0

Name	↑↓	Scope	↑↓	Compliance...↑↓	Resou...↑↓	Non-Compli...↑↓	Non-complia...↑↓

No assignments to display within the given scope

FIGURE 16-11:
Viewing an
Arc-managed
system's policy
settings.

3. **On the Basics tab of the Assign Policy blade, complete the form, and click Next to continue.**

Complete the following information:

- *Scope:* Make sure that this setting is set to your Azure subscription and your Azure Arc resource group.

- *Exclusions:* Use this control to exclude the Ubuntu system from this policy. The time-zone policy you're about to assign is for Windows systems only.

- *Policy Definition:* Search the built-in policy definitions for the one named Configure Time Zone on Windows Machines.

- *Assignment Name* (optional): You can give the policy a custom name, if you want. By default, the name is set to the policy definition name.

- *Policy Enforcement:* The options are Enabled and Disabled. You want to use this policy, so ensure that it's set to Enabled.

4. **On the Parameters tab of the Assign Policy blade, choose your desired time zone from the Time Zone drop-down list, and then click Next to continue.**

In this scenario, you're assigning all systems to Pacific time: UTC – 8 hours in the United States and Canada.

5. **On the Remediation tab of the Assign Policy blade, create a remediation task, and then click Review + Create to continue.**

Policy can do much more than simply audit compliance. Here, select the Create a Remediation Task check box to instruct Azure to set the Windows server's time zone to match your policy definition.

REMEMBER

Make sure that the Policy to Remediate drop-down list is set to your policy. Azure creates a managed identity to provide a security context for the remediation task. By default, Azure grants the managed identity temporarily.

TECHNICAL STUFF

A *managed identity* is a special-purpose Azure AD identity that acts very much like a service account in a local network environment. For more information about managed identities in Azure, read "What is managed identities for Azure resources?" at https://docs.microsoft.com/azure/active-directory/managed-identities-azure-resources/overview.

6. **Click Create to submit the deployment.**

You can follow up on policy remediation status by navigating to the Windows server's Policies blade, selecting your policy, and switching to the Remediation Tasks tab (see Figure 16-12).

I checked the time zone on my Windows Server VM, and sure enough, it was set from the Central time zone (my original time zone) to Pacific.

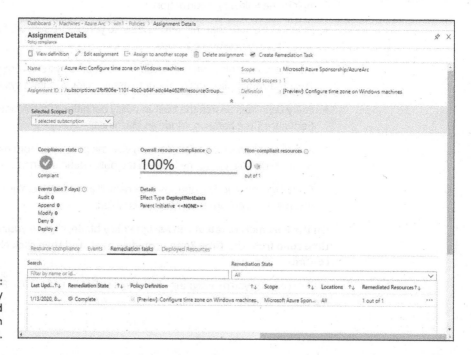

FIGURE 16-12: Verifying policy compliance and remediation status.

Implementing taxonomic tags

You can create a taxonomic tag set for your Arc servers. Specifically, you define a tag called env:arc on your Ubuntu VM.

Follow these steps to assign a taxonomic tag to an Arc (or native Azure) resource:

1. **On the Machines - Azure Arc blade, select your Linux VM.**

   The VM's Overview Settings blade appears.

2. **Select the Tags setting in the Settings list.**

3. **Define the env:arc tag, and then click Save to save your changes.**

   Note that taxonomic tags are name:value pairs. You simply type the tag name and tag value; alternatively, you can reuse previously defined tag names and/or values.

   Figure 16-13 shows the finished configuration.

For more information on taxonomic tags, see the nearby sidebar "What can you do with tags in Azure?"

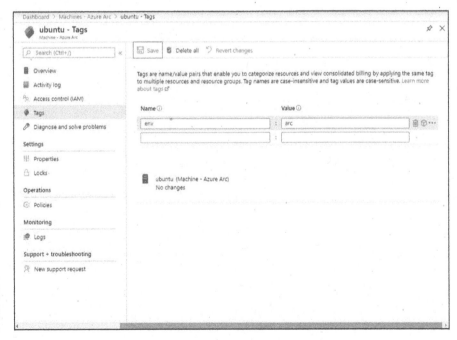

FIGURE 16-13:
Applying taxonomic tags to an Arc resource.

TECHNICAL STUFF

WHAT CAN YOU DO WITH TAGS IN AZURE?

Most businesses need to manage multiple Azure deployments and track cost and utilization separately for each environment. At first blush, the resource group seems to be the most appropriate container for these tracked deployments. The reality, however, is that most cost centers also span entire Azure subscriptions.

Thus, by applying taxonomic tags to your resource groups and resources, you can aggregate Azure resources throughout your environment and then report on them, using tools such as Azure Monitor, Azure Cost Management, and Azure Log Analytics. For best practices on tag use in Azure, see "Resource naming and tagging decision guide" at https://docs.microsoft.com/azure/cloud-adoption-framework/decision-guides/resource-tagging.

6

The Part of Tens

Getting to know the top ten Azure advanced technology areas to watch

Finding out how to optimize your Azure environment (and save money, too)

IN THIS CHAPTER

» **Keeping abreast of Azure platform features**

» **Remaining current with Azure product updates**

» **Discovering new industry trends that are being integrated into Azure**

Chapter **17**

Top Ten Azure Technology Opportunities to Watch

Microsoft is not your everyday enterprise IT vendor. Few companies can invest over $20 billion into their product lines, with over half of the spending being invested in cloud-first initiatives in a single calendar year. As you read this chapter, you'll quickly realize the following ten trends are industry-wide, but in this dog-eat-dog world, Microsoft leads the pack in research and development dollar spending to build the best-in-breed cloud platform. As you review the key ten areas that keep Microsoft on its toes (and many businesses up at night), recognize that the criticality and maturity of each area vary widely.

TIP

This chapter presents cutting-edge concepts, some of which may not be generally available just yet. Microsoft takes about six months to a year to make a technical capability generally available. Once the capability is generally available, Microsoft doesn't just freeze efforts and move on to the next. It releases updates constantly to improve the platform. That said, significant updates are often announced quarterly or at major conferences. Watch out for major events and big press releases to keep yourself up to date.

Focus on Hybrid and Multi-Cloud

Most organizations cannot simply pull the plug on all on-premises and data application resources. It takes time to transform IT infrastructure, as the quality of service and security are essential for operational continuity. That's why the modern organization looks to secure their infrastructure in stages. With *hybrid cloud computing*, you can secure on-premises data and applications based on your public cloud providers' operational maturity. As your data is ready to transition, you can interconnect the legacy infrastructure with your cloud solution providers' infrastructure to scale.

It's also not uncommon for organizations to use many cloud solution providers. Consider this all-too-common scenario. You may host your organization's cloud infrastructure in Microsoft Azure, but your organization has chosen enterprise resource planning (ERP) software hosted exclusively in Amazon Web Services (AWS). In this case, your technology strategy now falls into the bucket called *multi-cloud*. The modern organization is quite agile, which means it supports services to fit its individual business needs using many cloud service providers.

Whether your organization has one workload in Microsoft Azure or hundreds, you can integrate with other cloud solution providers offering distributed multi-cloud, on-premises, or by utilizing edge computing in conjunction with Azure services such as Microsoft Azure Arc.

Increase Usage of Event-Driven Serverless Containers

Cloud apps and microservices are rapidly being hosted in fully managed serverless containers. Unlike traditional infrastructure services like Azure Kubernetes Service (AKS), an event-driven serverless container app is specifically built for microservices and those functions that require quick scalability based on HTTP traffic events or background jobs.

As more organizations push for their developers to build apps based on loosely coupled programming languages, often low-code or no-code environments, an Azure Event-Driven Container App can help deploy these new service options. Event-driven serverless container apps sit on top of open-source projects that include pre-built runtimes. The Event-Driven Container leverages technology based on the Kubernetes Event-Driven Autoscaling (KEDA) framework, an industry-neutral Kubernetes architecture supported by Microsoft and IBM/Red Hat, among other vendors.

Whether you are Microsoft, AWS, Google Cloud, or another cloud platform leader, serverless container services are commonplace. What differentiates Microsoft Azure from the pack, though, are those vendors who offer Platform as a Service (PaaS) like control of deployments, making it easier for organizations to manage tools to a minimum. There is no doubt that managing a Kubernetes cluster can be a full-time job; therefore, containers have promised to quickly scale more minor services up and down at a moment's notice. The developer should not worry about infrastructure. Instead, the focus can be on the code's innovation and rapid application enhancements.

Rapid AI and Edge Adoption

Microsoft is heavily investing in artificial intelligence (AI) tools, edge, and cloud platform convergence. The next generation of AI-enabled applications, most of which will be hybrid, can run just about anywhere your data is housed. With services like Azure Stack Hub, your organization can bring a trained AI model to the edge. Once discovered, you can integrate the AI model with any application that supports low-latency intelligence. The result will be continuous feedback that is trained for improved accuracy without requiring additional tools. Even local applications will mature over time. So long as you have a connection to Azure Stack Hub, you can be sure that an edge application connected to Azure will mature over time.

Emphasis on Zero Trust Cloud Security

Look at the news daily, and you'll hear of some internet security breach or exploit that takes down an organization's IT infrastructure. As workloads move to the cloud, your organization has likely been a victim (somehow) of an attempted cyberattack. And guess what? You may not even know about it. How is it then that vendors such as Microsoft protect your infrastructure? With Zero Trust cloud security.

Zero Trust is a security model that assumes that any inappropriate action against a cloud environment such as Azure is likely a breach. Therefore, each request made is treated as though it is from an uncontrolled network. As organizations move their authentication and authorization-based technologies from the data center to the cloud using enterprise solutions such as Azure Active Directory, consider the principles of verifying explicitly, using least privilege access, and assuming breach in the security architecture design for all cloud resources.

With Zero Trust, these three concepts should always be applied regardless of cloud workload type:

>> **Verify explicitly.** Always authenticate and authorize data sources based on all data endpoints, not just specific data endpoints.

>> **Use least privilege access.** Users should be given access when they require the access, period! That means limiting users who need Just-In-Time and Just-Enough Access. Such limitations mean establishing risk-based policies and data protection practices that tighten any possible access unless a user requires such control.

>> **Assume a breach.** Assume that you are under attack. Don't be lax by letting go of critical security controls. Always minimize the blast radius. Protect operations with segment access. Consistently implement a robust end-to-end encryption program. Leverage analytics (and let's be honest, Azure has tons) to gain visibility of potential threats. Use tools such as Azure Defender to monitor your threat posture while driving threats away via detection and improving defenses manually.

Transformation through Hyper and Intelligence Automation

Picture this: A million data sensors feeding a Microsoft Azure SQL Server database every minute. Most data points fit the normal range of acceptably, but now and then, you'll have the needle in the haystack. Oops. As big data only grows, finding those ambiguous data points collected within Azure Cloud services can be tricky. Because a human is incapable of detecting everything, to evaluate the large volume of data collected means putting hyper and intelligent automation solutions in place. Whether the data set is with the development and operations team (DevOps) or is production-ready, Azure allows organizations to infuse AI automation into virtually every environment. When organizations can become more self-adaptive, resilient, and efficient, they experience more extraordinary digital transformation.

Microsoft is quickly building cloud intelligence into every solution. The project name, AIOps, uses AI and machine learning (ML) to build and operate cloud compute environments, including all relevant services at scale. The goal is simple: workload efficiency and effectiveness in support of systems, customers, and DevOps.

TECHNICAL STUFF

Microsoft hopes to build intelligence into every IT solution, from data to analytics:

>> **AI for systems** intends to self-control and adapt practices with less human reliance.

>> **AI for customers** intends to leverage AI and ML patterns to create custom-tailored user experiences, leading to user satisfaction across cloud services. In other words, Microsoft hopes for a strong transition from the data center to the cloud-first by building customer experiences tailored to a user's personal needs.

>> **AI for DevOps** intends to take its AI and ML solutions portfolio and tailor it to the ongoing software development lifecycle. By reducing the need to code and test constantly, Microsoft hopes organizations can achieve higher worker productivity while supporting complex solutions requiring little hands-on interaction from humans.

Bringing Data Analytics Mainstream

Data Analytics in 2022 is the equivalent of the database in the 1990s. Every big vendor jumped on the relationship (and non-relational) database wagon as enterprise applications required structured storage. Fast-forward twenty-plus years, these data solutions now house millions, if not billions, of records. As you discover in Chapter 10, a host of IoT and Big Data Analytic tools help you sort out data glut. Count on Microsoft to add to the portfolio over time. The portfolio, among the most comprehensive in the enterprise IT industry, will only grow from its current baseline, as shown in Table 17-1.

TABLE 17-1   **Data Analytic Offerings in Microsoft Azure**

Azure Data Product	Key Capability
Azure Synapse Analytics	Azure's shared data integration platform combines extract transport load (ETL), data integration, warehousing, and big data analytics under a single umbrella
Azure Databricks	Leverages the Apache Spark analytics platform, optimized for Azure
Azure HDInsight	The fully managed Hadoop and Spark service, optimized for Azure
Azure Data Factory	The data integration service to orchestrate and automate data movement

(continued)

TABLE 17-1 *(continued)*

Azure Data Product	Key Capability
Azure Machine Learning	Microsoft's premier elastic AI development solution spanning the cloud and the edge
Azure Stream Analytics	The real-time data streaming process for IoT devices
Azure Data Lake Analytics	A pay-per-job analytics service for those requiring security and auditing
Azure Analysis Services	Microsoft's enterprise analytics engine built exclusively for as-a-service workloads
Azure Events Hub	Azure's hyper-scale telemetry service that collects, transforms, and stores event-based data
Azure Data Explorer	Azure's data exploration service
Azure Data Share	A point-solution that allows for data sharing with external organizations
Azure Time Series Insights	An IoT analytics platform to monitor, analyze, and visualize vertical-based IoT data at scale
Azure Chaos Studio	Azure's data engineering experimentation platform for reviewing targeted large datasets
Microsoft Graph Data Connect	Azure's high-throughput connector to transport Microsoft 365 datasets into an Azure tenant

Maturing of IoT and Cognitive Services

Look around you right now. You'll likely spot at least one device in your current room that is collecting data. Where does this data inevitably go? Somewhere in the cloud, but to get to the cloud requires internet access. Depending on your location, remote updates and assuring security may be prohibitive. Microsoft recognizes the need to be "always-on" and "always ready." That's why it's built a two-pronged approach to ensuring Internet of Things (IoT) services and cognitive (ML/AI) services remain available.

With Azure IoT Edge, Microsoft allows IoT devices with intermittent access to the Internet to buffer outbound devices with local telemetry. That means that until there is a reliable Internet connection, data can be stored indefinitely on the sensor (so long as space remains available, of course). Once a reliable connection is achieved, the IoT data is uploaded with all the original attributes. This is possible because targeted deployment configurations specify which container applications can support a given device. The key to this architecture is only allowing devices registered with Azure IoT Hub to confer data between the telemetry data point and a given Azure-hosted endpoint.

IoT devices are not the only solution that is always-on, always-learning. With Azure Cognitive Services, Microsoft allows developers to access an enormous library of intelligence algorithms and integrate such features into apps, websites, bots, and IoT sensor-based products. Cognitive solutions allow apps to automate hearing, seeing, and speaking functionality through one or more Software as a Service (SaaS) offerings.

Microsoft is not limiting cognitive services to web-based solutions exclusively. In the first half of 2022, Microsoft began supporting local support of cognitive services using containers. And this is likely the tip of the iceberg for service options, including Computer Vision, Face, and Text Analytics. As of this edition of *Azure For Dummies,* many Cognitive Services, especially those that offer containerization options, are available for specific operating systems such as Linux x64. Furthermore, the products remain in a constant public beta due to ongoing product enhancements and investments in the AI/ML portfolio.

When you bring Azure IoT Edge and Cognitive Service Containers together, your organization can build IoT Solutions that allow for local AI processing where Internet connectivity may be spotty. Your organization will not need to rely on external services to produce data. Activity can be processed locally and securely via the cloud at speed and scale.

Building Vertical Solutions in the Cloud to Accelerate Innovation

It should be no surprise that Microsoft is laser-focused on vertical industry solutions within Azure Cloud. The need for tailored cloud offerings for industry verticals such as healthcare, government, supply chain, and finance became even more evident during the early days of the COVID-19 pandemic. In early 2021, Microsoft announced its public preview of the Microsoft Cloud for Healthcare. As touted by Microsoft, this will be its first industry vertical cloud offering with data analytics, collaboration, and operations assets.

Microsoft hopes to build on top of enterprise applications such as Dynamics 365 Marketing, Dynamics 365 Customer Service, Dynamics 365 Finance, Dynamics 365 Operations, and Power Platform assets, notably Power BI and Azure IoT, to craft focused industry offerings. Combined with core business productivity applications such as Microsoft 365 (which includes SharePoint) and Microsoft Teams, the Azure vertical solutions will gain traction in the future.

ON THE WEB

To review the vertical solution portfolios available to date, go to https://www. microsoft.com/industry.

Pushing Low-Code and No-Code Development

Thanks to AI– and ML–based technologies, Microsoft has moved away from its heavy push for all development to be completed in Visual Studio. In 2020, Microsoft invested billions of dollars in large language models to run in Azure. To Microsoft, Azure isn't just a cloud platform but an AI supercomputer. You'll find heavy integration of natural language processing and AI models such as the GPT-3, built by OpenAI, and DeepSpeed library. Both libraries are making their way into Azure and core Microsoft products over the next few years. Whether it is obvious or not is another story!

While the GPT-3 and DeepSpeed library are still in research for use within Azure Services, hence private preview, Microsoft is already integrating GPT-3 into many of its core product offerings, including the Microsoft Office, Microsoft Power Platform, and Microsoft Dynamics product families.

You can build robust applications quickly using Azure and AI integration under the Microsoft low-code/no-code application portfolio, Power Platform. A few years ago, you had to be a trained developer to analyze data, extract information, and create custom apps or workflows. No longer! With Power Platform, you get a low-code/no-code development platform that allows enterprise and novice developers to drag and drop components as well as connect them with a lightweight API.

REMEMBER

Low-code and no-code modular approaches enable a developer, experienced or novice, to quickly create targeted applications with a limited need to write code. Whether you are a business analyst, small business owner, data scientist, or professional developer, you can create applications without having to know a single programming language or how to translate machine code into something meaningful. And most of the automation controls to build these applications are grounded in the Microsoft Azure Services portfolio.

Environmental Sustainability

The most prominent IT vendors, including Microsoft, have committed to environmental sustainability globally. Some, like Microsoft, have committed to a carbon-neutral footprint within the next five to ten years. At Microsoft, they recognize the herculean effort it takes to ensure that climate protections are enforced. That's why you'll notice more Azure core platform capabilities and services be notated with sustainability and environmental detail over the next several years. The goal is to ensure that environmental waste is minimized while protecting precious resources such as our water supply and reducing deforestation during the construction of data center operations. Microsoft has committed to the following four metrics:

>> Use 100 percent renewable energy by 2025.

>> Be "water positive replenishment positive" (replenish more water than used) by 2030.

>> Attain global zero-waste certifications by 2030.

>> Achieve net-zero deforestation for any new project completed by Microsoft.

Microsoft has recently benchmarked the impact of migrating from on-premises to Azure for those organizations looking to expedite their environmental sustainability initiative. Organizations that move to the Azure Cloud report an increase in energy efficiency by 93 percent on average and 98 percent carbon efficiency. Given Microsoft's commitment to environmental sustainability, these metrics will likely only increase over the next few years.

ON THE WEB

To read the Microsoft White paper on "The Carbon Benefits of Cloud Computing: a Study of the Microsoft Cloud," go to www.microsoft.com/download/details.aspx?id=56950.

Chapter **18**

Ten Ways to Optimize an Azure Environment

I f you've reached this chapter in excitement trying to cut costs on your cloud computing infrastructure, you are indeed not alone. Cloud computing is sold as a significant cost saver by enterprise IT vendors. Truth be told, though, it can get as pricey as operating in the data center, if not more. If you treat Azure like you've treated the data in that filing cabinet found in the back office, you will spend big money unnecessarily.

Why spend more than you need to? Why give your cloud infrastructure more horsepower if the workload doesn't require such resources? In this chapter, you discover ten ways to optimize your cloud (and save money too).

Leverage the Stop-Start Button for Virtual Machines

It does not matter whether you are a cloud rookie or a cloud administrative superstar. We all make this error now and again. Why keep the lights on if your cloud workload does not require 24/7/365 always-on support? Turn your virtual machine (VM) off to reduce energy expenditure. Better yet, when the VM isn't running, you only pay for the storage utilized in Azure, not the VM itself. Think about it like this. During a given month, there are about 720 hours, give or take. Your organization is using a VM perhaps 72 hours a month. Would you rather pay for the lights to stay on for 72 or 720 hours? Unless there is a good reason not to power down the VM, we should assume that you'd instead be interested in being billed for 10 percent utilization and not 100 percent.

Rightsize Capacity and Storage

When an organization moves from its data center to the cloud, a fraction of the capacity is likely utilized. Why? You must buy more capacity and storage to handle those off-chance peak loads. Once you move your workloads to the cloud, you can significantly reduce costs by rightsizing server capacity. Rightsizing is a mechanism to control costs and optimize resources.

Azure has many tools for you to see system performance and capacity utilization. You can select the smallest virtual instance to support your business need as a cloud administrator. Once selected, you can put levers to increase capacity and demand should a peak occur. Otherwise, your status quo capacity remains, which enables you to save money by not having to keep your environment at overcapacity.

A classic example of when rightsizing is appropriate is exemplified by a CPA firm. During tax season, your cloud utilization and capacity will inevitably spike, perhaps as much as 100 percent. But what about the remaining nine or ten months? Capacity is significantly lower, which means that lower static usage indicates an opportunity for savings. With Azure, rightsizing the environment helps you realize those cost savings immediately.

Use Spot and B-Series VMs

Some workloads are used once and a while. Why would you want to pay full price, if not a premium, for a workload used incidentally? That is why Microsoft has come up with a cost-efficient option: one for VMs that always need to be on but tend to be idle most of the time. Because VMs remain a dominant portion of cloud usage, Microsoft recognized that many systems require minimal specifications to run and are often idle with slight periodic usage. These VMs incur the entire price burden because they are always on. The Azure B-Series of VMs, also known as burstable VMs, allow the environment to always be on, with occasional peaks in usage. Using a burstable environment can reduce your cost by about 40 percent. How is that? You are charged a slight premium for your uptime usage but virtually nothing for periods where capacity is dormant.

Another cost-saving option for those workloads that need to always be on but can handle interruption now and again when Azure reaches peak capacity is the use of Spot Virtual Machines. Consider spot instances if a workload does not have a mandatory period where a task must be done. Use cases where Spot Virtual Machines are appropriate to include are development, testing, quality assurance, advanced analytics, big data, and machine learning/artificial intelligence with minimal operational interruption should the VM stop for a short time.

Tidy Up Your Azure Environment

It's unlikely that you or your organization want to pay for things not used. Unfortunately with Azure and other cloud platforms, making environment updates often has an unintended consequence, leaving garbage behind. Now garbage may sound like a strong word, but there is truth to this, as deleting a resource such as a VM may not clean up the remainder of the resources created when the initial VM was configured. Deleting a resource such as a VM still leaves the storage drive, the IP address, and network interfaces lingering in the Azure Resources folder. Here are some ways to tidy the house:

>> **Disks:** You should look at disks that are not attached to VMs, meaning extraneous disks that are collecting dust in the Azure resource directory. Such behavior is especially true when you replace a disk with a different storage option or even delete the entire VM. To locate the unused disks, go to the list of all disks. Look at the owner column. A name should be assigned to the disk. If you find the value empty, the disk is ripe for removal.

>> **IP addresses:** Like with a telephone number, you pay for being issued an IP address. Locate your IP address pool, and search for the column Associated To. If you can't find what the IP address is associated with, it means the address has been abandoned. Again, no usage of a resource, but you are still paying for the IP address makes no sense. Therefore, delete the IP address!

>> **Network Interfaces:** You can also find what network interfaces are being used and abandoned, like the IP Address. By searching the column Associated To, look to see if the Network Interface has any ties to existing resources. If the column remains empty, you can safely remove the Network Interface resource.

While not exhaustive, these three resources lingering around can potentially double your invoice unnecessarily. Other resource types may be abandoned, too, but these three are the key to tidying the house and saving money.

Avoid Disaster with Azure Backup

A worst-case scenario for most Azure users is when a VM in your production environment crashes and you forget to create a backup. Azure has a backup service called Azure Backup that supports single VM or multi-VM instance recovery.

TECHNICAL STUFF

Regardless of the VM instance recovery mode, the Azure Backup will need to install an extension on the VM agent running the workload. Those VMs created using the Azure Marketplace almost always include the agent once running. For environments created manually, you'll likely need to install the agent.

You must enable the backup using Azure Backup within Azure Backup Center. Just because the agent is installed in the environment does not mean it automatically starts. To enable Azure Backup for a single or multi-instance environment, go to the VM. In the navigation pane, locate Backup under Operations and follow the prompts to complete the Backup configuration.

You can set the backup schedule as frequently as you desire. When you set up the initial backup, a backup extension is installed to establish the snapshot parameters for your virtualized instance. If you have multiple VMs, you'll have the Windows Volume Shadow Copy Service (VSS) take a copy of the app-consistent instances. Initially, a full backup is made. For subsequent backups, only those changes in the environment will be captured in the snapshot.

REMEMBER

>> Backups are done for each VM disk in parallel.

>> Once an initial backup is complete, Azure Backup only reads and transfers the changed blocks.

>> Snapshot data may take some time to transfer to the data vault. For a daily backup, this means that within 24 hours of your snapshot capture your daily backup is compiled into the data vault.

Monitor Your Spending with Azure Cost Tools

Microsoft enables you to watch your cloud spending using a variety of tools. Under Cost Management and Billing, you can analyze your spending on a day-by-day basis or across a more extended period. Microsoft even provides forecasting tools to tweak your environment if you see a resource cost rise more than anticipated. If your organization has a cloud budget, you can create alerts and budget notifications to enforce spending limits or warnings. Controlling spending can be done by selecting the Cost Management and Billing Pane and then selecting the Cost Analysis, Cost Alerts, or Budgets option in the secondary navigation pane.

Maximize Azure Autoscaling and Hybrid Use Benefits

You can spend a lot of money if you maximize your cloud environment's capacity unnecessarily. For example, you may procure a higher-end CPU-based VM that is always-on. Yet, your peak capacity for the entire year may not be more than a week. Why spend extra money for the extra fifty-one weeks? You shouldn't! With autoscaling, you set the parameters in Azure Cloud Services, Mobile Services, Virtual Machine Sets, and Platform as a Service (PaaS) applications to perform based on demand. Some apps may require more CPU capacity, while others may require memory-intense support. Take, for example, your enterprise application that runs like a workhorse Monday through Friday from 8:00 a.m. to 6:00 p.m. However, from 6:01 p.m. to 7:59 a.m. each day, as well as on the weekends, traffic comes to a trickle. You can use autoscale to support your services for optimal performance by scheduling when the environment should respond in advance.

Another way that organizations can better scale (and save money) with Microsoft Azure is by using their existing software licensing benefits. You can turn these licenses on and off based on needs like autoscaling. Such benefits are called Azure Hybrid Use Benefits.

When provisioning a virtual environment or a new SQL Server license in Azure, you will likely pay hundreds if not thousands of dollars per month for the new license entitlement. However, if you are part of an organization with an end-user license agreement via Software Assurance for Windows Server or SQL Server, consider applying the pre-purchased license to the Azure environment to reduce your Azure Cloud spend. And these licensing options are not just limited to Microsoft products. You can also bring Red Hat and SUSE Linux licenses to Azure.

Use Elastic Database Pools

There are some use cases where you'll want to put a lightweight database on your VM because the volume of data is fractional. And that is perfectly okay. What happens, though, when your database experiences unexpected spikes in usage? Can your virtualized environment handle the performance peaks and valleys? Most vendors, including Microsoft, offer elastic pooling with select databases. With Azure SQL Database, you can scale multiple databases simultaneously to handle varying and unpredictable demands. The database in an elastic pool sits on a single server. However, the database shares several resources based on a pre-determined price. When utilizing SQL Database elastic pools, a Software as a Service (SaaS) developer can optimize their performance based on their known budget and capacity requirements.

TIP

It used to be that a developer would provide a single database for each customer or application. The problem is that each customer and application have different needs, especially usage patterns. Either the organization over-provisions based on their known peak usage or under-provisions to save money, but the performance at peak intervals takes a hit. It would be best to choose elastic pools to solve this problem so that you get the performance and resource allocation only when needed.

Promote Cloud-Native Features First

Understandably, your organization might resist moving its entire data platform to the cloud. What if you could reduce spending by guaranteeing performance and gaining greater visibility of your data and operations?

That's the goal when you strive for a cloud-native first architecture. Instead of keeping those data center environments alive, organizations that shift to a cloud-native first mindset build and run scalable applications in a combination of public, private, and hybrid cloud environments. The organization leverages containers, service meshes, microservices, and APIs to support the software development lifecycle. Enabling cloud-native features within a system of varying capacity can support resilience, manageability, and scalability. Within these environments, if you combine robust automation, engineers can make frequent updates to the platform with minimal risk and costs.

Better yet, if most of your applications are built utilizing PaaS resources in Azure, your team can forego the expense of cloud administration in favor of developing innovative applications because Microsoft does all of your cloud administration.

Purchase Azure Capacity Using Reservations

Willing to commit to a marriage with Microsoft for one to three years? If the answer is yes and you can predict capacity requirements, why not purchase services in advance? Doing so can save you as much as 72 percent over three years. With on-demand capacity reservations for Azure, your IT organization can reserve compute capacity for specific virtual environment requirements. So long as there is a long-term commitment where you know you will use compute capacity in any public Azure region, you can lock in potential savings.

TIP

Once your capacity exceeds the on-demand reservation spend threshold, you'll be billed using the Azure price sheet unless your organization has an enterprise license agreement with attached discounts.

Organizations often adapt to Azure Capacity using Reservations because you lock in prices for the long term while also ensuring that your organization gets service level agreement guarantees at a substantial discount. You can't beat getting a discount for committing beyond a monthly period.

Index

E

edge applications, 373

80 percent services, 1, 17

Elastic Compute Cloud VM instances, 100

elastic pools, 198, 386

elasticity, 9–10, 26

environmental sustainability, 379

event-driven serverless containers, 372

extract, transfer, and load (ETL) management. *See* data analytics

F

file service, 52

compared to other storage types, 65

creating, 65–66

viewing properties of, 60

function apps, 180, 183–188

actions, 182

creating, 184

creating functions, 186–187

defined, 155–156

defining functions, 184–186

events, 182

logic apps vs., 182

settings configuration, 188

testing, 188

triggers, 182–183

G

gateways

local network gateways, 356–357

planning and configuring, 95–96

on-premises gateways, 354–355

virtual network gateways, 355–356

GCP (Google Cloud Platform), 11–12, 144

General Data Protection Regulation (GDPR), 299

generalization, 103

general-purpose v1 storage accounts, 53

general-purpose v2 storage accounts, 53

geographies, 37

georedundant storage (GRS), 54

georeplication, 15, 203–205

Git

configuring, 159–160

creating repositories, 161–163

defined, 159

distributed version control, 308–309

GitHub, 311–314

asset searches, 311–312

GitHub Actions, 312–314

GitHub Marketplace, 312–313

GitHub vs. Azure DevOps, 312

GitHub Labs, 309, 311

GoDaddy, 173

Google Cloud Platform (GCP), 11–12, 144

governance tools, 285–302

Azure Advisor, 301–302

Azure Policy, 292–298

assigning policies, 296–297

creating policies, 295–296

policy definition structure, 293–295

policy lifecycle, 295

testing policies, 297–298

governance, defined, 359

security, privacy, and trust compliance, 298–300

Azure Trust Center, 300

documentation, 299–300

standards, 299

taxonomic tags, 285–292

adding programmatically, 288–289

adding via Azure portal, 287–288

API access, 292

common tagging patterns, 287

cost reporting, 291–292

removing, 289–290

reporting via, 290–292

government clouds (sovereign clouds), 37

GPT-3, 378

Gremlin, 208

GRS (georedundant storage), 54

guest-level monitoring, 126

H

Hanselman, Scott, 172

Hardware Security Modules (HSMs), 245–246

hello-world container, 133–135, 140–142

Henriksen, Justin, 198

high availability, 54, 106–107

Hot access storage tier, 56, 62

hybrid cloud model, 353–358, 372

ExpressRoute, 357–358

overview, 13–14

site-to-site VPNs, 354–357

hyper and intelligent automation solutions, 374–375

Hypertext Transfer Protocol (HTTP), 30

I

IaaS. *See* Infrastructure as a Service

IBM Cloud, 11

idempotency, 58, 117

Identity as a Service (IDaaS), 16

About the Author

Jack Hyman is the founder of HyerTek (www.hyertek.com), a Washington, D.C.-based technology and training services firm specializing in cloud computing, business intelligence, learning management, and enterprise application advisory needs for federal, state, and private sector organizations. During his extensive IT career, Jack has led U.S. federal government agencies and global enterprises through multiyear technology transformation projects. Before founding HyerTek, Jack worked for Oracle and IBM. He has authored many books, provided peer-review guidance for scholarly journals, and developed training courseware with an emphasis on Microsoft technologies. Since 2004, he has sat on the faculties at George Washington University, American University, and the University of the Cumberlands. Jack holds a Ph.D. in Information Systems from Nova Southeastern University.

Dedication

To my children, Jeremy and Emily: I hope you always love learning as much as I do.

Author's Acknowledgments

Many folks were involved in getting the second edition of *Microsoft Azure For Dummies* into your hands. Thanks to Executive Editor Steve Hayes and Senior Managing Editor Kristie Pyles for giving me the opportunity to write this book (and so many other For Dummies projects over the years). A great big thanks to Project Editor Katharine Dvorak for keeping me on track throughout this project. A hearty thanks to Technical Editor Sarah Guthals for ensuring that the content in this edition remained accurate and technically sound. Also, thanks to Carole Jelen of Waterside Productions for bringing me yet another exciting project to share with the world. And finally, thanks to my wife, Debbie, and kids, Jeremy and Emily, for allowing me to take on yet another extensive book project.

Publisher's Acknowledgments

Executive Editor: Steven Hayes

Senior Managing Editor: Kristie Pyles

Project Editor: Katharine Dvorak

Technical Editor: Sarah Guthals

Production Editor: Tamilmani Varadharaj

Cover Image: © ZinetroN/Shutterstock